"Rick Hanson's seven steps of awakening are a remarkable presentation of how the brain, mindfulness, and meditation are interconnected. There is a surprise perhaps for some in his take on nirvana, but you have to read the book to find out what it is!"

SHARON SALZBERG, AUTHOR OF *LOVINGKINDNESS* AND *REAL CHANGE: MINDFULNESS TO HEAL OURSELVES AND THE WORLD*

"Combining a deep understanding of both neuroscience and Buddhist practice and philosophy, Rick Hanson has beautifully created a fascinating synthesis that shows how to train the mind to transform the brain toward health and flourishing."

DANIEL J. SIEGEL, MD, *NEW YORK TIMES* BESTSELLING AUTHOR OF *AWARE: THE SCIENCE AND PRACTICE OF PRESENCE* AND *MIND: A JOURNEY TO THE HEART OF BEING HUMAN*; EXECUTIVE DIRECTOR, MINDSIGHT INSTITUTE

"Dr. Rick Hanson, one of the pioneering thought leaders of our time, has distilled essential practices into a simple, yet powerful road map to the highest happiness."

SHAUNA SHAPIRO, PhD, AUTHOR OF *GOOD MORNING, I LOVE YOU: MINDFULNESS AND SELF-COMPASSION PRACTICES TO REWIRE YOUR BRAIN FOR CALM, CLARITY, AND JOY*

"Filled with wise and beautiful ways to train the heart and mind."

JACK KORNFIELD, PhD, AUTHOR OF *A PATH WITH HEART*

"A brilliant and unprecedented offering, *Neurodharma* will guide you to the upper reaches of your potential as a human being."

DEEPAK CHOPRA, MD, *NEW YORK TIMES* BESTSELLING AUTHOR OF *YOU ARE THE UNIVERSE* AND *METAHUMAN*

"With brilliant clarity and skill, Rick Hanson weaves the warp of ancient contemplative practice and the weft of modern brain science into a seamless whole, based on his long experience as a practitioner and teacher. Accessible and gentle, there is deep wisdom here from which all may benefit."

MARK WILLIAMS, DPHIL, EMERITUS PROFESSOR OF CLINICAL PSYCHOLOGY, UNIVERSITY OF OXFORD; COAUTHOR OF *THE MINDFUL WAY WORKBOOK*

"Rick Hanson has spent the last several decades honing the art and studying the neuroscience of awakening to the heights of our human potential. The result—*Neurodharma*—is mind-blowing. It is also a tremendous relief for this working mom of four. I now have a practical path for my spiritual growth and wellbeing that I can pursue from the carpool lane or my office, bedroom, or kitchen. Hurrah!"

CHRISTINE CARTER, PhD, AUTHOR OF *THE SWEET SPOT* AND *THE NEW ADOLESCENCE*

"In *Neurodharma*, Rick Hanson displays his mastery as a teacher. He shares his personal journey, rich with personal challenges and transformative experiences, illustrating how these practices may unburden and free the reader from the seductive dangers of ego, competition, and acquisition that dominate contemporary culture."

STEPHEN W. PORGES, PhD, FOUNDING DIRECTOR OF THE TRAUMATIC STRESS RESEARCH CONSORTIUM AND DISTINGUISHED UNIVERSITY SCIENTIST, KINSEY INSTITUTE, INDIANA UNIVERSITY; PROFESSOR OF PSYCHIATRY, UNIVERSITY OF NORTH CAROLINA

"Rick Hanson has a rare ability to inspire us to our fullest potential while giving us practical, actionable tools for our everyday lives."

MARIE FORLEO, AUTHOR OF *EVERYTHING IS FIGUREOUTABLE*

"Simultaneously inspirational and practical, this book vividly brings the Buddha's teachings to life, providing a step-by-step guide to awakening. Weaving together modern neuroscience, years of clinical experience, and deep personal practice, Dr. Hanson guides us through the whole journey, from beginning mindfulness techniques to transcending our conventional sense of self. It's a must-read guide for beginners and experienced practitioners alike."

RONALD D. SIEGEL, PsyD, ASSISTANT PROFESSOR OF PSYCHOLOGY, PART-TIME, HARVARD MEDICAL SCHOOL; AUTHOR OF *THE MINDFULNESS SOLUTION: EVERYDAY PRACTICES FOR EVERYDAY PROBLEMS*

"Rick Hanson takes you on an inspiring tour of our very human capacities for contentment and kindness. This book sparkles with actionable practices, scientific delights, and deep, focused reflection upon what is truly the highest happiness. Reading *Neurodharma* will change your life in enduring ways."

DACHER KELTNER, PHD, PROFESSOR, UNIVERSITY OF CALIFORNIA, BERKELEY; FOUNDER, GREATER GOOD SCIENCE CENTER; AUTHOR OF *BORN TO BE GOOD*

"Reading *Neurodharma*, I felt a profound sense of relief and peace wash over me. The book masterfully explains how our brains function and how we can leverage this understanding to be more authentic, present, and emotionally balanced, even in the face of extreme adversity. Both fascinating and practical, *Neurodharma* breaks down complicated neurobiological processes and outlines a simple path to mental freedom."

LORI DESCHENE, AUTHOR OF *TINY BUDDHA'S WORRY JOURNAL*

"In this fascinating, compelling, and eminently *practical* book, Rick Hanson uncovers the physics, psychology, and neuroscience of *be here now*, and reveals the things you can do right now to achieve this most sought-after and life-enhancing state of mind."

DANIEL J. LEVITIN, PHD, PROFESSOR EMERITUS OF PSYCHOLOGY AND NEUROSCIENCE AT MCGILL UNIVERSITY; AUTHOR OF *THIS IS YOUR BRAIN ON MUSIC, THE ORGANIZED MIND,* AND *SUCCESSFUL AGING*

"*Neurodharma* is a brilliant synthesis of the most helpful contemplative practices and the emerging science of the mind and brain. In these pages you hold a precious experiential education, a unique and accessible guide to living your best life."

ELISSA EPEL, PHD, PROFESSOR, UNIVERSITY OF CALIFORNIA, SAN FRANCISCO; COAUTHOR OF *NEW YORK TIMES* BESTSELLER *THE TELOMERE EFFECT: A REVOLUTIONARY APPROACH TO LIVING YOUNGER, HEALTHIER, LONGER*

"This eloquent and pioneering book is a gem. Wise, practical, and brilliant, full of humor, guidance, and a warm heart, this is a book that will be a companion for life."

SUSAN POLLAK, MTS, EDD, COFOUNDER, CENTER FOR MINDFULNESS AND COMPASSION, CAMBRIDGE HEALTH ALLIANCE/HARVARD MEDICAL SCHOOL

"With a light and steady hand, Dr. Hanson guides our steps on paths of ancient wisdom. In simple, clear, practical (and playful) language, he shows us the practices of an awakened, compassionate, joy-filled life. And if the going gets difficult, he assures us there is no rush, and that everything we need is already present. I am very grateful for this book."

ANDREW DREITCER, PhD, PROFESSOR OF SPIRITUALITY, CO-DIRECTOR OF THE CENTER FOR ENGAGED COMPASSION, CLAREMONT SCHOOL OF THEOLOGY AT WILLAMETTE UNIVERSITY

"A wise, practical, scientifically grounded, and surpassingly friendly guide to becoming who we can be. *Neurodharma* is a terrific book, and Rick Hanson is who you want by your side, supporting you as you meet your challenges and celebrating you as you embrace your experience."

JAMES S. GORDON, MD, AUTHOR OF *THE TRANSFORMATION: DISCOVERING WHOLENESS AND HEALING AFTER TRAUMA*; FOUNDER AND EXECUTIVE DIRECTOR OF THE CENTER FOR MIND-BODY MEDICINE

"Integrating body, heart, and mind, his systematic approach is wise, compassionate, beautifully human, and accessible to all. This book is a guide to the freedom that is hiding in plain sight, waiting to be discovered."

FRANK OSTASESKI, AUTHOR OF *THE FIVE INVITATIONS: DISCOVERING WHAT DEATH CAN TEACH US ABOUT LIVING FULLY*

"Rick Hanson has done something you'd think would be impossible: lain out an entire and complete spiritual path from beginning to end in a single book. The fact that it's brilliant, funny, profound, understandable, and effective is icing on the cake. And the 'neurodharma' angle is amazing. I highly recommend this powerful book."

MICHAEL W. TAFT, AUTHOR AND TEACHER

"Dr. Hanson has a rare and remarkable ability for synthesizing the deep wisdom of the great spiritual teachers with a clear understanding of modern neuroscience, to offer us practical tools for making our lives more peaceful, loving, and whole."

ROBERT D. TRUOG, MD, PROFESSOR AND DIRECTOR OF THE HARVARD MEDICAL SCHOOL CENTER FOR BIOETHICS

"In this engaging and accessible yet profound work, Rick Hanson has written a road map for liberating the mind from suffering and realizing the highest happiness. He shows that peace is possible not only for long-time practitioners but also for anyone who sincerely applies these principles and practices. Well done!"

JAMES BARAZ, COAUTHOR OF *AWAKENING JOY: 10 STEPS TO HAPPINESS*; COFOUNDER OF SPIRIT ROCK MEDITATION CENTER

"This book is an inspiring yet grounded description of self-transcendence and an accessible guide to both profound experiences and the daily dynamics of living well."

DAVID BRYCE YADEN, PhD, DEPARTMENT OF PSYCHOLOGY, UNIVERSITY OF PENNSYLVANIA

"This is is a treasure and a milestone in the exploration of our highest potential. Dr. Hanson walks the reader on the path to true happiness, skillfully leading them gently deeper and higher to potentially ultimate spiritual attainments. I have not seen such a clear and uncluttered but comprehensive approach, so available to the western trained mind, in any other single text I have read over many years. There is a taste of true experience here, and he has my deepest gratitude and admiration for this accomplishment."

RICHARD MENDIUS, MD, NEUROLOGIST

"Wonderfully written, this is a delightful, easy-to-read, and informative guide to training our minds and brains for the personal and common good. If you wanted one guide to happiness and wisdom, this would be it."

PAUL GILBERT, PhD, OBE, AUTHOR OF *THE COMPASSIONATE MIND* AND *LIVING LIKE CRAZY*

"Rick introduces us to our minds as if we were strangers meeting for the first time. With astonishing clarity, he shows us where all the buttons and levers in the brain are. We learn how to focus our own mind, calm it, heal it, and reroute it away from negative roadblocks and dead ends onto the open highway of happiness. He helps us to free ourselves."

RUBY WAX, MA, OBE, AUTHOR OF THE BESTSELLING *HOW TO BE HUMAN: THE MANUAL*

"I love *Neurodharma*. This heartfelt, smart, and wise book illuminates the heart of Buddhist psychology with the latest in affective neuroscience in a very accessible and practical way. It also offers a number of user-friendly guided meditations that will support you to grow in wisdom and compassion."

BOB STAHL, PHD, COAUTHOR OF *A MINDFULNESS-BASED STRESS REDUCTION WORKBOOK (1ST AND 2ND ED.), LIVING WITH YOUR HEART WIDE OPEN, CALMING THE RUSH OF PANIC, A MINDFULNESS-BASED STRESS REDUCTION WORKBOOK FOR ANXIETY,* AND *MBSR EVERYDAY*

"Marrying science with spiritual practices, bestselling author Rick Hanson shares seven principles to awaken, enlighten, and discover true happiness. . . . While meditation, mindfulness, and other spiritual practices, including those in his *Neurodharma*, are truly transformational, the goal is to move from passing states of peace and calm into lasting change in our everyday, waking life."

ELEVATED EXISTENCE

"The book has a nice structure, presenting both science and classical spiritual approaches to awakening. [Hanson]'s set the book up to feel like a retreat, presenting concepts in chunks and following them up with guided meditations. . . . The more we learn about how our brains work, Hanson shares, the more assuredly we can travel up the path toward the mountain of enlightenment."

SPIRITUALITY & HEALTH

"This highly accessible primer on the neuroscience of Buddhist psychology and meditation will appeal to novice and expert meditators alike."

PUBLISHERS WEEKLY

NEURODHARMA

New Science, Ancient Wisdom, and
Seven Practices of the Highest Happiness

RICK HANSON, PhD

HARMONY
BOOKS
New York

Published in the United States by Harmony Books, an imprint of Random House, a division of Penguin Random House LLC, New York.
harmonybooks.com

Harmony Books is a registered trademark, and the Circle colophon is a trademark of Penguin Random House LLC.

Originally published in hardcover in the United States by Harmony Books, an imprint of Random House, a division of Penguin Random House LLC, New York, in 2020.

Library of Congress Cataloging-in-Publication Data is available at
https://lccn .lac.gov /2019050403

ISBN: 978-0-593-13548-8
Ebook ISBN: 978-0-593-13547-1

Printed in the United States of America

Book design by Meighan Cavanaugh
Cover design by Pete Garceau
Cover art by Leyn/Getty Images

4 6 8 10 9 7 5 3

First Trade Paperback Edition

For my teachers

Train yourself in doing good that lasts and brings happiness.
Cultivate generosity, the life of peace,
and a mind of boundless love.

ITIVUTTAKA I.22

CONTENTS

--- · ---

Part One

EMBODIED PRACTICE

1

MIND IN LIFE

If, by giving up a lesser happiness,
one could experience a greater happiness,
a wise person would renounce the lesser,
to behold the greater.

DHAMMAPADA 290

've hiked a lot in the mountains, and sometimes a friend farther up the trail has turned and looked back and encouraged me onward. Such a friendly gesture: *Come join me ... watch out for the slippery ice ... you can do it!* I've often thought about those moments while writing this book, which is about the heights of human potential: about being as wise and strong, happy and loving, as any person can ever be. If those heights are like a great mountain, *awakening* is the magnificent journey that carries you along toward the top. Many real people have gone very far up—the great sages and teachers throughout history as well as others no one has heard about—and I imagine them turning with a sweet smile and beckoning us to join them.

Those who have climbed this mountain come from different cultures and have different personalities, but they all seem alike to me in seven ways. They are mindful; they are kind; they live with contentment and emotional balance through even the hardest times; they are whole and authentic; they are present here and now; they speak of feeling connected with everything; and a light shines through them that does not seem entirely their own.

You might have your own examples of inspiring people you've heard about, or whose words you've read or listened to, or perhaps even met. These individuals are models to us of what is possible. I've known some of them myself. They are down-to-earth, humorous, realistic, and supportive—not the cartoonlike stereotype of exotic characters in caves making cryptic pronouncements. They have no interest in celebrity. Some have taken a spiritual approach, while others have been secular. Their realization is genuine, and it's the result of the *path* they've traveled, not some unique transformation that's unattainable for the rest of us. Through their own example, they demonstrate that wonderful ways of being lie ahead, that accessible paths lead onward, and that much as their own efforts were fruitful, ours can be, too.

And remarkably, you can see some of their qualities already deep down inside yourself, even if they're sometimes covered over by stresses and distractions. These ways of being are not reserved for the few. They are opportunities for all of us—and we'll be exploring how to develop them in these seven practices of awakening:

- steadying the mind
- warming the heart
- resting in fullness
- being wholeness
- receiving nowness
- opening into allness
- finding timelessness

There are many traditions, which are like many routes up the mountain of awakening. Nonetheless, on each of these routes, we find the same steps taken again and again: steps of steadiness, lovingness, fullness, wholeness, nowness, allness, and timelessness. This is some of the most profound and perhaps sacred territory there is. It is ultimately beyond science and logic, so words about it can be loose, metaphorical, and poetic.

The complete development of these seven ways of being marks the pinnacle of human possibility, which could be called enlightenment or full awakening. Meanwhile, even the first simple sense of them is very useful in everyday life. For instance, while dealing with stressful challenges, it's so good to rest in the fullness of feeling *already* peaceful, happy, and loved. And whether it is for the beginning of the path or its end, today we have an unprecedented opportunity to explore a kind of reverse engineering of awakening that is grounded in the living body.

Aiming High

Neuroscience is a young science. Still, we can study the examples of those who have gone far up the mountain and ask: How do you *do* that? What must be happening in your body so that you stay centered when things are falling apart around you? What changes in your brain help you be compassionate and strong when others are hurtful or threatening? What is the underlying neural basis for engaging life without any sense of craving, without any sense of greed, hatred, or delusion?

There aren't yet neurologically definitive answers to these questions. We don't know everything. But we do know more than nothing, and emerging science can highlight and explain plausibly beneficial practices. And when the science is unclear, we can still use reasonable ideas and methods from modern psychology and the contemplative traditions.

One of the things I find most inspiring about the great teachers throughout history is their invitation for full awakening. The routes they've charted travel from the dusty plains into the foothills and mountains and then highest peaks of enlightenment. Even in the early stages, you can find real benefits for everyday well-being and effectiveness. I'm writing for people like me, "householders" (not monastics) who have limited time for formal practice and need tools they can use right now. While I've been meditating since 1974 and long for the heights, numerous people have gone farther up than I, and you'll see some of them quoted here. My focus is more on the process of practice than on the eventual destination, with the hope that you will find this useful on your own path. Still, the ultimate possibility is the complete liberation of mind and heart, with the highest happiness and most sublime peace.

As we move up the trail, it steepens and the air gets thinner. So it helps to have a guidebook. For this, sometimes I'll turn to the penetrating analysis of the mind offered by the Buddha. My own background is in the Theravadan tradition, which is practiced widely in Southeast Asia and increasingly in the West; it is sometimes called insight- or *vipassana*-oriented practice. This tradition is grounded in the earliest record of the Buddha's teachings, the Pali Canon (Pali is an ancient language related to Sanskrit). I also have deep respect for and much interest in how Buddhism has evolved in its Tibetan, Chinese, Zen, and Pure Land streams.

I'm not trying to present Buddhism as a whole, which is a rich and complex tradition that's evolved over many years. Rather, I'm adapting and applying key ideas and methods for our practical purposes here. For these and for everything else in this book, I think the Buddha himself had some lovely advice: *Come and see for yourself* what rings true and is useful over time.

A Neurodharma Perspective

The Buddha didn't use an MRI to become enlightened. Many other people have also gone far along their own paths of awakening without advanced technologies. Still, 2,500 years after he walked the dusty roads of northern India, scientists have discovered many things about the body and the brain. The Buddha and others have explored the *mental* factors of suffering and happiness. During the past couple of decades, we've learned a lot about the *neural* basis of these mental factors. To ignore this emerging understanding seems antithetical both to science and to Buddhism.

> The dharma—understanding, peering into the nature of reality—is not specific to Buddhism. The dharma is truth. And the only choice we really have is whether to try to be in relationship with the truth or to live in ignorance.
>
> REV. ANGEL KYODO WILLIAMS

When I use the word *dharma*, I simply mean the truth of things. This is both the way things actually are and accurate descriptions of them. Whatever the truth is, it is not the property of any tradition; it's for everyone. *Neurodharma* is the term I use for the truth of the mind grounded in the truth of the body, particularly its nervous system. Neurodharma is of course not Buddhism as a whole. Nor is it necessary for Buddhist (or any other) practice. I just think it can be helpful. We will use this approach to:

- explore seven ways of being that are the essence of awakening
- learn about their basis in your own brain
- use this understanding to strengthen them in yourself.

Even a little knowledge about your brain can be very useful. It's a goofy metaphor, but I imagine driving a car and suddenly seeing clouds of steam coming out of the front with red lights flashing on the dashboard and needing to pull over and stop. If I don't know anything about what the car is made of and how it works, I'm pretty stuck. But if I know about the radiator and the type of fluid it needs to keep the engine cool, then there are things I can do to get back on the road and prevent this in the future. The car is like the body. Thousands of years ago, no one knew much about it. But today we can draw on the knowledge we've gained over the centuries about our neural "engine."

For starters, this knowledge is motivating: when you know that your practices are actually changing your brain, you're more likely to keep doing them. Really taking your body into account can also draw you into a sense of thankfulness for the physical processes that have led to this moment of consciousness. Understanding what is happening in your brain while experiences are moving through your mind sharpens your mindfulness and fosters insight. You can lighten up about the passing show of consciousness when you recognize that it's being made by many tiny, swift cellular and molecular processes...without any sort of master engineer hiding in the background and continually flipping all the right switches.

In its basic design, we've all got the same brain. A neurodharma perspective offers a common framework for understanding the ideas and tools in clinical psychology, personal development (a broad term for other secular approaches), and the wisdom traditions. It can help us prioritize and use key tools we already have. For example, research on the brain's evolved *negativity bias*—which we'll learn more about in chapter 3—highlights the importance of emotionally positive experiences such as gladness and kindness. A greater understanding of the neural "hardware" can even suggest new approaches to our mental "software," such as neurofeedback. It also helps to individualize practice. When you consider your temperament—perhaps distractible, perhaps anxious—as a perfectly normal variation on the human brain, it's easier to be self-accepting and to find the practices that are most suited to you.

This approach invites us to work backward from important experiences such as feeling happy and content and explore their basis in the brain. We can know ourselves both subjectively and objectively—from the inside out and from the outside in—and neurodharma is where these two meet. At the same time we can respect what we don't know and avoid merely intellectual practice. I try to remember the Buddha's advice to steer clear of the "thicket of views" about theoretical matters, and to focus instead on the practical *how* of ending suffering and finding true happiness here and now.

A Path That Progresses

The seven themes of this book—steadiness of mind, warmth of heart, and so forth—have been explored in many ways by many people in many traditions. They involve experiencing what is out in the open and not hidden: we can be more mindful and loving, we can afford to crave less, we are innately whole, this moment is the only moment there is, and each person exists interdependently with everything else.

These ways of being are accessible to all of us, and their essence is available without years of rigorous training. I'll offer suggestions for how you can have a greater sense of them in everyday life as well as guided meditations that will go deeply into these experiences. You can also weave them into activities you're already doing, such as going for a walk. You don't need a background in science or meditation to develop a greater sense of contentment or kindness, or the other ways of being we'll be exploring. Even ten minutes a day, spread out here and there, can make a difference—if you do the practice, day after day. As with anything, the more you put into it, the more you will get out of it. What gives me both trust and hope is that this is a *path* we can walk step after step through our own efforts, not a magical quick fix.

Unless you're already living on top of the mountain of awakening—and I'm not there myself—there remains something to do. How should we do it?

GOING WHILE BEING

There are two approaches to this question. One emphasizes a *gradual* process that includes reducing unhappiness and growing compassion, insight, and equanimity. The other focuses on recognizing an *innate* perfection in which there is nothing to gain. Both of these approaches are valid, and they support each other. We need to heal and grow, and we can stay in touch with our deep true nature along the way.

In the mind, it takes a while to uncover who we already are. There is a saying: "Gradual cultivation...sudden awakening...gradual cultivation...sudden awakening..." As Milarepa, the Tibetan sage, described his life of practice: *In the beginning nothing came, in the middle nothing stayed, and in the end nothing left.* Meanwhile, a sense of your innate wakefulness and goodness is inspiring and encouraging, and it helps you keep going when things are boring or hard.

> On the long, rough road,
> the sun and the moon
> will continue to shine.
>
> THICH NHAT HANH

In the brain, trauma and ordinary neurotic crud are embedded in neural circuitry, which takes time to alter. Developing happiness, emotional intelligence, and a loving heart also requires gradual physical changes. At the same time, when you are not rattled or distressed, your brain settles into its innate resting state. Then it recovers from bursts of activity and releases neurochemicals, such as serotonin and oxytocin, that support a positive mood and kindness toward others. This is our neuropsychological home base: to be calm, contented, and caring. No matter how disturbed by stress and sorrow, we can always come home.

LETTING BE, LETTING GO, LETTING IN

Developing a greater sense of fullness, wholeness, and other aspects of awakening involves three kinds of practice. First, you can simply *be with* whatever you're experiencing: accepting it, feeling it, perhaps exploring it. As you be with it, your experience may change, but you're not trying to nudge it one way or another. Second, you can *release* what is painful or harmful, such as by easing tension in the body, venting feelings, challenging thoughts that aren't true or helpful, or disengaging from desires that hurt you or others. Third, you can *grow* what is enjoyable or useful: developing virtues and skills, becoming more resilient, grateful, and compassionate. In a nutshell: *let be, let go, let in.* If your mind is like a garden, you can observe it, pull weeds, and plant flowers.

Of these, letting be is most essential. It's where we start, and sometimes it's all we can do: just ride out the storm of fear or anger without making things worse. And as practice matures, increasingly we simply be with the next moment as it arises and passes away and becomes something else. But this is not the whole of practice. We can't only be with the mind, we must work with it as well. For example, most of the Eightfold Path in Buddhism involves letting go and letting in, such as releasing "unwise" speech and replacing it with wise speech. While there are pitfalls in working with the mind, such as getting caught up in "fixing" oneself, there are also pitfalls in *not* working with the mind. For instance, I've known people who are good at observing their own minds . . . and also chronically unhappy as well as unskillful with others. We shouldn't work with the mind in order to avoid being with it, nor be with the mind to avoid working with it.

Letting be, letting go, and letting in form a natural sequence. Perhaps you recognize that you've gotten resentful about something, and you explore this experience and let it be as it is. At some point it feels natural to shift into deliberately letting go, and you relax your body, help feelings flow, and step back from troublesome thoughts. Then, in the space made by what you've cleared away, you can let in what could be beneficial, such as self-compassion. Over time, the strengths you develop inside yourself will help you let be and let go even more fully. And to explore this further, you might like to try the meditation in the box, which also contains suggestions for doing experiential practices in general.

LET BE, LET GO, LET IN

In this meditation and in the other practices in this book, I'll offer different ways to relate to your experiences and to have ones that could be beneficial. Not all of my suggestions will click for you, and please find approaches that do work for you. For example, you might like to move your body to evoke a particular feeling, or to focus on certain images, or to use words that are different from mine. What's important are the *experiences* we're having, not the methods we use to find our way into them. If it's challenging to have an actual sense of something—such as the feeling of letting go—that is

(continued)

very normal. I've had these challenges myself. If you feel frustrated or self-critical, this is normal, too. You can simply acknowledge it to yourself—such as "frustrated with this" or "being self-critical"—and then return to whatever you are practicing.

If it is hard to get in touch with something, just make a note of it and, if you like, come back to it later. It takes time and repetition to experience the ways of being that we'll be exploring—especially their depths. It really is like climbing a mountain. It's slow at times because it's steep! Not because you're doing it "wrong" or because you can't keep making your way up. Please go at your own pace and, as a teacher told me many years ago, keep going.

You could do the practice below as a kind of meditation. You can also do it informally, in the flow of life, when something— I'll call it the "issue"—is stressful or upsetting. Adapt it to your needs, and take as much time as you like.

LET BE

Find something simple that helps you stay present, such as the feeling of breathing. Take some moments to feel increasingly centered. Let sounds and sensations, thoughts and feelings, pass through awareness. Know what it's like to be with experiences without resisting or holding on to them.

When you're ready, focus on the issue, especially your experiences related to it. Be aware of thoughts you have about it . . . emotions related to it . . . perhaps naming them softly to yourself, such as "tightening . . . worry . . . irritation . . . softening . . ." Accept these thoughts and feelings, letting them flow, letting them be . . .

Whether it's pleasant or painful, try to accept your experience as it is. If something is overwhelming, focus on breathing or anything else that is calming and soothing . . . You are still here, you are okay . . .

Be aware of body sensations related to the issue . . . wishes and wants and plans related to it . . . Letting them be, letting them flow . . .

You can explore deeper layers, such as hurt or fear beneath anger . . . younger parts of yourself . . . Feeling it all . . . letting it all be . . .

LET GO

When it feels right, shift into releasing. Be aware of any tension in your body related to the issue, and let it ease and soften and relax. Let feelings flow . . . perhaps imagining them leaving you like a little cloud each time you exhale . . . Recognize any inaccurate, exaggerated, or limiting thoughts, and disengage from them . . . letting go . . .

Be aware of desires related to the issue, such as unrealistic goals or understandable longings that are just not going to be fulfilled . . . and breath after breath, let these go . . . You can also let go of unhelpful ways of speaking or acting . . . Breath after breath, let it go . . . let it all go . . .

LET IN

Then focus on what could be useful, wise, or enjoyable. Perhaps there is a sense of comfort or reassurance that would feel good to open to . . . or gratitude, love, or self-

(continued)

compassion ... taking it in as you inhale ... receiving
whatever is good into yourself ...

Perhaps there is a spaciousness in your mind, like the sky
after a storm passes ... There could be an easing in your
body ... Stay with these experiences ... giving yourself over
to them ...

You might invite a sense of strength or determination ...
You could identify thoughts or perspectives about the issue
that are true and helpful ... and open to any intuitions or the
voice of inner wisdom ... There could be a growing clarity
about how you'd like to act in the days ahead ...

Let whatever is helpful sink in ... all these good things
establishing themselves in you ... Let them spread inside
you ... all these good things sinking into you ...

How to Use This Book

This book is about cultivating seven ways of being that are the essence of awakening. We develop them by *practicing* them: repeatedly experiencing them, from a taste all the way to a full immersion. They're not esoteric or out of reach. They are grounded in your body, and they are the birthright of each one of us.

> Allow the teachings to enter you as you might
> listen to music, or in the way the earth
> allows the rain to permeate it.
>
> THICH NHAT HANH

This chapter and the next one provide a foundation of information about your brain and how to approach practice in general. Then we'll explore the first three ways of being—steadiness, lovingness, and fullness—which form a natural cluster. These are fundamental aspects of awakening, and vital to engage even if they already seem familiar to you. For example, resting in fullness is about developing a bone-deep sense of peacefulness, contentment, and love—no small thing in itself—which also reduces the "craving," broadly defined, that causes so much suffering and harm for ourselves and others.

The next three ways of being—wholeness, nowness, and allness—group together as well. These emphasize insights into the deep nature of all our experiences—which, amazingly, is also the deep nature of every atom in the universe. These insights usually begin conceptually, and that's all right; many deep teachings involve a penetrating understanding of the mind. If you encounter an idea that doesn't seem clear, pause to consider how it could apply in your own experience. Chewing on these ideas will gradually make them a part of you. And if a later topic such as allness seems too abstract, just go back to previous chapters to find your footing again.

The last way of being—timelessness—is an exploration of what could be _unconditioned_, distinct from phenomena such as events and emotions that are "conditioned" by their causes. For example, a rainstorm occurs due to conditions in the atmosphere, and a storm of anger happens because of conditions in the mind. This is a big topic, and we can approach it in three ways. First, it could be about gradually "unconditioning" our habitual—and painful and harmful—reactions to things. Second, it could be about entering into an extraordinary state of mind within ordinary reality, in which the usual conditioned constructions of experiences seem to cease. Third, it could be about something that is truly transcendental, beyond conditioned ordinary reality. The chapter on finding timelessness includes all three approaches. This is the deepest practice of all, and you are welcome to engage it in any way you like.

Each of these subjects could be a book of its own. I've focused on what I think are key aspects for personal practice, particularly those for which there's relevant neuroscience, and placed many comments and citations in the reference notes. There's a vast literature about these topics that's full of strong opinions, including about the proper translations of important words. In these chapters you'll see the path I've taken, and you can find other approaches in the notes.

I'm writing from the limited perspective of a middle-aged, middle-class, white American man, and there are many other ways to talk about and practice with this material. I have inevitably left out important approaches to practice, but this does not mean I don't value them. If you recognize points I've written about elsewhere, just skim them or take a fresh look. The first time a key term is used, it's italicized. When you see a non-English word as the source for a quotation—such as Dhammapada or Itivuttaka—it is from the Pali Canon. The chapters conclude with a section called Good Practice, which offers additional suggestions for everyday life; the exception is the last chapter, which is all about applying what you've explored in the days to come.

This book is structured like a retreat, with both presentations of ideas and guided meditations. The ideas are important because they help us understand ourselves better, bringing insights that free us from needless suffering and conflict. This understanding is about deep matters, so it can take time and effort. I first heard many of these teachings more than forty years ago, and they still perplex and fascinate me. I'm still chewing on them.

The meditations are very important, too, and I encourage you to do them. You could read them slowly and take time to get a feeling for them. Or record them in your own voice for yourself, or perhaps listen to me in the audio version of this book. In later meditations, I usually won't repeat basic instructions given in the earlier ones; if you have any difficulty, just look back at the first chapters. The more often you have a beneficial experience and the longer and deeper these experiences are, the more you'll build up the neural substrates of happiness, love, and inner strength.

FURTHER READING

Buddha's Brain (Rick Hanson with Richard Mendius)

The Hidden Lamp (Florence Caplow and Susan Moon, eds.)

Mind in Life (Evan Thompson)

Realizing Awakened Consciousness (Richard P. Boyle)

Reflections on a Mountain Lake (Ani Tenzin Palmo)

As you practice, sometimes you'll be trying to get something going in your own mind—such as a stability of attention—while observing what actually happens. It's normal to struggle occasionally; this is why we must practice. I've seen teachers underestimate their students, and I don't want to do that. I have taken many friends up into the mountains, and the essence is similar: *Check it out, where we're going is pretty amazing... here is our route, it's a good one ... we've got to climb it ourselves, we better get moving.* Our pace is going to be brisk, but these paths have been walked by many others before you, and you can have confidence that you can walk them yourself. I've been walking them, too—and sometimes falling off!—and I'll share my own bumps and lessons. Occasionally you'll want to slow down and catch your breath, to ponder and reflect and let the view sink in. This is how it's been for me, for sure. That the path is steep in places is part of what tells you it will bring you to wonderful heights.

Along the way, take care of yourself. When you open to the immediacy of this moment of experience, sometimes painful thoughts and feelings can arise. As your practice deepens and the edges soften between you and all things, you might feel disoriented. The more intense and far-reaching the territory you're exploring, the more important it is to be grounded and resourced internally. It's fine to slow down, step back, and focus on whatever feels stable, comforting, and nurturing. Some people are disturbed or distressed by psychological practices such as mindfulness, especially if there are underlying issues with depression, trauma, dissociation, or psychotic processes. Mindfulness, meditation, and the other practices in this book are not appropriate for everyone, not a treatment for any disorder, and not a substitute for professional care.

There is a process here, and you can take your time with it. Let it work on you in natural ways . . . let it work *with* you, and lift you and carry you along. Awakening proceeds with its own rhythms: sometimes slow growth, sometimes a plateau, sometimes sliding downhill, sometimes a breakthrough. And all the while there is the deep true nature of each one of us, whether it is gradually uncovered or suddenly revealed: aware, wise, loving, and pure. This is your true home, and you can trust it.

Good Practice

Here are some suggestions for bringing the ideas and methods in this chapter into your daily life. (I mean "good practice" generally—not as one single good practice.) These are not the only ways to explore this material, and you are welcome to add other practices of your own. In particular, please consider how you could add some of what I have not included myself, such as physical activities, spiritual or religious practices, teachings and tools from indigenous people around the world, making art, spending time in wilderness, music, and service.

Try to approach each day as an opportunity for *practice*. It's a chance to learn about yourself, manage your reactions, heal and grow. When you first wake up, you could establish the intention to practice that day. Then, as you go to sleep, you could appreciate how you practiced that day.

Bring to mind someone you respect. Perhaps it's someone you know personally, or whose words you've heard or read. Pick something that you find admirable about this person. Then see if you can get some sense of this quality already present in *yourself*. It might feel subtle, but it's real and you can develop it. For a day or longer, focus on bringing this quality into your experience and actions, and see how this feels. And then try this practice using other people you respect and other qualities you'd like to develop.

Every so often, slow down to recognize that life in general, and your body and brain in particular, are making this moment's experience of hearing and seeing, thinking and feeling. Wow!

When you want, just be with your experiences for a minute or more, without trying to change them in any way. This is the fundamental practice: accepting sensations and feelings and thoughts as they are, adding as little as possible to them, and letting them flow as they will. Overall, a growing sense of simply letting be can fill your day.

2

THE ENCHANTED LOOM

Think not lightly of good, saying, "It will not come to me."
Drop by drop is the water pot filled.
Likewise, the wise one, gathering it little by little,
fills oneself with good.

DHAMMAPADA 122

Two golden squirrels live in the trees outside my home, and I like watching them chase each other through the branches. They can't tell us how they feel, yet they're clearly hearing and seeing. A baby squirrel will recognize the smell of her mother, and later on she will fiercely protect her own children. In their squirrelish ways, these beautiful creatures have many experiences much like our own. And not surprisingly, the neural hardware that enables our human versions of hearing and seeing, learning and wanting, is present in similar forms in the inchlong brain of a squirrel.

Our own brain is much larger and more complex. It contains about 85 billion neurons, and they are connected together in a network with several hundred trillion nodes. Still, whether one is a squirrel or a human looking out a window, the experiences we are having depend upon what the brain is doing. A typical neuron fires many times a second, releasing neurochemicals into tiny junctions called synapses, several thousand of which could fit in the width of a single hair. As you read these words, millions of neurons inside your head are pulsing in rhythm together, producing waves of electrical activity. As the neuroscientist Charles Sherrington put it, the tapestry of our experiences is being woven by an enchanted loom. Some of the time we may be mindful of the body; all of the time we are body-full of mind.

Suffering and Happiness

What is in this mind, and what can we do about it? I grew up in a loving family in an American suburb; compared with many, I was very fortunate. Yet most of my memories as a child include a sense of much unnecessary unhappiness around me, in both the grown-ups and the kids. Nothing terrible, but a lot of tension, bickering, worry, and strain. As I grew older, left home, caught the wave of the human potential movement in the 1970s, and eventually became a psychologist, I learned that what had seemed like my own private unhappiness was in fact very common. It takes different forms, from the intense pain of trauma to a subtle feeling of unfulfillment. And between these extremes lie considerable anxiety, hurt, sorrow, frustration, and anger.

In a word, there is suffering, named by the Buddha as the First Noble Truth of human existence. This is not the whole of life. There are also love and joy, laughing with friends, and the comfort of a warm sweater on a cold day. Yet each of us must face the truth of suffering some of the time, and many of us face it all of the time.

Poignantly, much of our suffering is *added* to life. We add it when we worry needlessly, criticize ourselves to no good purpose, or replay the same conversation over and over again. We add it when we freeze up around an authority figure or feel ashamed of some minor fault. Life has unavoidable physical and emotional pains, and then we add suffering to them: thus the saying "Pain is inevitable, suffering is optional." For example, we get embarrassed about having an illness or drink too much to numb old wounds.

This add-on suffering is not accidental. It has a source: "craving," the sense of something missing, something wrong, something we must get. Most craving does not look like an addict searching for a fix. It includes getting attached to our own point of view, driving toward goals that are not worth the price, and holding on to grievances with others. It is chasing pleasure, pushing away pain, and clinging to relationships. This is the Buddha's Second Noble Truth—but happily we're not stuck there. Because we are the ones who make much of our own suffering, we are also the ones who can make it come to an end. This hopeful possibility is the Third Noble Truth, and the Fourth Noble Truth describes a path of practice that fulfills this promise.

These four truths begin with a clear-eyed look at the realities of life, whether in rural India thousands of years ago or in high-tech cities today. I grew up in Los Angeles, and in its entertainment culture and then later in parts of the self-help world, so I've seen a fair amount of happy-smiley pretense, fake it till you make it. But we need to be honest enough and strong enough to see the truth of our experience, the whole truth, including the discontent, loneliness, and unease, and the unfulfilled longings for a reliable, deep well-being. I once asked the teacher Gil Fronsdal what he did in his own practice. He paused and then smiled and said, "I stop for suffering."

This is where practice begins: facing suffering in ourselves and others.

But it's not where practice ends. The Buddha himself was described as "the happy one." As we'll see, wholesome, enjoyable experiences such as kindness are skillful means for both ordinary functioning and full awakening. When suffering falls away, what is revealed is not a big blank but a natural sense of gratitude, good wishes for others, freedom, and ease. The people I've known who are clearly far along are straightforward and fearless, endlessly patient, and openhearted. Whether their words are humorous or serious, soft or fiery, you sense behind them an undisturbable stillness. They stay engaged with the world and try to make it better while also feeling at peace in the core of their being.

The Natural Mind

How did they get this way? More to the point, how can *we* get this way? Let's look into our bodies for some answers.

The human body is the result of several billion years of biological evolution. About 650 million years ago, multicelled creatures began to appear in the primordial seas. By 600 million years ago, these early animals had become complicated enough that their sensory systems and motor systems needed to communicate quickly with one another: "Could be food . . . swim forward." So a nervous system began to evolve. Whether in an ancient jellyfish or in us today, the nervous system is designed to process *information*.

The "mind," as I mean it in this book, consists of the experiences and information that are represented by a nervous system. This might seem puzzling at first, but we are surrounded by examples of information being represented by something physical, such as the meanings of the squiggly shapes your eyes are scanning right now (or the meanings of sounds if you're listening to this book). As the Nobel Prize winner Eric Kandel put it:

> Brain cells have particular ways of processing information and communicating with one another....
>
> ...Electrical signaling represents the language of mind, the means whereby nerve cells...communicate with one another....
>
> ...All animals have some form of mental life that reflects the architecture of their nervous system.

When you are smelling coffee or remembering where you put your keys, your whole body is involved with making these experiences. At the same time, it is connected with the wider world. Still, the most immediate physical basis for our thoughts and feelings is the nervous system—particularly its headquarters, the brain.

Exactly how this happens—how patterns of light falling on a retina become patterns of neural activity representing patterns of information that become the sight of a friend's face—is still an open question. Nonetheless, thousands of studies on humans and other animals have established tight linkages between what we are feeling and what the brain is doing. In terms of the *natural* processes in ordinary reality, all of our experiences depend upon neural activity.

Every sensation, every thought and desire, and every moment of awareness is being shaped by three pounds of tofu-like tissue inside your head. The stream of consciousness involves a stream of information in a stream of neural activity. The mind is a natural phenomenon that is grounded in life. Major causes of both suffering and its end are rooted in your own body.

Mind Changing Brain Changing Mind

Scientists have been finding connections between helpful, even transformational experiences and underlying neural activity—and we can use these links between mind and body in practical ways. For example, in later chapters, I'll explain how you can activate neural factors of present-moment awareness, calm strength, and compassion. Over time, these useful mental *states* can be gradually hard-wired into your nervous system as positive *traits*.

This process of physical change occurs because all of our experiences involve patterns of neural activity. And patterns of neural activity—especially when repeated—can leave lasting physical traces behind. This is *neuroplasticity*, the capacity of the nervous system to be changed by the information flowing through it. (For major mechanisms of this process, please see the box that begins on the following page.) In a saying from the work of the psychologist Donald Hebb, *neurons that fire together wire together.* This means that you can use your mind to change your brain to change your mind for the better.

MECHANISMS OF NEUROPLASTICITY

It's long been recognized that any kind of learning—whether a child starting to walk or an adult becoming more patient—must involve changes in the brain. Neuroplasticity is not breaking news. But what *has* been revelatory is the recent discovery of how rapid, extensive, and enduring this neural remodeling is. These are the main ways it happens:

- sensitizing (or desensitizing) existing synaptic connections between neurons
- increasing (or decreasing) the excitability of individual neurons
- altering the expression of genes in the nuclei of neurons (*epigenetic* effects)
- making new connections between neurons
- birthing new neurons (*neurogenesis*) and weaving them into existing networks
- increasing (or decreasing) activity in specific regions
- reshaping particular neural networks
- changing the *glial cells* in the brain that support neural networks
- changing ebbs and flows of neurochemicals such as serotonin
- increasing *neurotrophic* factors that help neurons survive, grow, and connect with one another
- rapid changes in the *hippocampus* and *parietal* cortex in the first stages of new learning

(continued)

- "replay events" in the hippocampus that reinforce initial encoding
- transferring information from the hippocampus to long-term storage in the *cortex*
- increasing the coordination of the hippocampus and cortex
- general "systems-level" *consolidation* of learning in the cortex
- consolidation during slow-wave and rapid eye movement (REM) sleep

Recognizing that your mind is grounded in life—that it has an underlying biological basis—does not mean seeing yourself or anyone else as some kind of clockwork robot. Yes, the mind must be represented by a tangible nervous system—but it does not *reduce* to just those cells and gooey electrochemical processes. Your mind is more than the meat that makes it.

Imagine a conversation today with a friend about a funny event with her dog. As you talk, flows of information that have a logic of their own cascade through your nervous system, enlisting underlying neural activities for their representation. Suppose you speak again tomorrow about the same event: any information that is the same as today's will be represented by a different pattern of neural activity. Even a concept as simple as 2 + 2 = 4 will be known tomorrow via different neurons than it is known today. This means that many of our experiences proceed in ways that are *causally* independent of the underlying physical substrates that represent them. The mind has causal power of its own.

Mental activity and neural activity thus affect each other. Causes flow both ways, from the mind into the brain . . . and from the brain into the mind. The mind and brain are two distinct aspects of a single, integrated system. As the interpersonal neurobiologist Dan Siegel summarizes it, the mind uses the brain to make the mind.

FURTHER READING

After Buddhism (Stephen Batchelor)

The First Free Women (Matty Weingast)

In Search of Memory (Eric Kandel)

A Path with Heart (Jack Kornfield)

Saltwater Buddha: A Surfer's Quest to Find Zen on the Sea (Jaimal Yogis)

Train Your Mind, Change Your Brain (Sharon Begley)

Changing the Brain with Meditation

Let's consider the brain-changing effects of mindfulness and meditation. After just three days of training, *prefrontal* regions behind the forehead exert more top-down control over the *posterior* (rearward) *cingulate cortex* (PCC). This matters because the PCC is a key part of the *default mode network* that is active when we're lost in thought or caught up in "self-referential processing" (for example, Why'd they look at me that way? What's wrong with me? What should I say next time?). Consequently, greater control over the PCC means less habitual mind wandering and less preoccupation with oneself.

People in longer trainings that span a couple of months, such as Mindfulness-Based Stress Reduction (MBSR), develop greater top-down control over the *amygdala*. This almond-shaped region is close to the center of your brain, and it's continually monitoring your experiences for their relevance to you. The amygdala reacts like an alarm bell to anything that's painful or threatening—from an angry face to bad news on a medical test—and triggers the neural/hormonal stress response, so getting more control over it reduces overreactions. People in these trainings also grow more tissue in their hippocampus, a nearby part of the brain shaped like a little seahorse that helps us learn from our experiences. Activity in the hippocampus can calm down the amygdala, so it's not surprising that after a mindfulness training, people produce less of the stress hormone *cortisol* when they're challenged. They've become more resilient.

More experienced mindfulness meditators, typically with years of daily practice, have thicker layers of neural tissue in their prefrontal cortex, which supports their *executive functions*, such as planning and self-control. They also have more tissue in their *insula*, which is involved with self-awareness and empathy for the feelings of others. Their *anterior* (frontal) *cingulate cortex* is also strengthened. This is an important part of your brain that helps you pay attention and stay on track with your goals. And their *corpus callosum*—which connects the right and left hemispheres of the brain—also adds tissue, suggesting a greater integration of words and images, logic and intuition.

And then there are meditators with thousands of hours of lifetime practice. For example, experienced practitioners of Tibetan Buddhism—some who have already meditated for more than twenty thousand hours—demonstrate a remarkable calm before receiving a pain they know is coming, and unusually rapid recovery afterward. They also possess extraordinarily high levels of gamma-range brainwave activity: the rapid, 25- to 100-times-a-second synchronization of large areas of cortical real estate associated with enhanced learning. Overall, there's a gradual shift from deliberate self-regulation toward an increasingly natural sense of presence and ease during both meditation and daily life.

Scientists have also studied the brains of people who do Transcendental Meditation, Christian and Islamic prayer, compassion and kindness meditations, and other practices. As with any emerging field, this research will improve over time. Still, the results of many studies offer great hope. Even fairly brief practice could change areas of your brain involved with attention, body awareness, emotional regulation, and sense of self. Sustained long-term practice can alter the brain markedly. These changes of brain foster changes of mind, bringing greater resilience and well-being.

These findings about mindfulness and meditation are echoed in research on other kinds of mental training. Formal interventions such as psychotherapy and resilience programs can also change the brain in lasting ways, and so can informal practices of gratitude, relaxation, kindness, and positive emotion. There's a saying that your mind takes its shape from what it rests upon. Well, recent science makes it clear that your brain takes *its* shape from what you rest your attention on. Through having a sense, again and again, of steadiness, lovingness, fullness, wholeness, nowness, allness, and timelessness, you'll be weaving these qualities into your own nervous system.

SOME FAVORITE ONLINE RESOURCES

Access to Insight: Readings in Theravada Buddhism:
https://www.accesstoinsight.org/

Deconstructing Yourself:
https://deconstructingyourself.com/

Dharma Seed: https://www.dharmaseed.org/

Pariyatti: https://pariyatti.org/

Seven Steps of Awakening

We'll explore these ways of being in depth in the pages to come, but here you can get a sense of each one in a single meditation. For general information about how to approach experiential practices—including taking your time as we explore far-reaching and sometimes subtle subjects—please see page 13 in chapter 1, at the start of the Let Be, Let Go, Let In practice. For this meditation, I suggest you find a comfortable place where you'll be undisturbed and have enough time, at least twenty minutes. If you don't relate to the later steps, you can just come back to previous ones.

THE MEDITATION

Find a posture that is comfortable and alert. Be aware of your body, and let yourself be. As you focus on each theme in this meditation, you can let other things such as sounds or thoughts pass through awareness without pushing them away or following after them.

Steadiness. *Choose an object of attention such as the sensations of breathing or a word such as "peace," and stay aware of it. For example, if it's the breath, apply attention to the beginning of each inhalation and then sustain your attention to its full course, and do the same with each exhalation, breath after breath. Let your body relax ... your heart opening ... feeling more settled, calmer, and steadier ... staying with the object of attention ... Finding a stable sense of presence in the moment ... awareness spacious and open ... letting anything pass through it ... as you rest in a stable centeredness.*

Lovingness. *With an increasingly steadied mind, focus on warmhearted feelings as your object of attention. Be aware of people or pets you care about ... Focus on feelings of compassion and kindness for them ... staying simple, focusing on the feelings themselves ... Be aware of beings who care about you, even if the relationship is imperfect, and focus on feelings of being cared about ... feeling appreciated ... liked ... loved ... If other thoughts and feelings arise, let them come and go as you focus on a simple sense of warmheartedness ... As you breathe, there could be a sense of love flowing in and out through your chest and heart. Steadily warmhearted ... resting in love ... sinking into love as it sinks into you.*

Fullness. *Present with an open heart, focus on the sense of enoughness in the moment as it is ... enough air to breathe ... simply living, even if* *there is also pain or worry... Let yourself feel as safe as you can... safe enough in this moment... letting go of any anxiety... any irritation... finding a growing sense of peace. Also find gratitude for what you've been given... focusing on simple feelings of gladness and other positive emotions... letting go of any disappointment or frustration... any sense of stress or drivenness falling away... resting in a growing sense of contentment... Then touching again some feelings of warmheartedness... lovingness flowing in and out... letting any hurts ease and release, perhaps as you exhale... letting any resentments ease and release... any clinging to others falling away... resting in a growing sense of love... Take a little longer to rest in a general sense of fullness... a sense of peace and contentment and love.*

Wholeness. *Resting at ease in fullness, be aware of the sensations of breathing in the left side of your chest... the right side... and left and right together... being aware of the sensations in your chest as a whole... many sensations as a single experience... Gradually widen awareness of breathing to include your stomach and back... head and hips... arms and legs included... being aware of your whole body as a single field of experience... abiding as a whole body breathing... While remaining aware of the whole body, include sounds in awareness... hearing and breathing together. Then include seeing... feelings... and anything else in awareness... Accepting all that you're experiencing... opening to your whole being... accepting all the parts of yourself... all the parts of you as a single whole... widening further to include awareness... all of you as a whole... abiding undivided.*

Nowness. *As you abide as a whole, stay in the present... the sensations of each moment of breathing continually changing... staying present while letting go... remaining alert, experiences changing, things* *happening... with no need to follow them... no need to figure them out... simply being... now... finding a comfort in the present... a sense of going on being even as there is continual changing... Be aware of the continual arising of the next moment... Be at ease, you're all right... here in the present as it changes... receiving this moment... receiving now... resting at the front edge of now... and now.*

Allness. *Abiding now as a whole... breathing air flowing in and flowing out... inhaling oxygen from green growing things... exhaling carbon dioxide to them... each breath receiving and giving... what you're receiving becoming a part of you, what you're giving becoming part of other things... Letting these knowings become feelings of relatedness... of inter-being... with plants... and animals... and people... and with air and water... and mountains and all of this earth. All this flowing into you and you flowing out into it. Know you are connected with the moon and sun and all of space, all the stars everywhere... that what is happening now in the mind and body is related to everything else... every thought and thing is a wave in the ocean of allness. Let edges soften between you and anything else... feel a sense of the allness of everything... all experiences are passing waves in allness... allness enduring... so peaceful... only allness.*

Timelessness. *Abide... present... opening to intuition of what might be always unconditioned... not yet formed... always just before this moment... As ideas about this appear, let them go... settle back into a wordless sense of what might be not yet conditioned... distinct, fundamentally, from all conditioned mind and matter. An intuition, an intimation, perhaps a sense of possibility... spaciousness... stillness... abiding at the meeting of conditioned and unconditioned... what is conditioned is continually changing, what is unconditioned is not*

arising and passing away, thus eternal and timeless...Let go of
thinking, not trying to make anything happen...for the time being...
time passing in timelessness.

   When it feels right, come into a grounded sense of this moment...in
this body...in this place...perhaps moving your feet and hands...eyes
opening...perhaps breathing more fully. Touch again some feelings of
fullness...warmheartedness...living from them. You are here,
breathing and all right...being at peace.

Good Practice

When something is painful, stressful, or upsetting, try to slow down
to observe your reactions to this suffering. Ask yourself if you are
downplaying or denying the parts of life that are hard for you. See
what happens if you simply name your reactions to yourself, such as,
"This is tiring...that hurts...I'm a little sad...ouch." Along with
this basic acknowledgment, try to have feelings of support and compassion for yourself.

   Be aware of how you might be adding suffering to your day, perhaps rehashing resentments in your mind or getting stressed about
truly little things. It's really useful to be interested in how you make
your own suffering. And when you see yourself doing this, slow
down and see if you can make a deliberate choice to stop fueling and
reinforcing this add-on suffering. Old habits may take a while to
change, but if you make this choice again and again, gradually it will
become a new good habit.

   From time to time, consider how a particular experience could be
changing your brain bit by bit, for better or worse. When you know

this is happening, how might it shift the way you approach different situations?

Explore the seven ways of being—steadiness, lovingness, fullness, wholeness, nowness, allness, and timelessness—and try to get a clear sense of each one. Imagine or feel that they are already natural for you, already part of who you are.

Part Two

AN UNSHAKABLE
CORE

3

STEADYING THE MIND

Going down to a river that is flooded and turbulent,
if you are swept away by the current—
How can you help others across?

SUTTA NIPĀTA 2.8

began to meditate at the tail end of college, sometimes sitting in the hills of Southern California with my long hair and gold-rimmed glasses and bamboo flute. A little silly, perhaps, and still, something real would happen, a calming and quieting, and a sense of an untroubled awareness through which my troubles passed.

Over the next couple of decades, my meditations were inconsistent yet still a refuge when I was stressed. I got married, went to grad school, and became a father. And I eventually found myself in a meditation workshop with the teacher Christina Feldman. She asked us to describe our personal practice, and after we had all spoken, she asked a question that sent a jolt through the room: "But what about *concentration?*"

Concentration Power

Christina was referring to great steadiness of mind. To put this in context, there are three pillars of Buddhist practice: virtue, wisdom—and concentration. Concentration stabilizes attention and brings it to a laser-like focus that fosters liberating insight. In a parable I heard on a meditation retreat, you find yourself in a forest of suffering and see off in the distance a mountain of peaceful happiness. It's a relief to know that you don't need to cut down the whole forest, just carve a path through it. But how to do this? You could use a razor blade, but that would take forever. You could use a heavy stick, but it would bounce off the trees. Or you could make a sharp machete that combines the best of the razor blade and the stick, and with this tool make your way to the mountain. In this metaphor, the sharpness of the razor is insight and the power of the stick is concentration.

Like many others in that workshop, I'd never been taught concentration. But without it, it's easy to get distracted by one thing or another. So my meditations were pleasant and relaxing…but foggy and superficial. Additionally, I was missing out on what the Buddha said was *wise concentration*, which consists of four nonordinary experiences called the *jhanas*:

> Quite secluded from sensual desires, secluded from unwholesome states of mind, a person enters and abides in the first jhana, which is accompanied by applied and sustained attention, with bliss and happiness born of seclusion.
>
> With the stilling of applied and sustained attention, the person enters and abides in the second jhana, which has

inner clarity and one-pointedness of mind without applied and sustained attention, with bliss and happiness born of concentration.

With the fading away of bliss, the person abides in equanimity, and mindful and fully aware, still feeling happiness in the body, enters and abides in the third jhana, on account of which noble ones announce: "A person has a pleasant abiding who has equanimity and is mindful."

With the abandoning of pleasure and pain, and with the previous passing away of elation and distress, the person enters and abides in the fourth jhana, which has neither pain nor pleasure and purity of mindfulness due to equanimity.

As you can see, the jhanas are described in psychological, not mystical, terms. They are unusual experiences to be sure, but they're one of the standard steps on the Eightfold Path. In fact, in the Pali Canon there's a frequently repeated description of a process of awakening that begins with the four "form" jhanas described above. Then the process moves through four *very* nonordinary states—the "formless" jhanas—into the "cessation" of any kind of ordinary consciousness. This enables the awakening of *nibbana*. (I'll use this Pali term rather than the Sanskrit *nirvana*, which has taken on more general associations, such as, "Oh wow, that massage was nirvana.") This all might sound out of reach, but I've known several down-to-earth people who have trained in these meditations, had these experiences, and been deeply affected by them.

Christina's question and teachings pushed my practice to another level. My meditation became more focused, muscular, and fruitful.

During retreats, I began to enter the first three jhanas, with their extraordinary intensity and absorption. There are pitfalls in trying to strengthen your concentration—such as feeling frustrated at a lack of progress—but there are also pitfalls in downplaying one of the three major pillars of practice.

The jhanas are usually experienced only after guidance from knowledgeable teachers and many days on retreat. But even without entering the jhanas, we can develop greater steadiness of mind in everyday life, the focus of this chapter.

Skittery Attention

Steadiness of mind is important in daily activities, not just during meditation. We need to be able to keep attention on what's useful and shift it away from what's not. Attention is like a combination spotlight and vacuum cleaner: it illuminates what it rests upon while pulling it into the brain.

But managing it is challenging. One reason is the natural variation in temperament. At one end of this range, there are focused and cautious "turtles," and at the other end are distractible and spirited "jackrabbits," with lots of tweeners in the middle. As our human and hominid ancestors lived in small hunter-gatherer bands for several million years, these groups needed a full range of temperaments to deal with changing conditions and compete with other bands for food and shelter. These temperaments are normal and not a disorder—but it can be tough to be a jackrabbitty kid getting schooled in a curriculum designed for turtles, or to be a jackrabbitty meditator trying to use methods developed by turtles in monastic turtle pens to develop turtleness.

> We live in forgetfulness. But always there is the opportunity to live our life fully. When we drink water, we can be aware that we are drinking water. When we walk, we can be aware that we are walking. Mindfulness is available to us in every moment.
>
> THICH NHAT HANH

Meanwhile, modern culture bombards us with distractions, training us to keep chasing new shiny objects. We habituate to a dense stream of stimuli so anything less feels like trying to breathe through a straw. Understandably, a history of stressful, painful, even traumatic experiences keeps us scanning for new threats. And our circumstances—such as a challenging job or a health problem—can also hijack our attention. No wonder we have a "monkey mind"—attention like a chimp in a tower darting from one window to another: Sights! Sounds! Tastes! Touches! Smells! Thoughts!

To deal with these tendencies, it's very useful to *cultivate* particular mental/neural factors that promote concentration. But before we get into those specific factors, I'd like to cover the general skills of cultivation itself. These skills will also help you develop the other aspects of awakening that we'll be exploring in later chapters.

Cultivation

There was a turning point in my life when I was about fifteen. I had been pretty miserable for several years: nervous, awkward, withdrawn, and unhappy. It all seemed hopeless. Then I began to realize that no matter how bad things had been, I could always grow something good inside myself each day. I could become a little more able to talk with the other kids, and a little less afraid of them. I could get better at staying out of hassles with my parents. Bit by bit, I could get happier and stronger. I couldn't change the past, and the present was what it was, but I could always grow from here. This was so hopeful! There was something I could do. Whatever got developed each day would usually be small, but it added up over time. *Learning* is the strength of strengths, since it's the one that grows the rest of them.

Learning includes healing from the past, disengaging from bad habits and acquiring good ones, seeing things in new ways, and simply feeling better about yourself. It's about *lasting* change inside, so that you're not so dependent upon external conditions or buffeted by internal reactions. Situations and relationships come and go, and thoughts and feelings come and go, but you can count on what endures within you no matter what happens.

> The systematic training of the mind—the cultivation of happiness, the genuine inner transformation by deliberately selecting and focusing on positive mental states and challenging negative mental states—is possible because of the very structure and function of the brain.
>
> DALAI LAMA AND HOWARD CUTLER

LEARNING IN THE BRAIN

So how can you grow the good that lasts inside yourself? The essence is simple. Any kind of useful learning involves a two-stage process:

1. Experience what you'd like to develop.
2. Turn that experience into a lasting change in your brain.

I call the first stage *activation* and the second stage *installation*. This is *positive neuroplasticity*: turning passing states into lasting *traits*. The second stage is absolutely necessary. *Experiencing does not equal learning*. Without a change in neural structure or function, there is no enduring mental change for the better. Unfortunately, we typically move on so quickly from one experience to another that the current thought or feeling has little chance to leave a lasting trace. In working with others, we might think that something good will somehow rub off on the people we're trying to help. It may for some, though not very efficiently, and for many there is little or no lasting gain.

As a result, most beneficial experiences pass through the brain like water through a sieve, leaving no value behind. You have a good conversation with a friend or feel calmer in a meditation—and then an hour later it's like that never happened. If awakening is like a mountain, in some moments you may find yourself far up its slopes—but can you *stay* there, on firm footing? Or do you keep slipping back down again?

THE NEGATIVITY BIAS

On the other hand, stressful experiences tend to get woven into the nets of memory. This is the brain's *negativity bias*, the product of evolution in harsh conditions. To simplify, our ancestors needed to get "carrots," such as food, while avoiding "sticks," such as predators. Both are important, but imagine living a million years ago: if you don't get a carrot today, you'll have a chance at one tomorrow. Yet if you don't avoid every single stick today, whack, no more carrots forever.

Consequently, the brain scans for bad news, overfocuses on it, overreacts to it, and fast-tracks the whole package into memory, including its emotional and somatic residues. Cortisol, the hormone that accompanies stressful or upsetting experiences, sensitizes the amygdala and weakens the hippocampus. So the brain's alarm bell rings more loudly and the hippocampus is less able to calm it down, which fosters additional negative experiences and thus even more reactivity in a vicious cycle.

In effect, we have a brain that's like Velcro for painful, harmful experiences and Teflon for enjoyable, useful ones. This promoted survival for millions of years, but today it creates much unnecessary suffering and conflict.

Happily, you can compensate for the negativity bias—and also cultivate greater steadiness of mind and other important inner strengths—by focusing on the second, necessary stage of learning: installation. This is not positive thinking. You will still see problems, injustice, and pain. You're simply opening to whatever is beneficial in your experiences and taking it into yourself. In fact, by growing inner resources in this way, you'll be more able to cope with the hard things in life. And as you gradually fill yourself up inside, there is less basis for craving and the suffering it causes (more on this in chapter 5). Over time, your learning bears fruit and active cultivation fades away, like a raft that's no longer needed once you reach the farther shore.

HEALing YOURSELF

There may be some "incidental learning" from experiences without any deliberate effort. But you can really steepen your growth curve—the *rate* at which you are healing and developing—by deliberately engaging your experiences in simple ways that could increase the neural traces they leave behind. Here's a summary of how to do it, with the acronym HEAL.

ACTIVATION STAGE

1. Have a beneficial experience: Notice useful and/or enjoyable experiences that are already occurring, or create new ones, such as calling up a sense of compassion.

INSTALLATION STAGE

2. Enrich it: Sustain the experience for a breath or more; intensify it; feel it in your body; see what is fresh or novel about it; and/or find what is personally relevant in it.

3. Absorb it: Intend and sense that the experience is sinking into you, and focus on what is pleasurable or meaningful about it.

4. Link positive and negative material (optional step): Focus on something beneficial in the foreground of awareness while something painful or harmful is small and off to the side; if you get hijacked by the negative, drop it and focus only on the positive. This step is powerful, but it is optional

for two reasons: we can develop psychological resources by using just the first three steps, and sometimes negative material can feel overwhelming.

In the steps above, you're mobilizing different neural factors of social, emotional, and somatic learning. To highlight three of them:

- *Sustain the experience for a breath or more:* The longer that an experience is held in *working memory*, the greater its conversion into long-term memory.
- *Feel it in your body:* The amygdala and hippocampus work closely together. Experiences that are somatically and emotionally rich stimulate the amygdala. This increases its signals to the hippocampus and other parts of the brain that the experience is important and worth converting into a lasting change in neural structure or function.
- *Focus on what is pleasurable or meaningful about it:* As the sense of reward in an experience increases, so does the activity of two neurochemicals: *dopamine* and *norepinephrine*. This flags the experience for protection and prioritization as it moves into long-term storage.

You can use the HEAL steps for anything you want to cultivate. For example, during a meditation, you could focus on a sense of calm spreading inside you. Besides developing specific inner resources, this could help your brain become more sensitive to what's beneficial in general, in effect making it more like Velcro for *good* experiences and Teflon for bad ones. And as you grow the good inside, that could foster positive cycles in your work and relationships. As a proverb says, "Keep a green bough in your heart, and a singing bird will come."

> To keep thinking in wholesome ways will strengthen
> the tendency of the mind towards what is wholesome.
>
> BHIKKHU ANĀLAYO

Finding Your Place

Most of the times that you deliberately internalize beneficial experiences will be relatively brief, including with the practices in this book. You can also move through the HEAL steps in a more systematic way over several minutes or longer. Let's apply this approach to cultivating the feeling of being rooted and stable—which naturally helps to steady the mind.

To strengthen this sense of groundedness, you can tap into the neurologically ancient—and thus fundamental and powerful—process of locating yourself in a particular place. Around 200 million years ago, early mammals began evolving a hippocampus that could create *place memory*, which is at the foundation of much of our own learning today. Whether in ancient times or these days, we need to know where the food smells good and where it smells bad, where to find a friend and where to avoid a foe. When we don't know where we're at in a situation or relationship, attention understandably darts about, and it's hard to steady the mind. On the other hand, when you feel established in your place, you can draw support from it—as the Buddha is said to have done on the night of his awakening when he reached down to touch the earth. With a sense of grounding inside yourself, you can move out into life from this secure base.

For an experiential practice of this, please see the box on the next page.

FEELING GROUNDED

This meditation is structured in terms of the four HEAL steps. I will go into the details of each step, and you can adapt my suggestions to your needs. This is a cultivation practice, not simply observing your mind (which is a valuable meditation but not what we're doing here). As you try to have different experiences, you might find that this is easier to do with some than others. That's normal, and with practice you'll become more able to evoke particular experiences.

1. **Have:** *Find a comfortable location and be aware of what it feels like to settle into it. Be aware of the internal sensations of breathing . . . air moving through your nose and down your throat and into your lungs . . . chest rising and falling . . . Know that you are breathing here . . . as this body . . . in this place . . . Be aware of the support of the ground beneath you . . . Can you find a sense of stability . . . a sense of grounding? In general, focus on aspects of feeling grounded as your object of meditation.*

2. **Enrich:** *As best you can, stay with the sense of being grounded, breath after breath . . . When you like, deliberately intensify the sense of being grounded in a particular place, letting it fill your awareness . . . Explore different aspects of feeling grounded: look around and locate yourself in this setting . . . perhaps rubbing your feet on the floor, sensing the earth beneath them . . . with thoughts such as "This is my place, it's okay that I'm here" . . . Be aware of emotions related to being grounded,*

*such as calming, reassurance, confidence . . . aware of
desires related to being grounded, such as liking it or
intending to feel it more often . . . Notice new aspects of
feeling grounded, approaching this experience with a
sense of openness and not-knowing . . . Be aware of ways
that feeling grounded is relevant and important for you . . .*

3. **Absorb:** *Intend to receive a feeling of grounding into
yourself, sinking into it as it sinks into you . . . Sense that
this experience is spreading inside you like warm water
into a sponge . . . allowing it, giving over to it, letting it
in . . . Be aware of what feels good about being
grounded . . . what is enjoyable or meaningful about it . . .*

4. **Link:** *If you like, in this optional step, be aware of
memories or feelings of being unsettled or lost off to the
side while keeping a strong sense of groundedness in the
front of your mind. Widen awareness to include these two
things at the same time . . . maintaining a strong feeling of
groundedness, not being hijacked by feeling unsettled or
lost . . . There might be a feeling of groundedness
spreading out into any sense of anxiety or uncertainty,
easing and soothing it . . . Not getting caught up in
thoughts or stories, simply being aware of two things at
the same time . . . and allowing, even gently helping, a
feeling of being grounded to ease and perhaps eventually
replace any sense of being unsettled or lost . . .*

*As you approach the end of this practice, rest only in
feeling grounded . . . feeling yourself breathing in this place,
grounded and steady, here and now . . .*

Five Factors to Steady the Mind

In this section we'll explore five different ways to steady your mind. Each of them is organized as an experiential practice followed by an explanation of its neural foundations. After doing the practices one by one, you could go back and do all five in a row. As you become more experienced with these factors, you can draw on them whenever you like, not just while meditating. This section ends with a summary practice that integrates all of the factors and then offers the challenge of focusing steadily on your breath for five minutes in a row.

FURTHER READING

Buddha's Map (Doug Kraft)

The Experience of Insight (Joseph Goldstein)

The Little Book of Being (Diana Winston)

Mindfulness, Bliss, and Beyond (Ajahn Brahm)

Mindfulness (Joseph Goldstein)

The Mindful Geek (Michael Taft)

The Mind Illuminated (Culadasa)

Practicing the Jhānas (Stephen Snyder and Tina Rasmussen)

Satipatthana (Anālayo)

FOUNDATIONS OF PRACTICE

Before engaging in any practice, it helps to know why you're doing it. For example, why does steadiness of mind matter to you? Or why do you care about developing more compassion? You could name reasons to yourself or simply have a wordless feeling about them. More broadly, it helps to know why you practice at all. Please consider these questions: What do you hope to heal in yourself? What would you like to let go of? What do you hope to grow in yourself? You can also practice for the sake of others as well as yourself. Holding them in your heart as you practice can feel really sweet. How might your own healing and growth be a gift to those with whom you live or work?

During meditation, it's usually helpful to have chosen a specific object of attention. I think of it like a buoy in a warm tropical sea that you're resting your arm upon, staying in touch with it as the waves of experiences come and go, sometimes with beautiful strange creatures inside them, passing by but not carrying you along. In a *focused attention* practice, the object could be a specific sensation, emotion, word, or image such as the breath, compassion, "peace," or a memory of a mountain meadow. Here I'll usually refer to the sensations of breathing as the object of attention. You can be aware of them around the nose and upper lip, in your throat and lungs, chest or belly, or in your body as a whole. In *open awareness*, you take the ongoing flow of experiences as the object of attention, letting them come and go without being swept away by any of them. You could even *abide as awareness*, so that you are mainly experiencing awareness itself.

These three kinds of meditation—focused attention, open awareness, abiding as awareness—form a natural sequence. You could follow this progression during a single meditation or over the longer course of months and years of practice. I generally recommend beginning with focused attention practices. And these are not just for beginners. Focused attention practices are often the ones used for entering deep states of meditative absorption. Focusing on a specific object is so simple: you bring attention fully into it and become increasingly absorbed in it—and anything else is off purpose. If your mind wanders at all, you bring it back as soon as you notice this. Other thoughts, sensations, and images will naturally bubble up into awareness, but you rapidly disengage from them and do not feed or follow them. I like this instruction for focused attention I once heard on retreat from Eugene Cash: "Be devoted to the breath and renounce everything else."

It helps to choose an object that is stimulating enough to hold your attention, especially if your temperament is more jackrabbitty than turtle-ish. Being aware of the breath in the whole torso or body is more engaging than focusing on the upper lip. Walking meditation is more stimulating than sitting quietly. Emotionally rich and rewarding experiences such as gratitude or kindness also help to hold your attention. The specific object is just a means to the end of a meditation that is beneficial for you. So it's important not to be rigid about the object of meditation and to find one that serves the ends you care about. As your mind steadies, you can pick less stimulating objects that will further strengthen the "muscle" of attention.

Whatever your object is, try to remain steadily mindful of it. Be aware of the sense of *applying* attention to an object, like shifting a spotlight onto something. Also be aware of *sustaining* attention to an object—staying in touch with it continuously. For example, you can apply your attention to the beginning of an inhalation and sustain attention throughout its full course, and then apply and sustain attention to the exhalation…breath after breath. Especially if your aim in meditation is steadiness and concentration, it could help to monitor the very beginning of any distractions away from the object, and to disengage from these rapidly and return focus to the object. In effect, you can pay attention to attention—an aspect of *metacognition*.

In your brain, these processes of applying, sustaining, and monitoring attention—which are useful for everyday life, not just meditation!—draw on the anterior cingulate cortex and related prefrontal regions behind the forehead. With practice, your attention will become steadier and require less deliberate regulation, and neural activity in these areas will decrease. Focusing becomes easier the more you do it.

And with any practice, please adapt my suggestions to whatever works best for you.

ESTABLISHING INTENTION

Find a posture that helps you feel comfortable and alert. Be aware of your body, and choose your object of attention. (I'll refer to the breath.) It's natural for this object to move to the background of awareness when you focus on the factors of steadiness of mind that we're exploring, but try to stay in touch with it, even if lightly…Be mindful of breathing in when you are breathing in, and be mindful of breathing out when you are breathing out.

Now establish the intention to steady your mind. First, have a sense of giving yourself an instruction, with thoughts to yourself such as "Pay attention… stay with it…" There could be a sense of a determined part of yourself establishing an aim or purpose…Know what this kind of "top-down" intention feels like…

Second, imagine being someone who is very steady, very stable in their mind... Get a sense of already being very present, very focused... Let this way of being carry you along... Give yourself over to this intention to remain steadily aware of your object of attention... Know what this kind of "bottom-up" intention feels like...

Now allow these two kinds of intention to mingle together. With relaxed resolve, be committed to remaining steadily aware of breathing, breath after breath...

Top-down intentions engage the prefrontal cortex behind the forehead. This part of the brain is the primary neural basis for the executive functions, including deliberate control of attention, emotion, and action. This kind of intention is very useful, but it is effortful and thus vulnerable to *willpower fatigue:* it's tiring to have to keep telling yourself to do something. Additionally, the rewards of achieving the intention are deferred into the future, which can sap motivation. On the other hand, *bottom-up* intention engages your emotions and sensations, drawing on older and therefore more fundamental neural structures below the cortex. In this form of intention, you find a *felt sense* of what it would be like to have already fulfilled the intention, and then give yourself over to it. This feels rewarding already, and therefore more motivating. Instead of struggling upstream, you feel carried along.

EASING YOUR BODY

Be aware of your body... aware of breathing... allowing the body to rest... easing... taking several breaths in which the exhalations are longer than the inhalations ... letting your breath flow naturally ... letting it become softer ... lighter ...

If it's helpful, you could recall or imagine comfortable, relaxing settings, such as a beautiful beach ... a cozy chair ... being with restful companions ...

Let your body ease ... and calm ... and rest ... Breathing in, let the body be tranquil ... breathing out, let the body be tranquil ... breath after breath, tranquil and present ... remaining steadily present, with a body that is calm and restful ... being aware of how calm in your body supports steadiness of mind ...

Relaxation calms down the *sympathetic nervous system* (SNS) and reduces related stress hormones such as cortisol and *adrenaline.* These systems in your body evolved to fight against or flee from threats and to chase opportunities. When they get more active, your attention tends to jump around, which is at odds with steadying the mind. This is one reason why meditative traditions emphasize peacefulness and disengaging from stresses.

It's helpful to extend your exhalations because the "rest-and-digest" *parasympathetic nervous system* (PNS) handles exhaling while also slowing your heart rate, so longer exhalations are naturally relaxing. The PNS and SNS are connected like a seesaw, so as one goes up, the other comes down. As a general principle, increasing parasympathetic activity lowers the SNS arousal that can unsteady your mind.

ABIDING WHOLEHEARTED

Bring to mind one or more beings whom you care about ... Focusing on feelings of caring rather than anything complicated about the relationship ... perhaps a sense of compassion, friendliness, even love ...

Bring to mind the feeling of being with someone who cares about you ... perhaps a friend, a pet, or a family member ... Keeping it simple, focusing on feeling cared about ... feeling appreciated ... liked ... loved ...

Explore a sense of breathing warm feelings in and out of the heart area ... love flowing in as you inhale ... love flowing out as you exhale ... feeling open-hearted ... Being aware of how feeling wholehearted supports steadiness of mind ...

Warmhearted feelings are naturally soothing and settling. One source of this is the neurochemical *oxytocin*, which is released by the *hypothalamus* when you're feeling loving or close to others. Oxytocin activity in the amygdala can have an inhibitory effect, calming it down. As flows of oxytocin increase in the prefrontal cortex, the sense of anxiety usually decreases, which enables a greater stability of attention.

Caring about others is part of the *tend-and-befriend* response that can lower stress and thereby steady the mind. And feeling cared about is usually an indicator of protection and loyalty. During the many years that our human and hominid ancestors lived in small bands, being abandoned was a primal threat—so today, feeling cared about can increase your sense of safety, which adds to the impact of the next practice below.

FEELING SAFER

Help yourself feel as safe as you actually are . . . in this moment . . . in this moment . . . Be aware of protections around you, such as sturdy walls or good-hearted people nearby . . . Notice that you can still be aware of your setting even as you let go of needless fear . . . Be aware of strengths inside you . . . helping yourself feel calmer and stronger . . .

Be aware of any uneasiness . . . any unnecessary anxiety . . . and see if you can let that go . . . As you exhale, release fear . . . let go of worry . . . Notice what it is like to feel safer . . . not seeking perfect safety, simply helping yourself feel as safe as you actually are . . . Letting go of guarding . . . bracing . . . pushing away . . . Open to reassurance . . . relief . . . feeling calmer . . . more peaceful . . . Being aware of how letting go of fear helps to steady your mind . . .

We need to deal with real dangers, but much of the time we over-estimate threats—an aspect of the negativity bias—and don't feel as safe as we actually are. This makes us feel bad, and it wears down physical and mental health over time. Plus when we feel at all anxious, attention understandably skitters around, scanning the world—including relationships—and body and mind for what might go wrong. Helping yourself to feel reasonably safe calms the stress response system and helps you stay with the object of attention rather than look about for a tiger that might pounce.

FEELING GRATEFUL AND GLAD

Bring to mind one or more things for which you feel thankful . . . such as friends and loved ones who have helped you along the way . . . things you've been given . . . the beauty of nature . . . perhaps the gift of life itself . . .

Open to feelings of gratitude... and related feelings of gladness, comfort, perhaps happiness... If there are any feelings of sadness or frustration, that's all right... simply notice them—and then return your attention to things you feel grateful about...

Focus on feelings of gratitude and gladness as your object of attention... becoming absorbed in them and absorbing them into you... Perhaps there is a happiness about being with others... or a happiness for others... a warm-hearted happiness... Not chasing or grasping after positive feelings... more a gentle opening to them and receiving of them... Being aware of how peaceful well-being helps to steady the mind...

In the brain, steadiness of mind involves *stable* activity in the neural substrates of working memory, which include the upper-outer regions of the prefrontal cortex. They have a kind of gate that affects what is happening inside them. When this gate is closed, we stay focused on one thing. When this gate opens, new experiences flood into working memory, dislodging what was there. Steadiness in the mind means controlling this gate in the brain.

The gate is regulated by dopamine, a neurochemical that tracks expectations or experiences of reward. Ongoing dopamine activity indicates that something is worth paying attention to—which keeps the gate closed, so you stay focused on the object of attention. Dopamine activity decreases when things get less rewarding, which opens the gate to distracting stimuli. Consequently, to keep the gate closed and to prevent it opening, it helps to sustain experiences that are rewarding. Surges in dopamine related to the possibility of new rewards open the gate as well. So it is especially useful to experience a *strong* sense of gratitude or other positive emotions, since then dopamine levels will be at their ceiling already—and a gate-opening surge is less possible.

ALL FIVE FACTORS TOGETHER

Find a posture that is comfortable and alert...Establishing the intention of steadying the mind...Easing your body...Abiding wholehearted...Feeling safer...Feeling grateful and glad...

Focus on the sensations of breathing (or other object of attention)...Apply and sustain attention to each breath...staying steadily aware of the breath... If attention wanders, simply bring it back...Become increasingly absorbed in the feeling of breathing...

And now stay steadily in touch with breathing for five minutes in a row...

As you finish this practice, be aware of what greater steadiness of mind feels like...opening to the sense of steadiness...being steady...breath after breath...

Good Practice

For an hour sometime, observe the things that distract you from whatever it is that you want to focus on. Then consider what you could do to change external distractions, such as asking someone to be more thoughtful about interrupting your work unless it's really important. Also consider what you could do inside your mind to be less distractible, such as recognizing the "fool's gold"—the empty rewards—in much of what tries to grab your attention.

Be mindful of how the negativity bias shows up in yourself and others. Watch how you tend to over-focus on negative things and move quickly past positive ones. Definitely be aware of the negative when that's appropriate, but also make sure you stay aware of the good things around you and inside you.

Look for opportunities every day to slow down to internalize a beneficial experience. This is not just smelling the roses—as good as that is! It includes times you feel determined, cared about, committed to getting more exercise, or clear about a better way to talk with your partner. Stay with the experience for a breath or longer, sense it in your body, and focus on what feels good about it. It's like filling yourself up at one little oasis after another over the course of your day.

Commit to meditating each day for at least one minute. It could be the last thing you do before your head hits the pillow. But make it a real minute or longer, and do it every day.

When you meditate, include ten breaths or more of sustained attention to the breath or other object. In your mind, you can softly count up to or down from ten. If you're ambitious, try a hundred breaths in a row; to stay on track, you could extend one finger at a time after each group of ten.

In meditation, make room for emotionally positive experiences, such as feeling peaceful, loving, or happy. Don't chase or cling to these experiences, but welcome them and receive them into yourself. This will help to weave them into your nervous system while also steadying your mind.

4

WARMING THE HEART

With good will for the entire cosmos,
cultivate a limitless heart: above, below, and all around,
unobstructed, without hostility or hate.

SUTTA NIPATA 1.8

About twenty years ago I had the good fortune of joining the board at Spirit Rock Meditation Center and, soon after that, receiving an invitation to hear the Dalai Lama speak there at a conference. Since he's the head of state of Tibet, there was a high level of security around him, and guards with guns smiled and joked in the carnival-like atmosphere. Hundreds of people mingled together—Tibetans as well as teachers and monastics from Europe and America—most of us giddy with the occasion. With many others, I filed into a large room to await the Dalai Lama. After a few minutes, he entered with his translator and another man. He spoke mainly in English with his usual combination of friendliness, directness, and calm intelligence. At the time, I thought he gave a marvelous talk, but I don't remember any of it. What I do remember is the other man who came in with him. He was dressed in a gray suit and seemed unassuming, standing off to the side in the front of the room looking at everyone and smiling.

After a while I watched him more closely: he stood at ease like a dancer, filling out his suit like someone who'd been a linebacker on a small college football team, smiling and smiling, with eyes that kept scanning the room. I realized he was the Dalai Lama's bodyguard, the last line of defense. There was no sense of threat from him. He radiated a feeling of happiness and love. Meanwhile, it was clear he was completely capable, standing there wishing everyone well with hands relaxed at his sides and eyes that never stopped moving.

I've thought of him many times since. For me, he embodied practicing with a warm heart. He had a job to do, and it included a readiness to be strong and assertive if need be. But he was not aggressive or hostile. This teaching described him well:

> One is not wise because one speaks much.
> One is wise who is peaceable, friendly, and fearless.
>
> DHAMMAPADA 19.258

While awakening can seem focused on the internal world of the solitary individual, many of its most important elements are interpersonal. For example, on the Buddhist path, wise speech, wise action, and wise livelihood apply mainly to our relationships; there's a high value on compassion, kindness, and happiness for others; one of its Three Jewels is community (the others are Buddha and dharma); and the Bodhisattva ideal involves practicing for the sake of others. I've found a similar emphasis on love and service in other traditions, including secular humanism.

So how can we warm the heart and develop compassion and kindness, for our own sake and for that of others? Mindfulness is necessary, but it's not sufficient.

Studies of mindfulness and related meditations have found that these can alter neural networks for attention, self-awareness, and self-control. This is really good, but it doesn't directly strengthen key parts of the neural basis of compassion and kindness. Related but distinct networks handle these things. For example, pleasurable social experiences activate brain regions that help produce experiences of physical pleasure. Being generous, cooperative, and fair can stimulate neural reward centers. And social pain—such as rejection or loneliness—taps the same networks that underlie physical pain.

It is when we focus on warmheartedness itself that its aspects are most experienced in the mind and developed in the nervous system. Compassion-focused meditation stimulates specific parts of the brain involved with the sense of connection, positive emotion, and reward, including the middle *orbitofrontal cortex*, behind where your eyebrows meet. Long-term practitioners of lovingkindness meditation develop similar neurological reactions to seeing the faces of strangers and their own faces, with a growing sense of "you're like me." They also build neural tissue in key parts of the hippocampus that support feelings of empathy toward others.

Further, what is *not* compassionate and kind—such as hurt, resentment, or contempt—can loom large and persist in a person's mind. The brain is designed to be shaped by our experiences ... and especially by those in childhood ... particularly if they were painful and involved other people. The traces linger and can shadow your days. These physical changes in your brain are not reversed just by watching your mind. It takes deliberate practice to heal and to find new ways of being with others.

So let's see how we can grow compassion and kindness for others—and ourselves.

Compassion and Kindness

Very simply, compassion is wishing that beings not suffer, and kindness is wishing that they be happy. As wishes, these are forms of desire. Which raises an important question that we should address first: *Is desire okay?*

GOOD WILL

The Buddha made a useful distinction between two kinds of desire. First, there is healthy desire, such as trying to be more patient and loving. Second, there is the unhealthy desire—the "craving" mentioned in chapter 2—that causes so much suffering. For example, this kind of desire is active when we run away from or fight with what is painful, get driven about or addicted to what is pleasurable, or keep trying to impress other people.

So the issue is not desire per se but rather:

- Can we desire what is *beneficial* for ourselves and others?
- Can we pursue it with *skillful means?* For example, there might be a positive aim, such as helping a child to read, but if a parent goes about it with yelling, that's not skillful.
- Can we *be at peace with what happens?* Different parts of the brain handle *liking*—enjoying or preferring something—and

wanting, in the sense here of craving. This means it is possible to aim high and be ambitious without being consumed by pressure and drivenness (more on this in the next chapter). Sure, there could be disappointment about not achieving a goal, but there can also be acceptance—and enthusiasm for the next opportunity.

This is healthy desire in a nutshell: pursuing beneficial ends with skillful means while being at peace with whatever happens. In this way, we can certainly desire the welfare of all beings—including cats and dogs, strangers on the street, friends and family, and ourselves.

A SWEET COMMITMENT

A beautiful expression of this healthy desire is found in the Metta Sutta below. I'm translating *metta* as kindness, and the root of this word from Pali is "friend."

May all beings be happy and secure.
May all beings be happy at heart!

Omitting none, whether they are weak or strong,
seen or unseen, near or distant, born or to-be-born:
May all beings be happy.

Let none deceive another,
or despise anyone anywhere,
or through anger or ill will wish for another to suffer.

Just as a mother would protect her child,
     her only child, with her own life,
even so you should cultivate a boundless heart
     toward all beings.

You should cultivate kindness
toward the whole world with a boundless heart:
above, below, and all around,
unobstructed, without enmity or hate.

Whether standing, walking, sitting, or lying down,
as long as you are alert,
you should be resolved upon this mindfulness.
This is called a sublime abiding here and now.

This is such a lovely aspiration! And a strong encouragement to keep training ourselves and growing. It's a lifelong process to develop ever more kindness, compassion, and love.

AN ENNOBLING DEVELOPMENT

The Buddha is said to have offered Four *Noble* Truths—"noble" in the sense of excellent and honorable. But it is more accurate to translate them as the Truths of the Noble Ones. This difference is important, inspiring, and relevant for us today. Radically for his time, the Buddha said that it is not birth but intentional actions of thought, word, and deed that make a person truly noble. These are truths of noble beings because we are drawn to them by what is noble within us. And we develop additional noble qualities through practice. So I like to think of these as the Four *Ennobling* Truths.

In this spirit, one way to honor the best in yourself and develop it further is through cultivating compassion and kindness. You can do this informally, even with people you don't know, by silently finding good wishes for them as you pass on by. More formally, you could focus on warmheartedness as part of or all of a meditation. As we saw in the previous chapter, repeatedly "resting your mind upon" these experiences—staying with them for a breath or longer, feeling them in your body, and being aware of what's enjoyable and mean-ingful about them—will gradually weave lovingness into your ner-vous system.

Cultivating compassion and kindness sometimes involves the de-liberate creation of useful thoughts, feelings, and intentions. It's all right to nudge your mind for good purposes—which is a key aspect of resilience, healthy relationships, and spiritual practice. And if try-ing to create an experience is like trying to start a fire with wet wood, just settle into a simple awareness of breathing and the present moment—and perhaps try again later.

GOOD WISHES FOR EVERYONE

In the Theravadan tradition, there's a lovely meditation that offers four kinds of warm wishes for five types of people, and I suggest you try my adaptation of it in the box below. You can also bring this ap-proach into your daily life.

The four wishes are for others and ourselves to be "*safe, healthy, happy,* and *at ease.*" They can be expressed as soft thoughts, perhaps in rhythm with the breath, or simply as wordless feelings and atti-tudes. Feel free to find words that touch your own heart, including specific ones such as "May your pain lessen . . . may you find work . . . may you be at peace with this loss . . ."

The five types of people are *benefactor, friend, neutral person, oneself,* and *someone who is challenging for you.* The first three are usually straightforward, particularly the benefactor—someone who is easy to feel grateful and caring toward. Understandably, compassion and kindness for people who are challenging for you could be hard. It can help to start with someone who is just a little challenging. Then, if you want, you can try this practice with other people.

> Happy indeed we live, friendly amidst the hostile.
> Amidst hostile people, we dwell free from hatred.
>
> DHAMMAPADA 197

It can also be hard to have good wishes for yourself. It might work just to keep doing the practice while disengaging from any self-criticism. Over time, the repetition of the phrases could feel more real to you. And bit by bit, synapse by synapse, these experiences can be internalized to grow traits of acceptance and support for yourself.

Increasingly in daily life, you could find yourself resting in a sense of friendliness and caring...resting in love...love flowing in and love flowing out...lived by love.

A MEDITATION ON COMPASSION AND KINDNESS

Be aware of your body . . . grounded here . . . aware of sensations of breathing in your chest . . . Imagine the breath flowing into and out of your heart . . . You might place a hand on your heart . . .

Bring to mind one or more beings you feel good around . . . a friend, a family member, a pet . . . who appreciate you, like you, perhaps love you . . . focusing on the good feelings you have around them . . . If your attention moves to situations or issues, return your focus to the simple feeling of being with those who care about you . . . Open to these feelings, receiving them into yourself . . .

Choose a benefactor, someone you appreciate. While holding this being in your heart, explore saying these phrases to yourself: "May you be safe . . . May you be healthy . . . May you be happy . . . May you live with ease." Be aware of warm feelings . . . You can try other words . . . or simply rest in wordless caring and good wishes . . .

Try this with a friend, someone you like, perhaps love . . . "May you be safe . . . May you be healthy . . . May you be happy . . . May you live with ease." Let feelings of compassion and kindness fill your awareness . . . Feel them spreading inside you . . .

Try this with a neutral person, perhaps a neighbor or coworker, or a passing stranger in the street . . . Find compassion and kindness for this person . . . "May you be

(continued)

safe . . . May you be healthy . . . May you be happy . . . May you live with ease."

Try this with yourself . . . "May I be safe . . . May I be healthy . . . May I be happy . . . May I live with ease." If you like, you can use your own name, perhaps imagining that you are sitting in front of yourself . . . You might have a sense of these warm wishes sinking into you, as if you are receiving them into yourself.

Try this with someone who is challenging for you, starting with someone who is only mildly so. It might help to imagine the core of this person, beneath the characteristics that are challenging, or perhaps this person as a child, even a very young child. We can have compassion and good wishes for people we disagree with or disapprove of . . . Try these wishes: "May you be safe . . . May you be healthy . . . May you be truly happy . . . May you live with ease."

And then simply rest in compassion and kindness . . . rippling outward from you, not aimed at anyone in particular . . . Rest in warmth and goodheartedness . . . and perhaps love . . . love sinking into you and you sinking into love . . .

The Bliss of Blamelessness

The Buddha was a parent, and his son, Rahula, came to practice with him as a young monk. As the sutta explains, one day the Buddha heard that Rahula, then perhaps seven or eight years old, had told a deliberate lie. He spoke with his son and said that he should always consider whether his actions were skillful and led to beneficial results. He told Rahula to reflect in this way before, during, and after all acts of thought, word, and deed. If an action was skillful and beneficial, fine; otherwise don't do it. (In my mind's made-up movie, I see this as a scene of high drama, and for comic effect imagine Robert De Niro playing the Buddha.)

> To attain...deep insight, we must have a mind which is both quiet and malleable. Achieving such a state of mind requires that we first develop the ability to regulate our body and speech so as to cause no conflict.
>
> VENERABLE TENZIN PALMO

This pillar of practice—*sila*, in Pali, which is usually translated as restraint or morality, and which I have called virtue—might seem like just an entry-level prerequisite: tick the boxes and then get on with "real" awakening. But actually, warmheartedness in action is a deep vital practice that confronts the worst in us and encourages the best in us. Doing the right thing—even when it's hard—develops mindfulness and wisdom, and brings "the bliss of blamelessness," knowing you've done all that you can.

> May I be loving, open, and aware in this moment.
> If I cannot be loving, open, and aware in this moment, may I be kind.
> If I cannot be kind, may I be nonjudgmental.
> If I cannot be nonjudgmental, may I not cause harm.
> If I cannot not cause harm, may I cause the least harm possible.
>
> LARRY YANG

In the heat of the moment, though, this is not always easy—especially if you're swept along by impulsiveness or ill will. Here's where knowing a bit about your *vagus nerve complex* is helpful. Its two branches originate in the *brain stem*, and the more ancient one heads downward to regulate the viscera, including your heart and lungs. The older branch is involved with the parasympathetic nervous system, which is relaxing and restorative, and slows the heart rate as you exhale. The more recently evolved branch weaves upward into the ears, eyes, and face, and is a key part of the brain's *social engagement system*. Because these are two branches of a single neural network, activity in one ripples into the other. This means, first, that easing and settling your body can help you be calmer and kinder with others. Second, feeling more compassionate and loving can help you be more centered and even-keeled, and in better control of yourself. For a practice that brings groundedness and warmheartedness together, please see the box below.

GROUNDED WARMHEARTEDNESS

Take some full breaths and feel your body calming . . .
Wherever you are, help yourself feel a solid footing in this
place. You could touch the chair or the ground, and remind
yourself that it is all right to be here. Find a posture that gives
you a sense of relaxed stability . . . presence . . . dignity . . .
Feeling at ease, imagine a line running through you from the
center of the earth up to the sky, so that you are both rooted
and uplifted . . . As you breathe, feel more and more grounded.

Be aware of the sensations of breathing in the area of your heart . . . Find a simple warmhearted feeling, perhaps by bringing to mind someone you care about . . . Be aware of these warm feelings along with the sensations of breathing in the area of your heart. Warmhearted feelings could include compassion . . . friendship . . . happiness . . . loyalty . . . love . . . perhaps radiating outward from you in all directions.

Be aware of feeling both grounded and loving . . . grounded with an open heart . . . Be aware of how groundedness enables love to flow freely . . . and how lovingness is calming and strengthening . . . Breath after breath, grounded and loving . . .

There are those who do not realize that
    one day we all must die.
But those who do realize this settle their quarrels.

DHAMMAPADA 6

NOT HARMING OTHERS—AND YOURSELF

Living with a warm heart certainly includes trying not to harm others. To do this, these practical guidelines from the Eightfold Path have been helpful to me and many others:

- *Wise speech* is well intended, true, beneficial, not harsh, timely, and, ideally, wanted.
- *Wise action* avoids killing, stealing, sexual misconduct, and using intoxicants.

- *Wise livelihood* avoids commerce in weapons, human trafficking, meat, intoxicants, and poisons.

Non-harming also includes not hurting *ourselves*—but this may be harder to see, and a lower priority. Yet of all the beings in the world, the one whose suffering you know best and can most relieve is yourself. You can bring the same clarity and moral force to not harming yourself that you bring to not harming others. For example, you can say "stop" to yourself before drinking something you'll regret later, much as you can say "stop" to someone who keeps interrupting you. For a structured practice of this, please see the box.

HOW WE HURT OURSELVES

You can do this practice in your mind, through writing, or by talking with another person. Imagine feeling the same tender concern for yourself that you would for a dear and vulnerable friend, and then ask yourself the first question below. After an answer comes to you, ask yourself: "If so, what would it look like to stop doing this, and what would change as a result?" Then continue to the next question.

- Have I been killing anything that is alive within me—such as passions, feelings, longings, or creativity?
- Have I been allowing others or my own habits to take precious time, attention, or energy from me, against my true wishes?
- Have I been using sexuality in ways that have harmed or lessened me?

- Have I been lying to myself about anything, such as how I really feel around someone, or how fulfilling my work actually is, or how much it costs me to live with dreams deferred for another month or year?
- Have I been letting toxins into my body and mind, such as drugs or alcohol, the gradual accumulations of not-great foods, or the dismissive judgments of others?

A GIVING HEART

Besides the absence of the bad, warmheartedness in action involves the presence of the good. Many ethical principles are expressed through negation—for example., thou shalt not kill—but it's also valuable to consider them in terms of affirmation. For instance, you could explore how to give life through planting trees or protecting children, or how to replace a harsh tone with encouragement and praise.

Generosity is rare in the animal kingdom, since in most species it lowers the odds of individual survival. But as our ancestors lived and evolved in small bands, altruism helped others with whom they shared genes. And as the brain gradually grew larger—tripling in size over the past several million years—our ancestors became more able both to appreciate and reward one person's giving, and to criticize and punish another person's freeloading. This promoted positive cycles of social and moral evolution whose traces are now woven into our DNA.

> If people knew, as I know, the results of
>   giving and sharing,
> they would not eat without having given,
> nor would they allow the stain of stinginess
> to obsess them and root in their minds.
>
> ITIVUTTAKA 26

Most expressions of generosity are not about money. People offer attention, encouragement, and patience many times a day. Nonetheless, sometimes we withhold when it would be so easy, actually, to listen quietly for another minute or to offer a word of appreciation or simply a look that says, "I'm with you." You could pick a key relationship and then for a day be a little more generous with that person and see what happens.

Toward yourself, consider how you might be stingy with praise, sparing of comfort, withholding of mercy. Through processes of *social learning* in childhood, we tend to internalize the dismissiveness and disdain of others and then do that to ourselves. It's normal—yet still sad. To make a shift in specific ways, you could give yourself a time each day that's just for you or consciously slow down when you start to feel pressured or stressed. And more generally, you could cultivate self-compassion.

Self-Compassion

Compassion involves sensitivity to suffering, a caring response, and a desire to help if one can. Self-compassion simply applies all this to *yourself.* Studies show that self-compassion has many benefits, including reducing self-criticism and increasing resilience, a sense of worth, and a willingness to try new things and to be ambitious. Extending compassion to yourself will not make you self-centered. In fact, it usually has the opposite effect. For example, we naturally tend to get preoccupied with ourselves when we're in pain, particularly if we've been wounded by others. The balm of compassion soothes our hurts and losses and eases the heightened sense of self that often comes with them, such as taking things very personally. Nor is this wallowing in self-pity. Self-compassion usually takes just a few moments, and then you move into more active forms of coping. When things are hard, we start with compassion for ourselves, but it's not where we stop.

It can feel easy to have compassion for others yet hard to give it to oneself. This is where the sense of *common humanity* is so helpful: we all make mistakes, we all feel stress and worry and hurt, and we all need compassion. Life fractures everyone, as Leonard Cohen writes:

> There is a crack, a crack in everything
> That's how the light gets in

THE BITTER AND THE SWEET

Compassion is bittersweet: there is the bitter of the suffering and the sweet of the caring. If you get overwhelmed by the suffering, including your own, then it's hard to sustain the caring. So try to help the sweet be larger than the bitter in your mind. You can do this by focusing on a sense of tender concern, warmheartedness, loyalty, and support in the foreground of awareness, while having a sense of whatever is painful off to the side.

If you get hijacked by the suffering and related thoughts and feelings, try to disengage from that for a while. Recenter in simple grounded beneficial experiences such as feeling your feet on the floor or looking out a window. Then find again the sense of your own strong and warm heart, and whenever you're ready, return to an awareness of the suffering, holding it with compassion.

FURTHER READING

Radical Compassion (Tara Brach)

Born to Be Good (Dacher Keltner)

The Mindful Path to Self-Compassion (Christopher Germer)

Real Love (Sharon Salzberg)

Say What You Mean (Oren Jay Sofer)

Self-Compassion (Kristin Neff)

You Just Don't Understand (Deborah Tannen)

A PRACTICE OF SELF-COMPASSION

In addition to practicing self-compassion informally from time to time, you can cultivate it as a trait through more formal practices. For example, Kristin Neff and Chris Germer have developed the rich and effective Mindful Self-Compassion program. You can also meditate on self-compassion. There are different approaches; here's a practice I've found to be quite powerful.

*Be aware of your breathing, finding a sense of ease and grounding...
finding a simple sense of being for yourself...*

*Bring to mind the feeling of being with someone who cares about you...
Help yourself recognize caring that is real, then open to feeling cared
about... Bring to mind others who care about you... Receive the sense of
being cared about into yourself...*

*Bring to mind someone whom you care about. Be aware of their burdens,
losses, perhaps injustices... and their stress and pain and suffering...
and find compassion for them... perhaps with soft thoughts such as
"May you not suffer... May you find work... May your medical
treatment go well" ... perhaps with a hand on your heart. It's fine if
other feelings are present, such as kindness or love... Perhaps bring
other beings to mind and find compassion for them... Sense compassion
sinking into you as you sink into it...*

*Knowing what the experience of compassion is like, apply it to yourself.
Be aware of your own burdens, losses, injustices... and your stress and
pain and suffering... and then find compassion for yourself... Focus on
good wishes for yourself and feelings of warmth and support, with a
sense of the suffering present but off to the side of awareness... perhaps
with soft thoughts such as "May I not suffer" or something more specific
like "May I not worry so much... May I find a partner... May I come
to peace with this loss" ... perhaps with a hand on your heart or
cheek... You might have a sense of compassion touching bruised, aching,
hurting, longing places inside... compassion sinking into you...
receiving compassion into yourself...*

*If you like, you could imagine yourself at a younger age, perhaps a time
that was particularly hard for you. Be aware of the challenges faced by*

that younger you ... and how they landed on you, and what it felt like ... And then find compassion for that younger being, perhaps visualizing yourself "over there" ... sending good wishes, understanding, warmth, and support ... perhaps with specific thoughts, including ones that might have been so good to hear back then, such as "This will pass ... It is not your fault ... You will be okay." You may have a sense of this compassion being received into younger layers inside you ... perhaps with an easing of old pain.

Then let go of any focus on suffering and rest simply in a general sense of warmth and lovingness ... being aware of breathing ... allowing things to settle in your mind ... feeling at ease ...

Omitting None

Until about ten thousand years ago and the gradual introduction of agriculture, our human and tool-making hominid ancestors lived in small bands, typically with several dozen members. These bands often competed with one another for scarce resources. Bands that were better at cooperation and caring with "us"—at compassion, bonding, language, teamwork, trust, altruism, and love—were more able to pass on their genes. And bands that were better than others at fearing and fighting with "them"—at distrust, disdain, ill will, and vengeance—were also more able to pass on their genes. The benefits of both kinds of capabilities have been a major driver of the evolution of the brain over the past few million years.

TWO WOLVES

Consequently, to paraphrase a parable, in each person's heart are two wolves, one of love and one of hate, and everything depends upon which one we feed each day. The wolf of hate is in our nature. We can't kill it, and hating it just feeds it. Besides, it has characteristics that are sometimes useful. Anger is energizing, and it shines a bright spotlight on mistreatment and injustice. Many people have had their well-deserved anger suppressed or punished, including by systemic social forces. We need to make room for anger inside ourselves and to understand why we're angry. Similarly, we need to have room for anger in others, and to understand why they're angry—maybe with us.

Still, anger is a seductive and potent force. Most people don't like feeling anxious, sad, or hurt, but the hot rush of anger can feel so good: "It's your fault... *of course* I got mad... you deserve it!" In the brain, anger draws on dopamine and norepinephrine to feel rewarding for you. But other people could be reeling and making decisions with lasting consequences. Dumping anger on others is like throwing hot coals with bare hands; both people get burnt. Most of my mistakes in relationships have begun with my anger.

Nonetheless, anger itself is not ill will—the will to hurt, tear down, and eliminate. If anger is a yellow flag, ill will is full red. This aspect of the wolf of hate is sneaky and powerful. It's so easy to feel aggrieved, and then spiteful and vengeful. Or simply cast others aside: they don't matter, it's all right to use them, no need to take them into account. Martin Buber described two fundamental types of relationships: I-Thou and I-It. When we regard people as an "It" to our "I," it's easy to overlook, discard, or exploit them. Consider what it feels like to be "It-ed" by others—treated like someone who doesn't matter, who is just a means to their ends. That's what it feels like for them to be It-ed by us. Throughout history and in the world today, whether in one-to-one relationships or among groups and nations, the destructive potential of the wolf of hate is obvious.

We cannot remove this part of ourselves. But we can be clear-eyed about its origins and power, and mindful of how quickly it can start sniffing about and snapping at others. And we can restrain and guide it while feeding the wolf of love.

EXPANDING THE CIRCLE OF "US"

As soon as we make a distinction between one group and another, it's a slippery slope to favoring "us" and looking down on "them." In fact, the heightened sense of warmth and loyalty toward "us" that increases oxytocin activity in the brain can foster suspicion and hostility toward "them." In the extreme, the circle of "us" can shrink to the size of just one individual. For example, I've worked with couples in which each person stood isolated on a separate island. On the other hand, the circle of "us" can expand to encompass the whole world.

> As the earth gives us food and air and all the things we need, I give my heart to caring for all others until all attain awakening. For the good of all sentient beings, may loving kindness be born in me.
>
> MAUREEN CONNOR

With practice—such as in the meditation in the box below—we can see every being as "like me" in some way: "Like me, you feel pain; like me, you have hopes; like me, you will face death one day." As you expand your sense of relatedness, interactions with others stimulate more neural reward activity; as interactions feel more rewarding, we treat others better. The circle of "us" can include all of humanity (and if you like, all of life), soon to be eight billion of us on a rapidly warming planet. If enough people felt this way, there would still be competition and conflicts. But we wouldn't tear each other apart, and we'd live from that kindness which includes the whole world with a boundless heart, omitting none.

ALL OF US

Bring to mind a group that is easy to feel part of, such as a collection of friends or a team at work. Be mindful of the feeling of "us" . . . the sense in your body of being part of a group . . . When you know what "us" feels like, start expanding that circle. Begin with what's easy, widening it to include benefactors, loved ones, and friends . . . expanding further to include more and more people who are easy to feel a sense of "us" with.

Then keep expanding it to include those who are neutral for you. Be mindful of things you have in common with them . . . Perhaps think to yourself: "Like me, you love your children . . . Like me, you need water when you're thirsty . . . Like me, you want to live" . . . Keep focusing on a simple sense of "us" that includes more and more people.

Now start including people who are challenging for you . . . Look for what you have in common with people you

(continued)

disagree with . . . dislike . . . oppose . . . Know that you are not giving up your views or waiving your rights by finding what you have in common with them . . . Notice that widening the sense of us to include those who are challenging for you may help you feel calmer . . . and clearer about any actions you'll take . . .

Gradually extend the sense of us in widening circles . . . including everyone nearby . . . everyone within many miles . . . everyone in this country . . . widening to include every human being on earth in the single circle of humanity . . . our shared common humanity . . .

Gradually include all of life . . . the animals . . . the plants . . . the large and the microscopic . . . all living things together . . . one great single circle of life . . . resting in the ease of all of us . . .

Good Practice

As you begin your day, you could find a heartfelt intention to be helpful to others, practicing for their sake as well as your own. For example, you could think to yourself: "I will be loving today" or "May my practice serve others" or "For the sake of all beings, may I be awake in this life."

You might have a sense of an underlying lovingness that is innate in you (and in others as well). What does it feel like to rest in this innate kindness and caring? When you experience aspects of love, such as compassion, let these feelings sink into you. Explore the sense of lovingness flowing outward from you like the heat of a stove on a cold day, with others moving through this warmth. It's natural to be affected by others, but fundamentally your lovingness is *yours*, radiating outward independently.

Pick an area of your life such as work, or something more specific such as a project. Ask yourself these questions: Are my efforts aimed at what is truly *beneficial* for myself and others? Am I pursuing these aims *skillfully*? Can I be at *peace* with whatever happens? And then consider any changes you'd like to make.

In meditation, include some compassion and kindness practice, deliberately evoking warm feelings for others and focusing on them as your object of attention. You could read the Metta Sutta softly to yourself, perhaps reflecting on certain words or phrases.

For a day, or even just an hour, use only wise speech (that is, well intended, true, beneficial, not harsh, timely, and—if possible—welcome). In particular, be mindful of tone. And if you like, try this with someone who is challenging for you.

Pick people you do not know, such as people in line at a store, and in your mind take some moments to offer compassion and kindness to them.

Remember self-compassion. When you are burdened or stressed, slow down to bring caring and support to yourself. Make self-compassion a priority.

None of us deserves to be mistreated. Yet all of us will be mistreated. No one is so special as to escape mistreatment. This does not mean downplaying mistreatment but seeing it within a larger perspective—taking it less personally, and with a sense of common humanity with so many other beings who have been mistreated, too. Then, when you take appropriate action, it can be helpful to keep all this in mind.

Be mindful of whether you feel another person is a Thou to you—or an It. If you are regarding someone as an It, try to get a sense of them as a whole person, just like you in important ways. And if you get the feeling that someone is "It-ing" you, consider how you could respond—while remaining peaceable, friendly, and fearless.

5

RESTING IN FULLNESS

When touched by the ways of the world,
a mind that is unshaken, stainless, sorrowless, and secure:
This is the highest protection.

SUTTA NIPATA 2.4

n this chapter we'll be exploring what I feel is at the heart of the Buddha's own awakening: liberation from the craving, broadly defined, that is the deep source of so much of our suffering. From his awakening, the Buddha offered a teaching that can be approached not as four truths but as four *tasks*, to:

- understand suffering
- let go of craving
- experience the cessation of craving and suffering
- develop the path of awakening

These are opportunities for a whole life of practice! We encounter them throughout this book. Here I will focus on the first two.

In the Basement of the Mind

Understanding suffering means much more than having ideas about it. It means recognizing it with respect and an open heart, whether it is subtle or anguished, in yourself or in others. Sometimes it is in plain sight: your head is throbbing with a migraine, you're worried about your mother in the hospital, or there's the familiar shadow of weariness or depression. But much of our suffering is buried deep down, embedded in younger layers of the psyche.

WHEN YOU WERE YOUNG

Every child is particularly vulnerable during the first few years. One reason is that the primary neural trigger for experiences of stress and fear—the amygdala—is fully formed before most babies are born. This "alarm bell" in your own brain was ready to ring loudly as you took your first breath. Second, a nearby part of the brain that calms down the amygdala—the hippocampus—doesn't become completely developed until around the third birthday. The hippocampus is key to forming *episodic memories*—specific recollections of personal experiences—and its slow maturation is why we don't remember our earliest years. It also signals the hypothalamus to quit calling for more stress hormones ("enough already!"). The combination of a ready-for-action amygdala and a needs-years-to-develop hippocampus is like a one-two punch: young children are easily upset while lacking internal resources for calming themselves and putting events in perspective. Third, the *right hemisphere* of your brain got a jump start in development during your first eighteen months. This matters because that side of the brain tends to emphasize the perception of threats, painful emotions such as fear, and *avoidance behaviors* such as withdrawing or freezing... which intensify the negative effects of the amygdala-hippocampus combination.

So, like every young child, you needed *external* sources of soothing, comfort, and care. But early childhood is also a time when most parents are stressed and many are poorly supported and sometimes depressed. And the hour-after-hour, day-after-day events of your first few years were happening while your nervous system was especially vulnerable, and while the foundational layers of your psyche were being laid down.

The feelings, sensations, and longings in your younger experiences were internalized into *implicit memory* stores but disconnected from explicit recollections of the situations in which they occurred. Today this buried material lives on. And it can be reactivated by the type of cues that were also present way back then, such as feeling unheard, unseen, or uncared for. In later childhood and then adulthood, something similar can occur during traumatic experiences. The painful residues of events can get caught in the nets of emotional memory, but without context and perspective. The conscious mind may forget, but as Babette Rothschild wrote, the body remembers.

Suffering sinks deep. Thinking that mindfulness and meditation alone will remove buried material can lead to what John Welwood called a *spiritual bypass*—and a failure to accomplish the task of understanding suffering, including its deepest remains. That material is embedded in physical memory systems designed to hold on to their contents. To uncover and release it takes focused effort that certainly draws on mindfulness and self-compassion—a steady mind and a warm heart—but also uses specific skillful means as appropriate. These include different kinds of psychotherapy and self-help practices; please see the notes section for examples. There are good methods for bringing light down into the basement of the mind, and if we are to understand suffering fully, it is all right to use them.

SOOTHING AND REPLACING SUFFERING

One method you could explore on your own is the Link step in the HEAL process (page 98), in which you connect positive experiences to negative material to soothe and even replace it. As one example, you could focus on the feeling of being included in a group of friends while off to the side of awareness are sad feelings from being left out as a child. In the brain, the positive will tend to associate with the negative, and those associations will go with the negative material when it gets stored back into memory networks. In fact, for at least an hour after the negative material leaves awareness, there is a *window of reconsolidation* during which it is neurologically unstable. In this window, you may be able to disrupt the "rewiring" of the negative into your brain by refocusing occasionally on only the positive material. Each time you use linking might take just a dozen seconds, but with repetition you can gradually replace weeds with flowers in the garden of your mind.

The negative material could be thoughts, emotions, sensations, desires, images, memories, or a combination of these. With linking, you won't be denying or resisting this material. You are accepting it as it is while also bringing comfort, perspective, encouragement, and other forms of support to it—and to yourself—as you might with a friend who is suffering.

The negative material could come both from what's been *missing* for you as a child or an adult and from what's been wounding. The absence of the good can hurt as much as the presence of the bad. For example, I was not actively mistreated by other kids in school. But as a young-for-grade, quiet, and painfully self-conscious boy, I felt excluded by my peers and unwanted much of the time. This left an aching hole in my heart that I have gradually filled with many experiences—most of them brief but still real—of being befriended and valued. In other situations, a person could understandably feel let down by parents or others who should have been protectors and allies. So be sure to include what was—or is—missing for you in your understanding of your own suffering.

To do linking, begin by having a sense of the negative material, perhaps by naming it to yourself, such as "that memory of my boss yelling at me" or "this feeling of hurt." Then identify some positive material that could ease and soothe it—and perhaps, over time, replace it. For example, a feeling of calm strength is a resource for anxiety or helplessness; gratitude for what is good in your life could help with sadness or loss; and feeling appreciated or liked is useful for abandonment or shame. In linking, the negative material is kept small and off to the side of awareness while the positive is big and in the foreground. Or your attention could move rapidly back and forth between them. If you get pulled into the negative, drop it and focus only on the positive material.

Over the course of your day, when you're already experiencing something positive, you could imagine that it is touching, softening, and easing negative material to which it is well matched. (Later in this chapter you'll see more about which kinds of positive experiences are best matched to particular negative material.) Perhaps imagine that beneficial thoughts and feelings are sinking down into the hurting, longing places inside you. Or imagine that your wise and loving parts are communicating with younger parts of you. You could also deliberately create beneficial experiences and associate them to negative material, as in the practice in the box below.

USING THE LINK STEP

Before you begin, have a sense of both what the negative material is and what positive material could help with it. When you experience the positive material, take your time with the Enriching and Absorbing steps, the crucial "installation" phase of lasting learning.

The more intense or traumatic the negative material is, the more important it is to go slowly and take good care of yourself, and to get professional help if you need it. My suggestions here presume that you can explore painful material without being hijacked or overwhelmed by it. But if it does grab you, please stop the practice and simply focus on what helps you feel centered and comforted. For more on the process of linking positive to negative material, please see my book *Hardwiring Happiness*.

1. **H**ave an experience of the positive material. Recognize it if you're already feeling it. Or create an experience of it, such as by bringing to mind times and places you have felt it. Help it be present in your mind.
2. **E**nrich it by staying with this experience . . . and feeling it in your body.
3. **A**bsorb the positive material by intending and sensing that it is sinking into you like a warm, soothing balm . . . and being aware of what feels good about it.

4. Link it by being aware of only the *idea* of the negative material while also keeping the positive big and in the foreground of awareness ... Next, have more of a sense of the negative while still keeping it off to the side with the positive big and in the front ... Then see what it's like to bring the positive into contact with the negative, like a soothing balm for wounded places inside. Keep the positive more prominent and powerful. After a few breaths or longer, let go of the negative and rest only in the positive.

Is Life Suffering?

A central Buddhist teaching is generally translated as *All conditioned things are suffering.* "Conditioned" is a shorthand way of saying that something exists due to various causes; it didn't just pop into being out of nowhere. For example, a wooden chair is the result of many factors, including the trees it came from and the people who made it. The sensations of breathing are also the result of many factors, such as the circuitry of the nervous system and whether you just took a big breath. In turn, these causes are themselves conditioned by *their* causes ... ultimately widening out into the universe and back into time.

Are all conditioned things indeed suffering? I don't think so. If we are to fulfill the task—and opportunity—of understanding suffering, we need to unpack this teaching in order to find the way in which it is actually true. So I'd like to walk through different versions of it I've encountered.

Taken literally—"All conditioned things are suffering"—this statement cannot be true. *All* conditioned things can't be suffering. Suffering is an *experience*. A chair is a conditioned thing—a physical object—that cannot have an experience, and it cannot be an experience. So it would be wrong to say, "All chairs are suffering."

A related version of this that I've heard is "Life is suffering." Yet, is it? Experiences—at least as this word is normally used—require a nervous system. Plants and microbes do not have nervous systems. Therefore, they can't have experiences, so they can't suffer. Bones and blood and neurons don't suffer, either. This is not just semantics: suffering is not "out there" in physical objects or in life as a whole. Most conditioned things are *not* suffering. It can feel startling and freeing to recognize that suffering is just a small part of everything.

Let's suppose that the term *conditioned things* is meant to refer only to our experiences, and not to physical objects such as chairs. Then a version of this statement could be "All human experiences are suffering." Is this actually true?

There are times when the mind is filled with physical pain, grief, fear, outrage, depression, or other overwhelming kinds of suffering. I've had those times myself, and then it feels like suffering is all there is. There are also countless people who each day must bear pain, illness, loss, disability, poverty, hunger, or injustice. And in the blink of an eye something might happen—perhaps a car on the highway swerving into you, or a shocking betrayal by someone you've trusted—that changes the rest of your life. Suffering is certainly around us, and often if not always inside us. Compassion calls us to do what we can about it. And still—are *all* of our experiences suffering?

Suffering matters because it is a particular kind of experience—one that is unpleasant—so there must be other kinds of experiences.

The pleasure in eating a juicy peach is not itself suffering. Nor is virtue, wisdom, or concentration. Awareness *itself* is not suffering. Human experience certainly contains fear and grief, but that's not all it contains. Further, any experience, even a painful one, is highly pixelated, with many elements like the individual brushstrokes of a painting. Most of those elements are not themselves suffering. The redness of red, the knowledge that a ball is round . . . none of these is itself suffering.

These points may seem merely technical, but if we overlook what is *not* suffering, then we won't truly understand what *is* suffering. And we will miss out on experiences and resources that we could use both for increasing health and well-being and for reducing suffering. Recognizing suffering in yourself and others opens the heart and motivates practice. But these good ends are not served by exaggerating it.

So let's get even narrower and consider this statement: "Human experiences—even loving, beautiful, inspiring ones—always have some suffering in them." This seems a lot closer to what could be true—but why would pixels of suffering *always* be present somewhere in the movie of consciousness?

At this point it's helpful to think of suffering in a broader and looser way, as "that which is unsatisfactory or *unsatisfying.*" But we still need to clear away some underbrush. In the immediate moment of an experience—perhaps there is the smell of cinnamon or the recognition that a job is done—the smell or recognition is just what it is, and it is not *itself* unsatisfying. Some might say that it is the inevitable ending—the impermanence—of all experiences that makes them always unsatisfying. But *impermanence alone can't be the problem,* since some kinds of impermanence are welcomed; the impermanence of pain makes room for pleasure. And even if the ending of each moment of experience is a loss, it is balanced by the gain of each new moment that arises.

Yes, because all experiences are impermanent, they cannot be permanently, continuously satisfying. But this becomes a problem *only when we try to hold on to them.* The suffering, stress, or dissatisfaction is not inherent in experience itself or in its impermanence. It is inherent only in the *holding* on to experiences. It's good to slow down to appreciate the implications of this. We must still face the inescapable physical and emotional pains of life, and the inescapable transience of all experiences, but we need not *suffer* these as long as we can practice letting go instead of holding on.

How could we do this?

TWO KINDS OF HOLDING

There are two kinds of holding. First, we tend to hold on to what the Buddha called the four objects of attachment:

- pleasures (which can include resisting pain)
- views (such as opinions, beliefs, expectations)
- rites and rituals (which could be extended today to rules and routines)
- the sense of self

For example, I know what it's like to want some ice cream but then find that the container is empty; to have a strong opinion that no one should ever take the last bit of ice cream without seeing if I want some, too; to want a new rule about this in my home; and to feel annoyed that someone took "my" ice cream. This kind of holding is a form of craving, and you can observe it with mindfulness. Like everything else in awareness, craving increases and decreases, ebbs and flows. With practice, you can get more comfortable with letting go instead of holding on, which is a theme throughout this book. Also, as we'll see in the second half of this chapter, you can feel *already* full, already at ease, and therefore less driven to hold on to any moment at all. Even at its most intense, the first kind of holding is only a part of consciousness, not the whole of it. And with practice, this type of holding gradually releases.

But there's a second kind of holding that is inherent in life itself. Intrinsically, the nervous system is always attempting to stabilize and segment extremely dynamic and interconnected processes. To serve the life of the body it inhabits, the nervous system keeps trying to hold on to the patterns of activation that underlie each moment of experience . . . even as they keep dispersing and morphing into something else. When your mind is quiet and steady, you can really see this. It produces an ongoing subtle tension that is a form of suffering. This tension is not the only thing we experience, but it is part of everything we experience. In this particular sense, suffering is indeed an inherent feature of our lives. While we cannot remove this tension, since it is grounded in our biology, we can understand it, which brings a sense of clarity and calm. Additionally, if we can accept this property of the nervous system and not resist it, then we don't add suffering to suffering. This kind of holding is just what brains do. In this life, there is always some tension somewhere. But amidst and around it can be so many other things, such as an open heart, the undisturbed spaciousness of awareness, and thankfulness for the good that is real.

The Causes of Craving

The first kind of holding is the craving that causes most of our suffering. This raises a really important question: What causes our craving?

> Just as a felled tree grows again
> if the roots are unharmed and strong,
> so suffering sprouts again and again
> until the tendency to crave is rooted out.
>
> DHAMMAPADA 338

THREE CAUSES OF CRAVING

Our craving comes from three sources.

First, there are *social* factors such as insecure attachment and feelings of inadequacy, loneliness, envy, and resentment. Practices of *relationship* for these factors include compassion, kindness, and happiness for others.

Second, there are *visceral* factors based on a sense of needs unmet: something is missing, something is wrong. In Pali, the language of early Buddhism, the word for craving is *tanha*, whose root meaning is "thirst"—which is particularly apt for the drives that underlie these sources of craving. You can address them through practices of *fullness* that develop both specific inner strengths for meeting your needs and general feelings of enoughness and emotional balance.

Third, there are *cognitive* factors, due to thinking that:

- something is lasting when actually it is changing;
- something will be continually satisfying when actually nothing can be continually satisfying; or
- there is a fixed "I" or "me" inside when actually there is no fixed self inside.

Practices to address this source of craving focus on the *recognition* of these forms of ignorance and confusion.

THREE KINDS OF PRACTICE

These three kinds of practice—through relationship, fullness, and recognition—are equally important, and each one supports the others. We draw on steadiness of mind for all of them as well as insight—*vipassana* in Pali—which must be relational and embodied if it is to be truly liberating.

There's a natural rhythm in which we often begin with relationship-oriented practices, including moral conduct and self-compassion. As the heart opens and softens, we turn more to practices of fullness that develop resilience and equanimity. With this inner stability, there's a growing recognition of the cognitive factors of suffering. Then these realizations feed back into your relationships and sense of fullness in a positive cycle.

We focused on practices of relationship in the preceding chapter, and in this one we're exploring fullness. The later chapters emphasize practices of recognition.

People are naturally drawn to one aspect of practice or another, and that's fine. Still, it's useful to ask whether it would serve you these days to highlight other aspects, too. For instance, without fully addressing the social and visceral sources of craving, a person's practice can become overly analytical and dry, and not as fruitful as it could be. Further, just one aspect of practice can predominate in some settings. I like to ask myself: How might Buddhism have developed if its root teacher had been a woman and a mother rather than a man and a father? Or if householders had held greater institutional authority for the next 2,500 years? I'm not saying it would have been better, but it's worth considering how it might have been different. Truths are truths regardless of their messengers, but their *expressions* and the *practices* designed to realize them depend upon many factors, including gender, class, and history. There is a saying: Leave nothing out of your practice. In both our personal practice and in our institutions, we can ask: What—and whom—might we be leaving out?

> Any sensual bliss in the world,
> any heavenly bliss,
> isn't worth one sixteenth-sixteenth
> of the bliss of the ending of craving.
>
> UDANA 2.2

Embodied Craving

The deepest roots of craving are in biologically based *drive states* that we share with other animals, including simpler ones such as monkeys, mice, and lizards. The neurobiological hardware that is the basis of these drives emerged hundreds of millions of years ago, long before the capabilities developed for complex cognitive errors. The most fundamental causes of craving lie beneath these cognitive errors, both in the physical structures of the brain and in evolutionary time.

We enter a drive state when there is an invasive sense of *deficit* or *disturbance* in the meeting of an important *need*. As an embodied being, what do you need?

Broadly stated, the fundamental needs of any animal, including us, are *safety*, *satisfaction*, and *connection*. You might pause for a moment and reflect on how these needs appear in various ways throughout your day. The brain meets these needs through regulatory and motivational systems that, respectively, *avoid* harms, *approach* rewards, and *attach* to others. In order, these systems are loosely related to our *reptilian brain stem*, *mammalian subcortex*, and *primate/human neocortex*. For example, if you feel the need for connection with a friend after a misunderstanding, you could draw on capacities for empathy and language in the neocortex to attach to this person in ways that feel good to you.

Our needs are normal, and the neuropsychological systems that try to meet them are necessary. Awakening is not the end of needs, nor can it change the basic structure of the brain. The question is: Can we meet our needs wisely—and without craving and the suffering it causes? To answer this question, it's useful to know something about our neural hardware.

A HEALTHY EQUILIBRIUM

Three major networks in your brain help to keep you on an even keel amidst the waves of life. First, the *salience network* highlights need-relevant information. (Please see the notes section for the key parts of each of these networks.) Second, the *default mode network* is active when we are daydreaming or ruminating, dwelling on the future or the past, or preoccupied with ourselves. Third, the *executive control network* is involved with problem solving and decision making.

These three networks work together and influence one another. To summarize and simplify: when the salience network flags something that matters, it tells the default mode network to stop spacing out, while urging the executive control network to start figuring out what to do.

HEDONIC TONES

To evaluate challenges and opportunities related to each of your needs, these networks track the *hedonic tones* of your experiences. The sense of something as *unpleasant* highlights the need for safety, and the sense of something as *pleasant* highlights the need for satisfaction. Along with a third hedonic tone, *neutral*, this summary of human life as boiling down to nothing more than avoiding pain and approaching pleasure is found both in the ancient teachings of the Buddha and in modern psychology.

But is this all there is to our lives? What about our need for connection, met through attaching to others? Experientially, our relationships have much more to them than only what feels unpleasant, pleasant, or neutral. And in them, we're motivated by much more than just avoiding pain, pursuing pleasure, and skipping past what is neither. Warm feelings of connection increase oxytocin activity in your brain, and releases of this neurochemical have a powerful influence over the neural basis of pain and pleasure. Further, while living in small groups over the last several million years, our ancestors evolved a much bigger neocortex to meet their need for connection more effectively. Today we routinely draw upon aspects of the "social brain" to exercise top-down control over more ancient pain and pleasure systems embedded in the brain stem and subcortex.

If the need for connection is meaningfully distinct from the needs for safety and satisfaction, and if attaching is meaningfully distinct from avoiding and approaching, then it would be biologically adaptive for a fourth hedonic tone to evolve that is meaningfully distinct from unpleasant, pleasant, and neutral. I believe that this is in fact occurring, especially in the brains of the most social species of all: human beings. Let's call it the sense of things as *relational.* You can observe it in your own experience. While being with another person, first notice what feels neutral: not unpleasant and not pleasant; perhaps simply a neutral fact about them, such as they have an elbow. Then notice what is unpleasant that you want to move away from . . . notice what is pleasant that you want to move toward . . . and then notice what is not specifically unpleasant or pleasant but is a sense of being *in relationship with.* This fourth hedonic tone may be subtle in keeping with its possibly recent emergence in evolution, but you can be mindful of it and recognize its role in highlighting your need for connection.

MANAGING NEEDS BY CRAVING

When there is an invasive sense of a need insufficiently met, the brain initiates a neurohormonal stress reaction. The amygdala signals the sympathetic nervous system to prepare for fleeing or fighting, or the parasympathetic system for freezing. Simultaneously, it tells the hypothalamus to call for stress hormones such as adrenaline, cortisol, and norepinephrine. In the body, long-term projects such as strengthening the immune system are put on hold. At the same time, the cardiovascular, gastrointestinal, and endocrine systems are shaken. In the mind, depending on whether safety, satisfaction, or connection is challenged, there could be a sense of fear, frustration, or hurt.

In a nutshell, this is your brain on craving, a neuropsychological summary of the Second Noble Truth. Milder versions of this pervade everyday experience, yet still with craving at their core. I call this the *reactive* mode, or the Red Zone. It is certainly one way to manage challenges to needs. In Mother Nature's biological blueprint, it is designed to be a brief burst of activity that ends quickly... one way or another. But our modern ways of living—and our neurologically advanced capabilities to regret the past and worry about the future—routinely pull us into mild to moderate stress. Life in the Red Zone further depletes and rattles body and mind, which creates a greater sense of deficit and disturbance, fostering even more craving in a vicious cycle.

MANAGING NEEDS BY *NOT* CRAVING

But this is not the only way to meet your needs. Many actions of thought, word, or deed—such as taking in a view, murmuring sympathetically to a friend, or reaching for a fork—actually involve no experience of craving. There might be craving elsewhere in the mind at the time, but not regarding the action itself. It's very useful to observe this in your experience and know what no-craving feels like.

Further, when you feel *resourced* enough to meet your needs, you don't have to fire up into the Red Zone to deal with them. For example, while rock climbing I've been hundreds of feet above the ground hanging on to holds the width of a pencil—and having a ton of fun. The need for safety was definitely challenged, but there was also a sense of capability and trust in the rope and my partner. Similarly, you can pursue big goals with obstacles to satisfaction while simultaneously feeling confident and grateful. In relationships, you can cope with conflict by drawing on interpersonal skills and a sense of self-worth. *The crux is not whether a need is challenged but whether you feel sufficiently resourced to meet it.* External resources such as good friends also matter for meeting your needs, but what's out there in the world is not always reliable. The strengths inside you are with you wherever you go.

Most fundamentally, challenges can land on an underlying sense of needs *already* sufficiently met: a feeling of fullness and balance in the core of your being. Then your body is most able to protect, repair, and refuel itself. Meanwhile, there is a general feeling in the mind of peace, contentment, and love related to the needs for safety, satisfaction, and connection. Fear and anger, disappointment and drivenness, and hurt and resentment may still arise in awareness, but they need not "invade the mind and remain," as the Buddha described during his own preparation for awakening.

I call this the *responsive* mode, or the Green Zone. In it, there is little or no visceral basis for craving. Old habits of craving may remain, but their underlying fuel has been dramatically reduced. This is the resting state—the home base—of your body, brain, and mind. It is not the full ending of suffering in the Third Noble Truth, but it is certainly a strong foundation for it. And it is the biological and psychological basis for resilient well-being.

Whose mind, standing like rock, doesn't shake,
dispassionate for things that spark passion,
unprovoked by things that spark provocation:
When one's mind is developed like this,
from where can there come suffering and stress?

UDANA 4.4

Living in the Green Zone

Developing inner resources is like deepening the keel of a sailboat so that you're more able to deal with the worldly winds—gain and loss, pleasure and pain, praise and blame, fame and slander—without getting tipped over into the reactive mode—or at least you can recover more quickly. With growing confidence in these capabilities, you become more comfortable raising your sights in life and sailing even farther into the deep, dark blue.

To use a related metaphor from the Buddha, we all face inescapable physical and emotional discomfort: the "first darts" of life. Perhaps you stub your toe on a table or feel frustrated while stuck in traffic. But you don't need to add "second darts," such as kicking the table or pounding on the car's horn (which I've done).

As you build up the neural substrates of the responsive mode, your well-being becomes increasingly unconditional, less based on external conditions. And your development of virtue, concentration, and wisdom becomes easier as the fires of craving receive less fuel.

GROWING GENERAL STRENGTHS

Some psychological resources, such as curiosity and patience, have broad uses that are not specific to a particular need. A good example of this is a general mindfulness of hedonic tones. Just because something is unpleasant doesn't *inherently* mean we must flee it or fight it; just because it is pleasant doesn't mean we must chase it; just because it is relational doesn't mean we must cling to it; and just because it is neutral doesn't mean we must ignore it. But to have this freedom while resting in the Green Zone, we do have to recognize the hedonic tones of our experiences before the ancient machinery of craving reacts to them. Then there is a space between you and pain, pleasure, relatedness, and blandness, and in this space is the freedom to *choose* your response. This real-time tracking of hedonic tones is so useful that the Buddha made it one of the four parts of his fundamental summary of practice, the Foundations of Mindfulness.

You might decide to experience the hedonic tone as it is, simply being with it. Liking this, disliking that, feeling connected to this, feeling indifferent about that: all these can just flow through awareness. For instance, your knee might hurt during a sitting meditation. Instead of moving, you could observe the pain mindfully. Simply labeling experiences to yourself—such as "pain...worry... throbbing"—can increase activity in your prefrontal cortex while calming down the amygdala, thus helping you to have more self-control and less distress. Or you might choose to take action, but without any sense of pressure or upset: after noticing the pain in your knee, you could move a bit to ease it, or do walking meditation instead of sitting.

GROWING STRENGTHS MATCHED TO NEEDS

To develop specific resources for particular needs, consider these questions:

1. What need is challenged?

You can work backward from what you are feeling to identify the underlying needs at issue:

- Pain or the threat of it indicates a challenge to *safety*, often signaled also by a feeling of fear, anger, or helplessness.
- Losses and obstacles indicate a challenge to *satisfaction*, which could also be signaled by a feeling of disappointment, frustration, boredom, drivenness, or addiction.
- Separations, conflicts, and rejections flag a challenge to *connection*, also indicated by a feeling of loneliness, abandonment, insecurity, envy, resentment, vengeance, or shame.

2. What inner resource would help with this need?

It's very useful to identify one or more resources that are well matched to the need:

- Relaxation, noticing that you are basically all right when you are, feeling protected, and a sense of calm strength are key resources for *safety*.
- Gratitude, gladness, healthy pleasure, and a sense of accomplishment help with *satisfaction*.
- Feeling included, seen, appreciated, liked, and cherished are resources for *connection*; additional resources include compassion, kindness, assertiveness skills, and sense of worth. In the broadest sense, these are aspects of love.

- And no matter what, *love is the universal medicine.* This resource helps us feel safer, more satisfied, and more
  connected—remarkably, whether it is flowing in or flowing
  out. So if all else fails, or if you don't know where to turn or
  where to start, begin with love.

3. How could you experience this resource?

This is the first step to changing the brain for the better (summarized in the HEAL process, page 51). We must feel what we want to
grow. Notice any times in which you are already having a sense of
this resource or related factors. And consider how you could create
such experiences. Watch out for any tendency to overlook, down-
play, or push away your sense of this resource. Instead, think of these
experiences as precious nutrients for your mind.

4. How could you take in these experiences?

This is the second and *necessary* step of any lasting healing and
growth. But it's the one we tend to forget. So keep those neurons firing together so they have more chance to wire together. Stay with
the experience for a breath or longer, sense it in your body, and feel
what is rewarding about it. You are receiving it into yourself without
clinging to it.

These two steps are so simple and direct that it's easy to underestimate them. But they are the fundamental process of growing the
strengths inside that will help you meet your needs with less craving and suffering. The positive traits you develop will foster positive states, which you can use to reinforce your traits—all in an
upward spiral.

FURTHER READING

Awakening Joy (James Baraz)

The Craving Mind (Judson Brewer)

Hardwiring Happiness (Rick Hanson)

In the Buddha's Words (Bhikkhu Bodhi)

There Is Nothing to Fix (Suzanne Jones)

Trauma-Sensitive Mindfulness (David A. Treleaven)

Unlocking the Emotional Brain (Bruce Ecker et al.)

When Things Fall Apart (Pema Chödrön)

Why Zebras Don't Get Ulcers (Robert Sapolsky)

FEELING ALREADY FULL

In addition to growing specific resources, you can take in experiences of your needs being met, with a sense, broadly, of peace, contentment, and love. Because of our reptilian brain stem, mammalian subcortex, and primate/human neocortex, I jokingly think of this practice as "petting the lizard, feeding the mouse, and hugging the monkey." When you do this again and again, you develop an underlying felt sense of a sufficiency—not a perfection, but an enoughness—of needs met already, a sense of fullness and balance already woven into the body, into the visceral core of your being. It seems kind of magical to me: through internalizing experiences of needs met, you become more able to meet your needs with less sense of craving.

> There is no greater woe than discontent.
> There is no greater fault than the desire to obtain.
> Therefore, one who knows that enough is enough,
> always has enough.
> (Indeed! Indeed!)
>
> TAO TE CHING

Feeling like your needs are met *enough* usually brings some positive emotions, whose neural correlates can have very positive effects. For example, experiences of contentment lower stress by engaging the parasympathetic nervous system and decreasing activity in the fight-or-flight sympathetic nervous system. Feeling contented also involves *natural opioids*, which can reduce pain, bring you into the moment of enjoyment rather than craving a future pleasure, and help you connect with other people and weather separations from them. And consider what is happening in your brain when you feel loved or loving. Oxytocin activity increases, which has well-known benefits for bonding with others. Additionally, its heightened activity feels calming and reassuring, lowering anxiety while promoting openness, creativity, and the pursuit of opportunities.

So look for those little ways in the flow of life to feel a bit more relaxed, protected, strong, and at ease ... and a little more grateful, glad, and successful ... and a little more cared about and caring, and a little more loved and loving. One breath at a time, one synapse at a time, you can gradually develop an increasingly unshakable core inside yourself. The more often and deeply you do this, the greater the results. For a formal practice of this, try the meditation that concludes this chapter.

Peace, Contentment, and Love

I'll offer a variety of suggestions for this practice, but please find whatever works for you, and eventually rest wordlessly in a feeling of peace, contentment, and love. Take these experiences as your object of meditation, absorbing them into yourself as you become absorbed in them. You are resting your mind upon what draws your heart, helping yourself come home to your true nature.

As you do this practice, be mindful of ebbs and flows in the sense of craving, including subtle forms of drivenness, insistence, or pressure. Recognize that craving has the same nature as everything else in the mind: changing, made of parts, and coming and going due to various causes. Let yourself disengage from any craving, and let it pass away.

THE MEDITATION
Come into this moment . . . this body . . . this breath.

> **Peace:** *Notice that you are basically all right right now, that there is enough air to breathe, that you are basically okay . . . Let yourself feel as safe as you actually are . . . Know that you can remain aware of potential threats while also resting in a sense of calm strength and ease . . . Releasing uneasiness, worry . . . feeling more tranquil . . . releasing guarding, defending, bracing . . . Mindful of any craving related to safety falling away . . . Opening to a sense of peace.*

Contentment: *Bring to mind one or more things you feel grateful for . . . people and places you appreciate . . . things you feel glad about . . . Exploring the sense of enoughness already . . . Releasing disappointment . . . releasing frustration . . . Recognize that you can pursue goals without tensing up . . . letting go of any pressure or drivenness . . . Mindful of any craving related to satisfaction falling away . . . Opening to a sense of contentment.*

Love: *Bring to mind one or more beings you care about . . . who care about you . . . opening to feeling caring, with compassion or kindness or love for others . . . opening to feeling cared about . . . warmth and love flowing in and flowing out . . . Knowing you can still look for love while feeling a fullness of love inside you already . . . Letting go of any feelings of hurt . . . resentment . . . inadequacy . . . increasingly replaced by a resting in love . . . Releasing any clinging to others . . . letting go of any sense of needing to impress others . . . Mindful of any craving related to connection falling away . . . Opening to a sense of love.*

Coming home: *Find an integrated general sense of needs met already . . . a general sense of peace, contentment, and love together . . . Abiding at ease . . . receiving the next moment while feeling already full . . . Mindful of any craving being unnecessary . . . any sense of craving dispersing like wispy clouds in full sunlight . . . fading away . . . You're abiding at ease . . .*

Good Practice

Pick a person—it could be a passing stranger on the street or someone close to you, or even yourself—and be aware of some of what is painful, stressful, disappointing, irritating, or hurtful for them—in other words, their suffering. Then choose another person, and so on. This is about simply understanding suffering in an openhearted way, not about being overwhelmed by it or trying to fix it.

Establish a sense of calm strength and compassion for yourself. Then reflect on the life you've had, especially in childhood, and consider what might still be suppressed or minimized, down in the basement of your mind. Also consider how you could allow whatever you have pushed away to flow more freely in your experience. What could help you do this, and what might the benefits be?

Try taking a simple action, such as reaching for a cup, and observe this experience to see what in it *is*…and is *not* suffering.

When your mind is very quiet, try to recognize a subtle ongoing effort in it to hold on to what is fleeting.

For a period of time—a minute, an hour, a day—observe what is unpleasant in your experiences. Then observe what is pleasant. And then what is relational. You can also be aware of what is neutral. Additionally, watch what happens *after* the hedonic tone arises in awareness. Can you be with this hedonic tone, while perhaps taking skillful action of some kind, without being drawn into forms of craving? In other words, can you stay open to your experience while also *not* resisting what is unpleasant, grasping after what is pleasant, and clinging to what is relational? If craving arises, can you release it?

Identify a key psychological resource you would like to grow, such as self-compassion, sense of worth, or patience. Then deliberately look for opportunities to experience this resource; and when you are experiencing it, slow down to receive it deeply into yourself.

Each day, set aside at least a few minutes to rest in a genuine sense of peace…contentment…and love.

Part Three

--- · ---

LIVING INTO
EVERYTHING

6

BEING WHOLENESS

Flowers in springtime, moon in autumn,
cool wind in summer, snow in winter.
If you don't make anything in your mind,
for you it is a good season.

WUMEN HUIKAI

n our exploration of seven practices, we are moving on from the first three—steadying the mind, warming the heart, and resting in fullness—to explore four increasingly radical aspects of awakening. While these next practices—being wholeness, receiving nowness, opening into allness, and finding timelessness—might seem out of reach, in fact each of them is directly accessible with some focus and effort. For example, what I call "wholeness" includes ruminating less about worries and resentments, accepting yourself fully, and feeling complete as a person; these are down-to-earth benefits, and they are available to each one of us. In the spirit of the Buddha's encouragement to go as far you can in this life on your own path of awakening, let's give it a whirl and see what happens!

The Inner Theater

Some years ago one of my neighbors worked in the film industry doing special effects. He showed me a brief clip for one of his projects, of a whale swimming underwater, and he mentioned that the powerful computers at his company had worked overnight to render that single beautiful scene. It seemed remarkable to me that it had taken many hours for their equipment to create a few seconds of imagery that the brain could produce at any time in the theater of imagination.

The circuitry of this inner theater has been one of the major evolutions of the brain over the past several million years. It's an extraordinary capability that helped our ancestors survive, and it aids and enriches our lives today. But it has some drawbacks, and it's important to learn how to use it wisely and not let it use you.

MIDLINE CORTICAL NETWORKS

Imagine tracing a finger from the top of your forehead along the middle of your skull back toward where it starts to curve downward. Neural networks beneath your finger, running along the midline of the topmost regions of your brain, are loosely divided into two sections:

- the network toward the front, which is involved with solving problems, performing tasks, and making plans
- the default mode network (mentioned in the previous chapter) toward the rear and spreading to both sides, which is

involved with ruminating, daydreaming, and wandering attention

Both of these neural networks are engaged with *mental time travel* and a strong sense of self. We draw on them for what's called *affective forecasting; affective* is a psychological term that means "relating to moods, feelings, and attitudes." This forecasting involves imagining and evaluating different scenarios, such as considering how it would feel to talk with someone in a certain way or simply wondering, "What would taste good for dinner tonight?"

Pause for a moment and consider how much time you spend in the mental activities that draw on these midline neural networks. For most of us, it's a lot. Experientially, we're caught up each day in many mini-movies in which there is a kind of "I" observing various situations, people, events . . . and often a "me" to whom things are happening . . . with lots of thoughts and feelings about the show.

The evolution of these midline networks helped our human and hominid ancestors to get better at learning from the past and planning for the future. The brain's default mode seems to help it organize itself—and sometimes we just need a break to daydream, which can reveal creative connections and hopeful possibilities. These capabilities have brought many benefits. Still, they've come with a price.

For example, the midline networks enable depressive, self-referential thinking: "I keep messing up. Why am I so stupid/ugly/unlovable?" And when the default mode gets active, your mind can roam all over the place. Studies of people randomly pinged on their cell phone during the day indicate that the average person has a wandering mind about half the time. The more a person's mind wanders, the more it tends to tilt negatively, toward anxiety, resentment, regret, and self-criticism.

LATERAL CORTICAL NETWORKS

When you shift into another kind of experiencing—simply present in the moment as it is, not judging and evaluating, and with less sense of self—then activity in midline cortices decreases while activity in *lateral* networks on the sides of your head increases. This lateral shift includes greater activation of the *insula*, which supports *interoception*, the sense of internal body sensations and "gut feelings."

These networks activate primarily on one side of the brain. For a right-handed person, the left side of the brain is specialized for sequential processing—taking things step by step, part by part—and therefore for important aspects of language. Meanwhile, the right side of the brain is specialized for holistic, *gestalt* processing—taking things as whole—and therefore for imagery and visual-spatial reasoning. Consequently, the lateral networks of present-moment awareness—with a greater sense of experience as a whole—are more active on the side of the brain that does holistic processing, the right side for most people. (This is switched for many left-handed people, but the general idea is the same.)

We'll be exploring ways to stimulate and strengthen the lateral networks to foster a greater sense of wholeness. But first let's consider a key way that the midline networks promote a sense of fragmentation and suffering—and what we can do about it.

Feeling Divided

When your mind is focused on solving problems or is wandering about, attention keeps shifting from one thing to another. For example, suppose you see a cookie. The image of the cookie is now a "part" of your consciousness. Next, there is the wish to have the cookie—"Me want cookie!"—which is now a second part of consciousness. Then there is the thought "Oh no, cookies have gluten and calories, not for me"—and a third part is now in the mind. But then another part speaks up: "You've worked hard, you deserve that cookie, it's okay..." Parts interacting with other parts, often in conflict with one another. This is the *structure* of most of our suffering: parts of the mind struggling with other parts. Think of something that has bothered you recently and consider some of the parts of this experience, and how they pushed and pulled against each other. On the other hand, as a sense of wholeness increases, this inner division decreases, and suffering decreases as well.

In this common way of experiencing oneself—parts and more parts—it's all too easy to push away parts that feel vulnerable, embarrassing, "bad," or painful. It's as if the mind is a big house with many rooms, and some of them are locked up for fear of what's inside. As understandable as this is, it leads to problems. We make ourselves numb to keep the doors bolted shut. But the more repression, the less vitality and passion. The more parts we exile, the less we know ourselves. The more we hide, the more we fear being found out.

Personally, by the time I got to college, it seemed like most of the rooms of my own mind were boarded up. Over the years I've had to work on accepting myself—*all* of myself, every bit, the scared parts, the angry parts, the insecure parts. Through practicing what Tara

Brach calls *radical acceptance*—including accepting *yourself*—you can reclaim every room in your mind while still acting appropriately. In fact, it is by opening up these rooms that you can best manage whatever they contain. It's like drawing on two traditional healing tools of a physician: light and air. For a practice of this, please see the box. Accepting yourself will help you feel whole, and feeling whole will help you accept yourself.

ACCEPTING YOURSELF

Acceptance means recognizing that something exists as a fact whether you like it or not, with a feeling of softening and surrendering to this reality. Meanwhile, you can still make efforts to change things for the better.

Pick something pleasant, such as a cup you like, and explore the sense of accepting it. Do the same with something that is neutral for you, such as a patch of beige carpet, and accept it. Then pick something mildly unpleasant—perhaps an annoying noise—and help yourself accept it.

Know what acceptance feels like. Your body could relax and breathing could ease. There could be thoughts such as "It's just the way it is . . . I don't like it, but I can accept it." There could be perspective about the big picture and the many causes of whatever you're accepting. It might help to imagine friends or others who are with you and supporting you as you face what you're accepting. Be aware of the difference between a feeling of acceptance, which usually has a calming, a peacefulness . . . and a feeling of helplessness or defeat.

Pick a positive characteristic about yourself, such as a skill or good intention. Explore what it's like to accept this. Next, pick a neutral characteristic such as the fact that you are breathing, and accept it. Then pick something you think is mildly negative about yourself and explore accepting it. Gradually raise the challenge level and build the "muscle" of self-acceptance.

Let things bubble up into awareness, and explore what it feels like to accept them, such as: "Ah, an ache in my lower back, I accept this ... resentful feelings about someone, accepting these ... the sense of a young child inside, hello, little one ... some scary things down in the basement, wishing they weren't there but accepting them, too ..."

Look for sweet, admirable, passionate, tender, good things inside yourself, and take time to accept them. You might imagine bowing to these parts of yourself, welcoming and thanking them, and including them in all of who you are.

Then pick something inside that you are embarrassed or remorseful about, and explore accepting it. Start with something small while knowing that you can take responsibility for it and act wisely. Imagine that compassion, kindness, and understanding are touching these parts of you.

Let the walls inside you soften ... Let everything flow as it will ... Relax as a whole being ... being whole ...

Doing and Being

In a broad sense, the medial networks are for "doing" while the lateral networks are for "being." Researchers have not yet linked every single thing in the table below either to the midline or to the side of the brain. Still, in ourselves and in others, we can recognize a clustering of these states of mind into two groups that are quite distinct:

"Doing"	"Being"
focused on a part of the whole	aware of big picture; panoramic view
goal-directed	nothing to do, nowhere to go
focused on past or future	abiding in here and now
abstract, conceptual	concrete, sensory
much verbal activity	little verbal activity
holding firm beliefs	not-knowing, "seeing newly"
evaluating, criticizing	nonjudgmental, accepting
lost in thought, attention wandering	mindfully present
prominent self-as-object	minimal or no self-as-object
prominent self-as-subject	minimal or no self-as-subject
sense of craving	sense of ease
feeling fragmented	feeling whole

Of course, we need both doing and being to make our way in life. Depending on what the moment calls for, you can move back and forth between them and even weave them together. Nonetheless, modern schooling, occupations, technologies, and entertainments are a repetitive stimulation of the midline networks, which strengthens them. The midline and lateral networks affect each other through *reciprocal inhibition*: as one gets busy, it suppresses the other. The overtraining of the midline network creates a kind of dominance in which experiences of being—in the present as it is, not trying to gain or to resist anything—are often and quickly taken over by forms of doing.

Bottom line: many of us, me included, would benefit from getting better at being. It sounds kind of odd—but it's true! Okay ... *how?*

The Sense of Wholeness

Let's explore several ways to strengthen neural factors that foster a sense of wholeness. Then you'll be more able to rest in the peaceful strength of simply being whenever you like. And you can also have an underlying sense of being while doing one thing or another.

IN THE GREEN ZONE

The feeling of needs unmet will tend to increase midline cortical activity, whether it's tense problem solving centered in the front or negative rumination at the rear. (*Rumination* means rehashing things over and over; it's appropriate that the root of this word relates to a cow chewing its cud.) On the other hand, when you're resting in fullness, there's less fuel for these midline activations and more room for simply being. You're more able to tolerate pain without dividing yourself to fight with it, and more able to enjoy pleasure without dividing yourself to chase after it. You can linger in the present moment, with no need to go mental time traveling: this right now, just this, is complete and enough as it is.

SENSORY FOCUS

Problem solving and rumination usually involve *inner speech* that draws on regions in the *temporal lobes* on the *left* side of your brain if you're right-handed. Sensory awareness—the smell of a lemon, the touch of soft cotton—is nonverbal. So focusing on tastes, touches, sights, sounds, and smells naturally quiets left-brain inner chatter and this source of midline activity. At the same time, it could heighten activity on the *right* side of your brain, potentially stimulating the lateral networks there. Focusing on internal sensations that engage the insula, such as the feeling of your chest rising and falling as you breathe, is particularly helpful. Instead of spinning into a cascade of thoughts, you can stay grounded in your body—which adds the bonus of reducing emotional reactivity and depressive mood.

NOT KNOWING

It also helps to disengage from categorizing, conceptualizing, and evaluating—all of which stir up midline activity. For example, while hearing the traffic, can you let it be simply sound, without labeling it or having opinions about it? What's it like to see a bird and rest in the seeing alone?

Explore "don't know mind," recognizing things as they are without adding beliefs or expectations to them, and letting go of the need to be sure about everything. This might feel a little unsettling at first, but then you relax and realize you can move a glass and even talk with a friend with a sense of not knowing. It's like looking out at the world through the eyes of a young child, and receiving its freshness without laying a veil of thoughts over it. Each way you turn, the world can seem new again.

Also, you can practice what could be called "don't prefer mind." Sometimes we do need to recognize what is helpful or harmful, but much of the time we can step out of the frame of right/wrong, good/bad, like/dislike, that we lay on top of reality-as-it-is. And it's such a relief to stop doing this to *yourself.* To stop narrating your actions with judgments and criticisms, and to stop treating some parts of your mind as if they are bad while other parts are good.

There's nothing wrong with thinking per se, but it tends to crowd out so much else, while also reinforcing the differentiating and preferring that underlie craving and suffering. As you engage in everyday activities—walking, driving, shopping, talking with others—explore what it's like to add as little as possible to them: not labeling them, not talking to yourself about them, and not giving them meanings. This isn't resisting thoughts; it's simply not feeding and following them.

LET YOUR MIND BE

When we're performing tasks or simply lost in thought, there's an ongoing effort to connect things to make sense of them and control them. The teacher Tsoknyi Rinpoche has said that thoughts in themselves are not an issue—but problems come when we try to glue them to each other. Consider this meditation instruction: "Let go of the past, let go of the future, let go of the present, and leave your mind alone." So notice how it feels to let the many things appearing in awareness come and go without trying to connect them together. This is a shift into an effortless receiving of experiences. For example, be aware of breathing, and then notice how "receiving the breath" feels different from "reaching for the breath." Most of the time, we just don't need to be so busy inside our own minds.

GESTALT AWARENESS

The sense of things as a whole engages the right side of the brain and quiets the parts-separated-from-other-parts mental activities of the midline neural networks. Seeing is a good example of this. While the sight of a room contains many things, they can be perceived as a whole, unified scene. Similarly, you could regard your mind like a vast sky through which cloudlike thoughts and feelings are passing. When faced with a problem such as a relationship issue, ask yourself, "What is the larger space in which this is happening? What is the widest possible view about it all?"

With your body, you can explore being aware of it as whole. As a little experiment, notice the sensations of breathing in the front of your chest…in the back of your chest…then both at the same time…and notice if this awareness shifts your state of mind. (For an extended practice of this, try the meditation in the box below.) You can also explore the sense of your body as a whole while moving, such as when walking slowly or doing yoga.

You are the sky.
Everything else—
It's just the weather.

PEMA CHÖDRÖN

TRANQUILITY

As you feel more whole, your mind gets quieter. The noise and clutter fade to the background. Tranquility grows—which is one of the seven factors of awakening in the Buddhist tradition. And as you become more tranquil, you feel less divided against things that are disturbing and thus more whole. The cultivation of a genuine tranquility—not pushing anything away, simply coming to rest—is so important, especially in our very untranquil world. For example, the classic Mindfulness of Breathing Sutta (Majjhima Nikaya 118) suggests that we "breathe in, tranquilizing the body; breathe out, tranquilizing the body . . . breathe in, tranquilizing the mind; breathe out, tranquilizing the mind . . ."

You can think of your mind as like a murky pond. As it becomes more tranquil, the dirt in it gradually settles. This reveals the pure nature of the pond's water—never tainted itself by what was floating in it—and the beautiful jewels that have always been resting on its bottom.

A WHOLE BODY BREATHING

Find a comfortable position in which you can be relaxed and alert. Find a sense of calm strength . . . letting go of unnecessary anxiety . . . noticing you are basically all right right now . . . opening into peace. Be aware of things you're thankful for . . . feeling gratitude, gladness . . . a sense of enoughness in the moment as it is . . . opening into contentment. Finding warmheartedness . . . compassion and kindness . . . a simple sense of being liked and loved . . . opening into love flowing in and out, resting in fullness . . .

Be aware of various sensations of breathing throughout your body . . . Focus on your chest, recognizing multiple sensations of breathing there . . . Be aware of sensations in the front of the chest . . . in the back . . . both front and back at the same time. Be aware of sensations on the left side of the chest . . . on the right side . . . now both right and left at the same time. Be aware of your chest as a whole as you breathe . . . attention widening to include the whole chest . . . receiving the sense of your chest as a whole as you breathe.

If the sense of the whole fades, that's normal, and simply be aware of it again. In this focus on sensation, let thinking and verbal activity fall away.

In these ways, gradually expand awareness to include sensations of breathing in the diaphragm . . . and chest and diaphragm at the same time, as a single experience. Expand to include sensations in the belly . . . and back . . . internal sensations in the lungs and heart . . . the sensations of breathing in the torso as a whole, a single, unified field of sensations experienced continuously.

Include the shoulders . . . arms and hands . . . neck . . . head . . . Be aware of the upper body as a whole as you breathe. Expand awareness further to include sensations in the hips . . . legs . . . and feet. Be aware of your upper body and lower body at the same time, as a whole, as a single experience continuing . . . Include all the body's sensations in awareness . . . Abide as a whole body breathing.

Abiding as a whole body breathing, becoming more tranquil . . . letting sounds and thoughts come and go, leaving them alone as you rest in the sense of the whole body . . . not needing to make sense of anything, simply resting in breathing . . . a whole body breathing . . .

Unhindered

The natural movement of the heart is to open, let go, and love—and to release tension, straining, craving, and suffering. Yet this natural flow can be blocked or covered over by certain feelings and desires. These hindrances are both a result of craving and a fuel for it. They involve a part of the mind that is obstructing other parts. As they decrease, wholeness grows; as you develop your sense of wholeness, hindrances are reduced, as are craving and suffering. The Buddha identified five hindrances in particular, and being aware of them is an important step in developing greater wholeness.

THE FIVE HINDRANCES

Sensual desire: This hindrance is the stressful pursuit of lasting pleasure in passing experiences. (It can also be approached as the stressful resisting of pain; for simplicity, I'll focus on grasping after
pleasure.)

Ill will: This is the will for ill: a motivation to hurt and harm. It
includes hostility, bitterness, and destructive anger.

Fatigue and laziness: This is heaviness of body and dullness of
mind. There could be a sense of weariness, even depression, and
little motivation for practice.

Restlessness, worry, remorse: This is mental and physical agitation.
There's an inability to settle down, and one preoccupation or another has invaded the mind.

Doubt: This is not healthy skepticism but a corrosive mistrust of
what you know or what could be reasonably believed. There could
be a lack of conviction, an overthinking, a "paralysis by analysis."
This is a powerful hindrance, since anything can be doubted.

PRACTICING WITH HINDRANCES IN GENERAL

Be mindful of them. Hindrances are mental phenomena like any other,
with the same nature as all the rest: impermanent, made of parts,
coming and going due to their causes. We don't need to give them so
much power. They are empty of essence, like swirling clouds, not
bricks, and recognizing this can help you be less burdened by them.

Don't fuel them. Habits and reactions may arise, but you can stop
reinforcing them. Be mindful of rumination and disengage from it.
Don't join with the hindrance to impede or undermine yourself.

Appreciate what is not hindered. Refocus on whatever could be beneficial, such as a simple sense of gratitude. Be aware of wholesome, loving, wakeful aspects of yourself. When you are aware of them, they are naturally unobstructed.

FURTHER READING

The Deep Heart (John Prendergast)

Radical Acceptance (Tara Brach)

RESOURCES FOR SPECIFIC HINDRANCES

Here are some key resources for each of the hindrances.

Sensual desire: Focus on a sense of satisfaction *already*, such as in thankfulness, appreciation, and contentment. Also, when you want something—perhaps more dessert or a new sweater—be mindful of the pleasure you imagine you'll experience if you get it. Then compare the anticipated pleasure to what it *actually* feels like when you get what you wanted. Much of the time, the actual pleasure is nice, but it's not as great as you imagined. We can get oversold by our own minds. I think of this as the workings of a kind of inner advertising agency that may have evolved to motivate our ancestors to keep chasing the next carrot: "It will taste *so* good!" So be realistic about the pleasures you will truly get from fulfilling your desires, and then you can choose as you like.

Ill will: Recognize that resentment and anger are a burden on *you* even if they feel good in the moment. Be mindful of any feelings of hurt, fear, or grievance beneath the ill will; focus on these underlying feelings and try to accept them. Have compassion for yourself related to whatever has prompted the ill will. Bring to mind people you like, and focus on feeling compassionate and kind toward them ... and also see if you can feel cared about by them. Then try to find compassion for the person who has been challenging for you.

Fatigue and laziness: Get plenty of rest. (You can also explore the sense of a wakefulness that can include weariness or fogginess simply as experiences like any other.) Take some deep breaths with vigorous inhalations to engage the stimulating sympathetic branch of your nervous system. Listen to or read something inspiring. Move your body, go out into nature if you can, be enlivened by fresh air.

To overcome laziness and strengthen motivation, you could consider the rare and fleeting opportunity of your own life. I once heard these questions offered as a reflection from the Tibetan tradition: *Will I escape illness? Will I escape aging? Will I escape dying? Will I escape being separated eventually, one way or another, from all that I love? Will I escape inheriting the results of my own actions?* Personally, I think about all those who have helped me—as well as my own efforts in previous years—and want to make good use of their gifts ... and also do what I can to hand my own gifts forward in time, both to others and to the person I will be in a year, and on the last day of this life. This does not feel morbid, but grateful and joyful.

You can also imagine the rewards of whatever you'd like to motivate yourself about—such as meditating more or being less irritable with others—before doing it, while doing it, and after doing it. Try to get a feeling of the rewards (for example, relaxation, sense of worth) beyond just an idea of them. In your brain, this will tend to associate anticipated rewards with particular actions, and help you form new good habits.

> Tell me, what is it you plan to do
> with your one wild and precious life?
>
> MARY OLIVER

Restlessness, worry, remorse: Overall, try to understand what is making you feel restless, worried, or remorseful. Identify what seems valid to you. Keep letting go of what seems exaggerated or unnecessary. And make a realistic plan for what you could do about whatever seems valid. These steps are boringly obvious, but they really work.

Restlessness can come from feeling that something genuinely important is missing in your life or in your current practices. There have been times I should have listened more to what my restlessness was trying to tell me, rather than "sticking it out" year after year in a particular job or spiritual practice. Also consider your temperament; maybe you naturally need more stimulation to stay interested and focused. For example, in meditation, you could use more engaging objects of attention, such as gratitude or contentment.

Worry is related to our need for safety. Do what you can to address real threats. Meanwhile, try to have feelings of relaxation, determination, reassurance, and peacefulness whenever possible. By internalizing these experiences again and again, you will build up an underlying sense of calm strength that will help you worry less. Any time you get caught up in rumination, ask yourself if there is any value in it; if not, try to shift your attention gently but firmly to something else.

Remorse is related to our need for connection; related feelings are guilt and shame. These are big topics, and I won't be able to do justice to them here. See if it is helpful for you to do any of the following:

- Decide for yourself what is truly worthy of remorse.
- Take responsibility for whatever this is.
- Let yourself experience and gradually release the remorse and related feelings.
- Be clear about how you want to act in the future.
- Make amends and repairs as much as possible.
- Have compassion for yourself.
- Explore forgiving yourself.
- Try to have a sense of what *is* kind and honorable and worthy about yourself.

Doubt: Be aware of *mental proliferation*, thoughts spinning out in all directions. Come back to what is simple and undeniably clear: the experience of this moment and the things you know to be true. In the moment itself, there is nothing to doubt about *it*, since it is obviously here as it is. Disengage from excessive analyzing, judging, and thinking. Allow yourself to be uncertain, to wait and see, to run the experiments of life one way or another and observe the results.

FEELING UNHINDERED

In this meditation we'll explore feeling centered in awareness that is unhindered in staying present . . . centered in a spirit of acceptance that is unhindered in letting go . . . centered in fullness and balance unhindered by a sense of something missing, something wrong . . . in a sense of peace, contentment, and love that is unhindered by fear, frustration, or hurt . . . resting in and being carried along by an unhindered true nature . . . Here we go:

Relax . . . steadying the mind . . . warming the heart . . . Settle into and stabilize open, receptive awareness . . . unhindered in staying present . . . Find a sense of fullness and balance . . . nothing missing, nothing wrong . . . Open into a growing sense of peace, contentment, and love . . . unhindered by fear, frustration, or hurt . . .

Be aware of any ill will . . . and let it go, resting in feelings of safety, compassion, and being loved . . .

Be aware of any sensual desire . . . and let it go, resting in a sense of well-being already . . .

Be aware of any fatigue or laziness . . . and let it go, resting in a natural wakeful energy and clarity . . . and resting in a feeling of your own good intentions and aspirations . . .

Be aware of any restlessness, worry, or remorse . . . and let it go, finding a sense of calm, reassurance, and your own natural goodness . . .

Be aware of any doubt . . . and let it go, resting in clear knowing of the moment as it is . . . trusting what you know to be true, such as this chair, this breath . . .

Feel and trust in your underlying true nature . . . a natural wakefulness . . . goodness . . . peacefulness . . . uncovered, unhindered . . . unshaken, stainless, sorrowless, and secure . . .

Being the Mind as a Whole

The widest possible sense of wholeness is to be present as the mind as a whole. Everything is included in this whole: sights and sounds, thoughts and feelings, perspectives and points of view, and awareness itself. The mind as a whole is apparent all the time, but most of us don't often experience it as a whole, since we're usually preoccupied with one part of it or another. But when we abide as the mind as a whole, there is no strain. There may be pain, there may be sorrow, but when no parts of the mind are struggling with other parts, there is no craving and there is no suffering. Undivided, you feel at peace. The various contents of the mind keep changing, so they don't feel very reliable. But the mind as a whole keeps being the mind as a whole: it is stable as what it is, and therefore more reliable. Undisturbed, you feel at peace.

AWARENESS AND THE BRAIN

Awareness offers a direct path into a sense of the mind as a whole. Since awareness is a tricky word with multiple meanings, let's begin by clarifying it. First, you can be *aware of* something, such as the sound of a car or a lingering feeling of irritation after a tense conversation with someone at work. As I mentioned in chapter 3, types of meditation in which you stay continuously aware of a particular something—such as sensations of breathing—are termed focused attention practices. Second, you can practice open awareness, in which you observe passing experiences without judgments about them or attempts to influence them. Third, you can be aware of awareness, in which you turn awareness back onto itself. Fourth, you can abide as awareness, primarily experiencing its spacious receptivity, disengaged from whatever passes through it, with a growing sense of simply being awareness. (The first two kinds of awareness are relatively straightforward, while the next two take more practice.) In both meditation and daily life, there can be a natural movement from focused attention to open awareness to abiding as awareness. If something distracts you—an upsetting memory, a sound nearby—after you recognize this, you can reestablish focused attention and gradually return to open awareness and then abiding as awareness.

The first kind of awareness—awareness *of* something—is widespread among animals, even those with simple nervous systems. The frog is aware of a fly when it moves, and the fly is aware of light and shadow falling onto its multifaceted eyes. The frog or fly does not need to be aware of being aware or to have a sense of personal identity in order to be awake and alert and to react to its environment. Exactly *how* the frog is aware of the fly—and how we are aware of the frog—is still a thorny question in the science of consciousness. Nonetheless, the underlying neurobiology of awareness is becoming clearer (though many questions and controversies remain, and this is a simplifying summary). Initial rudimentary information about a stimulus is processed by "lower levels" of the nervous system and sent to "mid-levels" for further processing, then to "higher levels," where it is represented in neural substrates that enable what Bernard Baars has termed the *global workspace of consciousness.*

To use the notion of a workspace as a metaphor, imagine a meeting room in which different parts of the brain can efficiently share information with other parts. For example, perceptual ("What is happening?"), salience ("Does it matter?"), and executive ("What should we do?") systems can keep one another informed. The representing of information in these *neural correlates of consciousness* involves fleeting coalitions forming among many neurons along with related neurochemical processes. These are like physical eddies in a neurobiological stream representing eddies of information that enable eddies of experiences.

So far I've described awareness as a static field in which experiences occur, but that's only a simplifying metaphor. Since the physical basis of awareness is living and continually changing, awareness itself is dynamic, with shifting edges and qualities. Awareness is a *process*, not a thing; we are "aware-ing." In terms of ordinary reality, the awareness of a human (or a frog) is *conditioned*, meaning that it occurs due to causes, and it is not something that has an absolute unconditioned existence of its own.

> An attitude of open receptivity, free of any goal or anticipation, will facilitate the presence of silence and stillness to be revealed as your natural condition.... Awareness naturally returns to its non-state of absolute unmanifest potential, the silent abyss beyond all knowing.
>
> ADYASHANTI

ABIDING AS AWARENESS

Since awareness is ineffable and impermanent, clinging to it or identifying with it would give rise to suffering. Nonetheless, as long as you, ah, stay aware of this, a growing sense of abiding *as* awareness will naturally draw you into wholeness as you disengage from the many things—the parts and more parts—passing through awareness. Since experiences of "I," "me," and "mine" are just some of these many things, abiding as awareness also eases the sense of self, and thus reduces the suffering that comes from taking life so personally.

By resting in awareness, you could gradually take on some of its qualities. Since awareness can receive anything and hold anything, is never stained by what moves through it, and has no edges...you become more open and spacious, pure, and boundless yourself. Further, awareness is a field of possibility that is *like* what might be utterly unconditioned, transcending ordinary reality. As we'll see in chapter 9, "like" isn't the same as "is," but abiding as awareness may help develop an intuition of what could *actually* be unconditioned in the ultimate sense. And you might find that what seems on the surface to be just your own awareness is in its depths somehow transpersonal, vast, and timeless.

As you continue in this way, the apparent distinction between awareness and its contents gradually fades, and you realize that these are simply aspects of a single mind. Then you abide as the mind as a whole. There is a sound...and there is awareness of the sound... and really there is simply the mind as a whole. Not a subject separated from objects, not awareness separated from its contents: a unity, not a duality. Not two, one.

BEING UNDIVIDED

Find a feeling of warmheartedness . . . fullness . . . a sense of peace . . . contentment . . . love . . . Be aware of the sensations of breathing . . . and gradually include the whole body . . . abiding as a whole body breathing.

Resting as the whole body, be aware of sounds . . . and include them with sensations as a single whole experience. Gradually include sights with sounds and sensations as a single whole . . . include feelings in this whole . . . and thoughts . . . and anything else in awareness as a single whole experience.

Be aware of witnessing this whole experience . . . letting it pass before you in the streaming of consciousness . . . Then settle into awareness itself . . . Let go of effort and rest in clear, nonconceptual awareness . . . Let go of fears, let go of hopes, let go of the sense of self if it arises . . . Let go of what's past . . . Let go of the future . . . Let go of the present as it passes away . . .

Open into what is apparent . . . awareness and its contents occurring together as a single process, mind as a whole . . . Letting the mind be . . . Simply being yourself as you most fully are . . . continuously . . .

Be mind as a whole with everything included . . . a whole mind unfolding . . .

Simply be . . . nowhere to go, nothing to do, no one to be . . . experiences happening on their own . . . being carefree and open . . . releasing your mind, letting it be free . . .

Good Practice

Try a little experiment for an hour in which you count the number of distinct "episodes" in which your mind goes into negative rumination. Don't count times when you are thinking about something in a deliberate way or your mind is wandering pleasantly. You don't need to get an exact count; what matters is greater self-awareness. Then you can reflect on what you've observed, and what you'd like to do about it.

At different times, focus on sensations while disengaging from thoughts; thoughts may still come, but don't feed or follow them. You could also include hearing and seeing, while still disengaging from thoughts. Let this way of being sink into you so you can draw on it again.

While doing a routine activity such as washing dishes, explore the sense of approaching the objects as if you do not know what they are. You'll be seeing, holding, and moving them but without much conceptualizing about them. You can also bring "don't know mind" into other parts of your day.

Occasionally drop into a sense of your body as a whole.

Pick one thing that hinders the expression of what is healthy and wakeful and good in you. At first, look for something small and concrete. Then, for a day or more, focus on disengaging from and not fueling this hindrance... and enjoying what is released as a result. You can do this with other hindrances as well.

In meditation, explore open awareness and abiding as awareness. These may not come naturally at first, but with practice they will.

In meditation and at other times, get a sense of your mind as a whole.

RECEIVING NOWNESS

What can anyone give you greater than now,
starting here, right in this room, when you turn around?

WILLIAM STAFFORD

One of the most remarkable facts of existence is under our noses all of the time.

This is the Now of the present moment: endlessly ending, and endlessly renewed. Radically transient, yet always enduring. Much like a single point in a line is infinitely thin spatially, each moment of now is infinitely thin *temporally*—and yet somehow each moment contains all the causes of the past that will make the future. It's where—or better, when—we actually live, yet we hardly know our own home. Scientifically, the nature of now and time itself remains mysterious. But experientially, it is clearly valuable to rest in the present moment. As the scientist and Buddhist monk Matthieu Ricard has said: "One should learn to let thoughts arise and be freed to go as soon as they arise, instead of letting them invade one's mind. In the freshness of the present moment, the past is gone, the future is not born, and if one remains in pure mindfulness and freedom, potentially disturbing thoughts arise and go without leaving a trace."

Let's explore how to enjoy this freshness.

The Making of This Moment

Your experience of the present moment is based on the activity of your nervous system at that moment. So it's helpful to understand the underlying neural basis of the experience of nowness. Then, in the next section, we'll see how to use this understanding in practical ways.

THE PHYSICS OF NOW

Your brain and mind are in a particular state at any moment, and those states change over time. Sounds straightforward ... except that no one really knows what *time* is, or why it is—and *now* is even more perplexing. The greatest scientists in the world do not know for sure why there is a present moment or what it actually is. It is always now, yet it's unclear exactly how the universe makes time—or how time makes the universe.

Still, there are some good guesses, and I like this one from the physicist Richard Muller. Nearly 14 billion years ago, the big bang produced a universe with four dimensions—three of space and one of time—and *all* of them have been expanding ever since (the emphases are his):

> The Big Bang is an explosion of 4D *space-time.* Just as space is being generated by [this] expansion, so time is being cre-

ated.... Every moment, the universe gets a little bigger, and there is a little more time, and it is this leading edge of time that we refer to as *now*....

... By the *flow* of time, we mean the continual addition of new moments, moments that give us the sense that time moves forward, in the continual creation of new *nows*.

Get it?! I don't, entirely, yet it's still awe-inspiring to imagine that each moment of our lives is being made at the front edge of the expansion of the universe. Without telescopes, we can't see the creation of new space, but with each breath we can witness the creation of new time. If Muller's hunch is true, we are always in creation.

> For the time being the highest peak, for the time being the deepest ocean
> For the time being a crazy mind, for the time being a Buddha body
> For the time being a Zen Master, for the time being an ordinary person
> For the time being earth and sky
> Since there is nothing but this moment, "for the time being" is all the time there is.
>
> DŌGEN

WAKEFULNESS

To observe our expanding space-time universe, the brain begins by establishing a state of *vigilance*. While this might sound stressful, the root meaning of this word is "wakefulness," and that's the sense of it here. Suppose you're trying to remain attentive to whatever might happen next—let's say you're driving with a friend late at night on a twisting turning road through the mountains. Neural networks in the right hemisphere activate to keep you watchful mile after mile. And from time to time, the *locus ceruleus* in the brain stem sends pulses of norepinephrine throughout your brain. This stimulating neurochemical is like your friend saying, "Hey, stay awake!"

Meanwhile, your attention can focus on specific things such as what you're talking about with your friend. Deliberate sustained focus draws on the *upper attention network* on both sides of the brain. When you are in the "doing" mode discussed in the preceding chapter, particularly during goal-directed tasks, you're usually engaging this upper network.

ALERTING

Then let's say that something new occurs: a deer starts to run across the road in front of you. Photons bouncing off the deer's body land on your eyes and trigger a cascade of neural activity, and within a tenth of a second or so, you begin to be aware that something has happened, something has *changed*. In the brain, basic perceptual systems—in this case, mainly visual—are processing the first and simplest raw sensory data. But in that very first flash of a sight emerging into consciousness, you don't yet know exactly where it is or what it is or what to do about it.

ORIENTING

In the next few tenths of a second, there is a growing recognition of *where* the something that happened is located. The brain quickly tries to figure out, is it close or far away? As our ancestors evolved, the closer that things were, usually the more important they were as a threat, opportunity, or relationship. And within a second or two, there is a developing knowledge of *what* the something is: a shadow cast by the moon—or a vulnerable deer.

The process of alerting and orienting engages a *lower attention network* that's mainly on the right side of the brain. This lower network is inhibited by the upper attention network when you're focused on particular things. But when something new happens, it activates and takes over from the upper network to "update" the field of awareness. As the lower attention network comes online, it also quiets the default mode network; something new has arrived to disrupt any daydreaming or ruminating.

> They do not grieve over the past,
> nor do they yearn for the future.
> They live only in the present.
> That is why their faces are so calm.
>
> SAMYUTTA NIKAYA 1.10

EVALUATING

After you know that something has happened and where and what it is, then you need to start attending to what it *means*. Can you ignore it, or does it matter? Is it friend or foe? Is there room to swerve

around it? Within the first second, the brain's salience network—
mentioned in chapter 5—gets involved, highlighting what's relevant
and beginning to generate a hedonic tone about it, such as the unpleasant sense of alarm at a deer darting into the road in front of
your car.

ACTING

As you move into action, the executive control system (also described in chapter 5) gets engaged to direct your immediate
behavior—let's say you turn fast to the right to get around the deer.
After the crisis has passed—whew!—and you return to talking with
your friend, the upper attention network reasserts itself while the
lower attention network settles back into readiness for the next
new thing.

BRINGING THIS SEQUENCE INTO YOUR EXPERIENCE

It's remarkable how much can happen in just a few heartbeats. In the
example of the road and the deer, four major neural networks got
involved within a couple of seconds. The brain is so fast that it does
this routinely. An event with a deer is dramatic, but most instances
of alerting and orienting are small and ordinary and peaceful. For
example, you could get a text, hear someone speak, or have your cat
jump into your lap. When sitting in meditation with open awareness,
you could be recognizing continual changes in the stream of consciousness. You can observe alerting and orienting many times a day
in your own experience, especially as your steadiness of mind

strengthens. Try this with new sensations and sounds emerging into awareness, as well as with new thoughts and emotional reactions.

Consciousness is like a windshield as you move forward through time—or as time streams through you—and the process of alerting and orienting is the leading edge of that windshield. As you become more mindful of this, you can move closer and closer, experientially, to the front edge of the subjective now. This is as close as ordinary experience gets to the emergent edge of the objective now—and perhaps to the instant of creation of new time in our universe.

Being Here Now

Strengthening and stabilizing wakefulness, alerting, and orienting are powerful ways to help yourself come into and stay in the present moment—being here *now*, steadily. Experientially, this brings you closer to the very beginnings of the brain's constructing of the streaming of consciousness. It's like there's a spring coming out of a mountain, cool water bubbling forth, and you're continually present with the first emergence of the stream into the open air.

For everyday life, here are some practical suggestions for staying in the present moment. You could also try the meditation in the box on page 160.

WAKEFULNESS

This is an open readiness to receive whatever comes next. Whether you're sitting quietly in meditation or busily doing one thing after another, you can encourage wakefulness by remaining aware of the larger surround. As we saw in the previous chapter, a sense of the whole—the room or building you're in, the sky above, the overall context—stimulates networks on the right side of the brain, and this may support activation of similarly right-sided neural networks that promote vigilance.

> If we don't have now, we don't have much.
> It's actually all we've got.
>
> JAN HANSON

If you start to feel foggy or spacey, you could draw on the norepinephrine system for a surge of wakefulness. For example, bring to mind something that carries a sense of intensity, such as a memory of a time you were excited. Inhale a little more vigorously—engaging the sympathetic branch of the nervous system—with a feeling of rousing. If you are sitting, it's useful to sit up straight, not rigidly but as if an invisible string on the top of your head were gently tugging you up to the sky. You can explore a similar sense of being vertical when you're standing or walking. Uprightness in the body supports wakefulness in the mind.

ALERTING

Notice what it's like to be alerted by something such as the ringing of a phone or the initial perception of someone coming into the room you're in. In the first half second or so, there will be the bare knowing that something has changed, along with raw sensory information and perhaps a quality of surprise. You could also shift from focused engagement to a receiving of something new: look up from what you're doing, change gears to a different task, or try on a new perspective. As you become more familiar with the experience of alerting, you'll be more able to evoke the sense of it whenever you like.

Alerting is like the feeling of fresh air. To promote this *updating* of consciousness, it helps to cultivate curiosity, a welcoming of novelty, and a capacity for amazement and wonder.

Experientially, *a sense of wholeness and nowness seem to come together.* Neurologically, there could be some reasons for this. The sense of wholeness tends to reduce activity in the midline cortical networks that enable mental time traveling, helping you come into the present moment. The lower attention network promotes a quality of receptive global awareness that is the essence of wholeness. The lateral neural networks of wholeness and the lower attention networks of nowness are both centered in the right side of the brain, and the activation of one may foster activation of the other.

There's a sweet spot in which you can help two things to happen at the same time. First, relax, which supports an open and receptive awareness. Second, stay attentive to the arriving of the next moment. This combination is beautifully summarized in the town motto of Barre, Massachusetts, which is home to two major meditation centers: Tranquil and Alert. Imagine spending the minutes and days of your life in this way.

ORIENTING

Be mindful of the dawning recognition of where and what something is that comes on the heels of alerting. It's like hearing a sound in the city and in less than a second registering that it's across the street and is a bus pulling away from the curb. This is the feeling of orienting, and as you become more mindful of it, you can rest more stably in the sense of it.

Sometimes we do need to filter out incoming signals. But it's so easy to get mentally captured by an endless list of tasks. If you, like me, get caught up in doing and more doing, focused on one thing after another, try to engage the lower attention network—alerting and orienting and coming into the present—which will help you rest more in being. You'll still be able to work and accomplish tasks. If you are swept along by doing, it's hard to have a sense of being; on the other hand, when you feel grounded in being, you can still do many things, such as making dinner or talking with a friend. In a similar way, when we're lost in thought about what was or might be, it's hard to feel present here and now. But while feeling centered in the moment, you can still reflect on the past and plan for the future. With practice, being and doing become increasingly woven together, as we saw in the previous chapter. Much the same can happen with alerting and orienting and with evaluating and acting. But at first, most of us need to train the mind and brain to rest more in the here and now.

AT THE FRONT EDGE OF NOW

Find a posture that is comfortable, upright, and stable. You may wish to keep your eyes open. Remain aware of the larger surround: the room you are in, the whole that you are part of.

Be mindful of the sense of relaxed wakefulness . . . being tranquil and alert. From time to time, see what it's like to sit up a little straighter . . . to inhale more vigorously and fully . . . to bring to mind something that has a feeling of excitement.

Establish a sense of alerting. Be aware of the ongoing "arriving" of the initial sensations of breathing . . . continuously . . . Rest in awareness of sensations changing . . . Disengage from labels or concepts . . . With a feeling of ease, remain receptively present.

Be aware of a similar arriving of sounds . . . sights . . . thoughts . . . Open wide to whatever might next appear . . . allowing what comes next to be unexpected . . . perhaps finding a sense of wonder . . . delight . . . Being at the front edge, continually, of whatever is appearing in awareness.

Establish a sense of orienting. Observe the process of recognizing where and what sensations are . . . where and what sounds are . . . anything else appearing in awareness . . . As soon as you recognize where and what anything is, let go of it, letting it whoosh on by . . . without evaluating anything or needing to act upon it.

Stay with alerting and orienting . . . being present in the continual updating of consciousness . . . Such a peaceful place, the present . . .

The Parts of Experience

If an enchanted loom—the brain—is weaving the fabric of consciousness moment after moment, what are the major threads? For

one answer to this question, I've adapted a framework in the Pali
Canon that "deconstructs" the flow of experience into five parts:

1. *forms:* sights, sounds, tastes, touches, smells; basic sensory
   processes
2. *hedonic tones:* the quality of pleasant, unpleasant, relational,
   or neutral
3. *perceptions:* categorizing, labeling; identifying what something is
4. *formations:* a traditional term for all the other elements of
   experience, including thoughts, emotions, desires, images,
   and memories; expressions of temperament and personality; planning and choosing; and sense of self
5. *awareness:* a kind of field (or space) in which experiences
   occur

PARTS AND MORE PARTS

Each of these parts of experience can be divided further into smaller
and smaller parts. Even awareness can be divided, in the sense of
being aware of being aware. In effect, you can deconstruct your experience, recognizing that it is entirely *compounded,* made of parts
within parts within parts. This is not mere conceptual analysis.
When you are mindful of the many individual threads making the
tapestry of each moment, experiences seem lighter and airier, and
less substantial and binding. You also see how the little parts of each
experience are continually changing. Realizing again and again that
you can't grab on to any *part* of any experience, you gradually stop
trying to hold on to experiences in general, thus easing a fundamental source of suffering.

The parts of every experience come and go due to countless causes—most of them impersonal, originating out in the world and back in time—with no master filmmaker inside your head directing each scene. When you recognize the show in the theater of the mind in this way, you can take it less personally and feel less implicated in it and thus less weighed down by it.

> "All conditioned things are impermanent."
> Seeing this with insight,
> one becomes disenchanted with suffering.
>
> DHAMMAPADA 277

BEFORE SUFFERING

Your awareness of something *new*—such as your phone vibrating with a new text, a person coming round a corner as you walk down the street, or a strong sensation in your body—tends to move sequentially through the first four parts of experience. Initially there is the most basic sense that "something has happened"—form—followed by where and what it is is—perception—and the beginnings of what it means signaled by its hedonic tones. Then come various reactions to these three in the formations, which include pushing away pain and chasing pleasure, pressure and stress, ruminations and preoccupations, and me, myself, and I. In other words, *there is little or no craving, sense of self, or suffering in the first three parts of experience.*

This has huge implications. Resting in the sense of alerting and orienting—while focusing mainly on forms and perceptions—

minimizes your engagement with the formations and the suffering in them. It's like approaching the speed of sound with all its turbulence, and then moving past it into a peaceful quiet. Staying close to the emergent now, you're moving so rapidly into the future—or time is rushing by you so quickly—that you can't "hear" what has passed behind you, so you don't need to react to it. When you're this close to the emergent edge of now, things are changing too quickly for the machinery of craving and suffering to find much traction.

Additionally, when you come close to the present, you're less involved with the "craving for becoming." The neurological basis for this is really interesting. The brain is continually making predictions and then comparing what happens to them. For instance, when you reach for a cup, your brain anticipates how much it will weigh to use the proper amount of force to lift it. Then sensory feedback about how much it actually weighs is used to fine-tune your effort. Similar processes of predicting, experiencing, and then making new predictions happen in many ways small and large, such as in conversations and relationships.

It's striking to observe the ongoing production of expectations in your mind. It's useful for ordinary functioning, which is why a significant portion of the neural processing power in your brain, including in the *cerebellum*, is devoted to it. But it also tends to keep us living in an imagined future rather than in the present—the only place we can ever feel truly loved and at peace—and it sets us up for disappointment when expectations are unfulfilled. Plus this process of antici...pation is involved with constructing/imagining a sense of self—what will happen to "me"—which can lead to possessiveness, craving, and suffering (discussed in the next chapter).

> There is no past.
> There is no future.
> You are completely supported.
>
> ROSHI HOGEN BAYS

Certainly it's useful sometimes to have expectations or hopes. But we can get lost in becoming. So for a minute or longer, see what happens in your experience when you stay right in the present without any expectations at all: not knowing or trying to predict what will happen next. During this practice, it also helps to disengage from deliberate action, since the executive functions and *motor planning* are closely involved with the machinery of prediction. For an extended exploration of all this, try the meditation below.

PARTS PASSING BY

Relax . . . steadying the mind . . . finding warmheartedness . . . a sense of fullness . . . being aware of your whole body breathing . . . the sense of the whole expanding to include sounds . . . and sights . . . and thoughts . . . softening into wholeness . . . allowing all of yourself to be.

Stay present as a whole, recognizing that there are so many things in awareness . . . recognizing the simple sense of form, bare awareness of sensations and sounds and sights . . .

(continued)

recognizing perceptions of what things are . . . recognizing hedonic tones . . . recognizing formations of thoughts and feelings . . . recognizing awareness . . . so many things in the streaming of consciousness . . .

Recognize that these parts of the mind keep changing . . . letting them change . . . letting them happen with no deliberate effort . . . it's all right . . . the mind process keeps going . . . with countless parts . . . always changing . . .

Let go continually . . . staying close to the present . . . letting go of all parts . . . no need to label or understand anything . . . the present so vivid . . . letting go of expecting . . . not knowing what will happen next . . . feeling all right with this . . . letting go of becoming . . . the present moment so bright and vivid . . . abiding before any pressure or stress . . .

Let go of past and future . . . continually letting go . . . living on the surface of now . . . abiding in the stillness of now . . . as changes pass through it . . . still now . . .

Resting in Refuges

Coming right into the present moment can feel very peaceful. But it can also feel sad to recognize the ephemeral nature of every experience—even the most touching and important ones of all. It can feel frightening to observe the mosaic-like compounded nature of the mind and see how loosely glued together its pieces are, and how impersonally they keep coming and going. Experiences can feel empty of meaning and value. A sense of groundlessness might become despair. Why bother if the bottom keeps falling out and everything turns to dust?

As the felt recognition of impermanence deepens, it's useful to talk with teachers who are familiar with this territory, especially if you feel disturbed by it. Additionally, here are some ways to help yourself become more comfortable with endless endings:

- Observe the endless *arisings* of the next experiences.
- Stay aware of the ongoing livingness of the body, the breath continuing, the heart still beating. Focus on the feeling that you're basically all right right now, and now.
- Move your body to intensify its proprioceptive feedback that you're still "going on being," in the reassuring phrase from the pediatrician and psychoanalyst Daniel Winnicott. Take small deliberate actions, such as choosing to shift your weight in a chair, and focus on the sense of agency: you can be active when you want, you're not helpless or overwhelmed, and your mind's executive functions (for example, selecting and initiating action) are still working just fine.
- Get a sense of the earth beneath you, still here, still solid, still reliable. For example, rub or tap your feet on the floor, or go for a walk. I love the folktale about the Buddha's night of awakening, which says he was assailed by forces of evil and delusion but then reached down to touch the earth for comfort and strength.
- Enjoy simple pleasures, such as a bite of food or a sip of water. These are naturally soothing, and they tend to calm down the body's stress response systems. Also focus on basic feelings of warmheartedness, perhaps talking with people you care about.
- Draw on the practice of resting in fullness and opening to peace, contentment, and love.

> In truth we are always present.
> We only imagine ourselves to be
> in one place or another.
>
> HOWARD COHN

It's also helpful to have a sense of *refuges*—things that give you shelter, refueling, and inspiration—both to be comfortable with the transience of the present moment and as a resource in general. Refuges can be places, people and nonhuman animals, experiences, ideas, practices, and spiritual forces. For example, meditation is a refuge for me—and so are memories of Yosemite Valley while I'm sitting in a dentist's chair. You can find refuge in the skills and virtues and other wholesome qualities you've cultivated in yourself.

In particular, consider these key refuges:

- *Teachers:* Bring to mind the many teachers you've probably had, people who have touched you and helped you and made a difference in your life, perhaps extending back in time to the sources of a spiritual tradition. There is also the sense of "the teacher within": an inner knowing, the wakefulness and goodness deep down inside everyone, and the better angels of our nature.

- *Teachings:* Stories and folklore and myths, ethics and parables, the arts, science and psychology, and spiritual traditions around the world can offer useful wisdom. And there is what many teachings are fundamentally about: reality itself, the way it is—including its mysteries. The facts are a refuge even if you wish they were different: they offer solid ground, the suchness of things as they are.

- *The Taught:* This is the refuge of good company, fellowship with others who support your path and may be walking it with you. It includes friends you can talk with, formal communities such as a church congregation, monastics and others who are deeply committed, and the larger gathering of people—even worldwide—with whom you share a common cause or creed or practice.

FURTHER READING

Be Here Now (Ram Dass)

Buddhism AND (Gay Watson)

Emptiness (Guy Armstrong)

The Heart of the Universe (Mu Soeng)

True Refuge (Tara Brach)

You can engage refuges in different ways. A common approach is to "go to" or "take" refuge as something distinct from yourself. You could also recognize or imagine that you are *already* there, "abiding as" or "at home in" a refuge. You can simply be aware of a refuge, or think or speak words such as "I find refuge in _____" or "May I abide as _____." You could recollect the life and personal qualities of a teacher or other person you respect, perhaps with an inspiring sense of walking in their footsteps. There could be a particular occasion when you take refuge, such as when you begin a meditation, and you can turn to the sense of refuge from time to time over the course of a day. It's also powerful to focus on refuges in a formal way. For a practice of this, try the meditation in the box.

Whatever the details, the *experience* of refuge is what matters: the feeling of reassurance, relief, and support. You are letting yourself have this experience, and staying with it for a few breaths or longer, taking it into yourself so the sense of various refuges becomes gradually embodied in your nervous system. This is not craving refuge or clinging to it. It is simply opening into and receiving into yourself that which is healing and wholesome and nurturing and good.

A MEDITATION ON REFUGE

Find a posture that feels comfortable and alert. Be aware of breathing, and relax. Bring to mind one or more things that are refuges for you: a friend, a cup of tea, reading a good book, your family, a pet, a church or temple, or looking out over the sea. Open to the sense of being with a refuge, such as comfort . . . reassurance . . . protection . . .

Stay with the feeling of refuge . . . You could think to yourself, "I take refuge in _____," or "I abide as _____." Get a sense of entering into refuge . . . and refuge entering into you.

Explore the sense of your teachers as refuges . . . perhaps reaching back to particular individuals . . . Also be aware of a natural wakefulness and goodness inside you, and find refuge in this.

Explore the sense of teachings as refuges . . . the knowledge in science . . . the wisdom in different traditions, perhaps one that is particularly meaningful for you . . . feeling supported by good teachings, and grateful for them . . . Consider reality itself as a refuge . . . coming to rest in the way it is . . . letting go into the suchness of every moment . . . accepting the truth of things.

Explore the sense of good company as a refuge . . . people who are companions on the path . . . people who are dedicated to practice . . . perhaps communities you're part of . . . finding refuge in them . . . a sense of fellowship with people far and wide.

As you like, explore other refuges for you, and focus on the experience of them. Perhaps activities . . . settings . . . nature . . . spiritual forces . . . Stay with the feeling of refuge . . . the sense of calm strength as a refuge . . . lovingness as a refuge . . . awareness as a refuge . . . a feeling of sanctuary, protection, support . . . resting in refuge . . .

The Nature of Mind and Matter

Deep insight into the *nature* of all experiences can free us from holding on to them, and thus free us from the suffering this clinging causes.

So let's explore the nature of our experiences and the nature of the brain that is enabling them. These topics might seem merely, and boringly, intellectual—so it helps to remember that they are about who and what we *are*. Further, the nature of mind and matter is a deep refuge. Things change—and thus are unreliable sources of lasting happiness—but their nature does not. Realizing this nature—realizing your *own* nature—enables you to rest in it, at peace.

> In the deepest forms of insight, we see that things change so quickly that we can't hold on to anything, and eventually the mind lets go of clinging.
> Letting go brings equanimity.
> The greater the letting go, the deeper the equanimity...
> In Buddhist practice, we work to expand the range of life experiences in which we are free.
>
> GIL FRONSDAL

WHAT IS THE NATURE OF THE MIND?

The *mind* consists of the experiences and information represented by a nervous system. (There are other definitions of the mind, but this is the one that's been used in this book.) Your mind, my mind, everyone's mind, has these four characteristics. It is:

1. *impermanent:* Consciousness is a *stream*, a fluid process of change. Even something seemingly static like a pain in your knee has dynamic qualities. As soon as one moment of experience appears, it's replaced by another one. The mind that is represented by the nervous system of a particular body shares the fate of that body, which will eventually pass away.

2. *compounded:* Experiences are made of many parts. For instance, if you observe a worry, you'll see different aspects of

this experience, such as sensations, thoughts, desires, and emotions. More generally, information in the nervous system about any one thing must be distinct from information about other things.

3. *interdependent:* Our experiences exist and change due to *causes.* They don't occur on their own. The causes that make your mind in this moment could include what you were thinking about a few minutes ago, your personal history, the state of your body, and the fact that a mosquito just landed on the back of your neck.

4. *empty:* The first three characteristics above establish the fourth characteristic, that all experiences are "empty" of any permanent, unified, self-causing essence. That experiences are empty does not mean they are void. Thoughts, joys, and sorrows do exist, but emptily. The stream of consciousness exists while also being empty. The mind, including its unconscious elements, is empty.

In sum, it is the nature of any experience in particular and the mind in general to be impermanent, compounded, interdependent, and empty. All experiences are the same in their nature. Knowing that pain and pleasure have the same nature helps you not fight the one or chase the other. Try this the next time you're caught up in something painful or pleasurable: recognize the *nature* of that experience, and notice how this softens and eases your relationship to it.

WHAT IS THE NATURE OF THE BRAIN?

Since the mind is represented mainly by the brain, it's useful to understand its nature as well. Like the mind, the brain is:

1. *impermanent:* Each day, hundreds of new baby neurons are born in a process called *neurogenesis,* while other brain cells die naturally. There is ongoing rebuilding of existing connections between cells and structures within cells. New synapses form, while less used ones wither away. New capillary tendrils—the tiny tubes that supply blood to our tissues—grow and reach into particularly active regions to bring them more fuel. Individual neurons routinely fire many times a second. And molecular processes cascade like falling dominoes over the course of a single millisecond.

2. *compounded:* The brain has three major parts: brain stem, subcortex, and neocortex. These parts contain many smaller regions that do different things. Altogether, there are about 85 billion neurons inside your head, plus another 100 billion supporting glial cells. These neurons are connected in a vast network with several hundred trillion synapses. And the microscopic structures of cells and synapses can be divided even further into smaller and smaller parts.

> Interdependence means that a thing can arise
> only in reliance on other things.
>
> THICH NHAT HANH

3. *interdependent:* What happens in one part of the brain is affected by what is happening in other parts of it. Neuronal activity interacts with activity in the glial cells. The brain interacts with the rest of the nervous system . . . which interacts with the rest of the body . . . which interacts with the world . . . and so on.

4. *empty*: Based on the three characteristics above, the brain is "empty" of any permanent, unified, or self-causing essence. It exists—emptily.

To sum it up: we find the same characteristics of the mind also in the brain. It, too, is impermanent, compounded, interdependent, and empty.

THE MIND-BODY PROCESS

A thought and a neuron are different from each other, and still their nature is identical. Mind and matter, inside and outside, are the same in their nature. There is one nature of everything, expressed in all things.

In this body, your brain is making your mind. (More generally, the nervous system, body, nature, and human culture make the mind; we're focusing on the brain for simplicity, and because the most immediate physical basis of the mind is the brain.) At the same time, as we saw in chapter 2, your mind is making your brain, since mental activity enlists neural activity that leaves physical traces.

Sometimes it's useful to focus on just the mind or the brain. Still, they are two aspects of a single unified process. You are this process: a person with a mind and a body—whose nature is impermanent, compounded, interdependent, and empty.

> Everything is connected.
> Nothing lasts.
> You are not alone.
>
> LEW RICHMOND

SWIRLING STREAMING

Two friends and I once took canoes down the Green River in Utah, paddling and drifting for four days before joining the Colorado River on its way to the Grand Canyon. I'd never spent so much time on a river and became mesmerized by the eddies swirling through it. Some were standing waves above a boulder, others were whirlpools we skirted, and many were transient circular ripples on the surface. They were all dynamic and beautiful, and a deep metaphor for many things. Broadly defined, an eddy is a patterning of something that is stable for a time and then disperses. A cloud is an eddy of the atmosphere, an argument is an eddy in a relationship, and a thought is an eddy in the stream of consciousness.

One afternoon we saw dark storm clouds piling up in the distance, sparks of lightning flashing inside them, finally dropping a torrent of rain. Then one waterfall after another appeared on the stony cliffs above us, shooting out onto the river, itself a vast kind of eddy flowing through dark red sandstone banks formed from the shifting sediments of ancient seas.

Some eddies change more slowly than others. The storm passed in a few hours, but some of the marks it left in sandstone could last for thousands, perhaps millions, of years. From my canoe, I saw swirling currents passing over golden rocks worn smooth by time, and then a leaf carried along, and then a fly landing on the leaf. Eddies in eddies in eddies. Compared with a cloud, your body is a slow eddy. Still, most of the atoms in it today will be gone in a year and replaced by new ones.

All our experiences rest upon eddies of information represented by eddies of neural activity. Thoughts are quicksilver eddies of mind and matter, while the traces they can leave in memory last longer—

until the eddying body itself passes away. All eddies disperse eventually. Whether in the mind or the Mississippi, all eddies have the same nature: impermanent, compounded, interdependent, and empty.

To function, the body and its mind must try to stabilize what is changing, to unify what is made of parts, and to partition what is connected. It's necessary to try, but we will inevitably, continually, poignantly fail. Craving or clinging to any particular eddy is therefore a certain prescription for suffering.

So love the eddy, and be the stream.

Let go into the larger streaming of consciousness, easing into wholeness as we've explored. Let go of the eddies that have passed on by a minute ago...a year and more ago...and come into the present, receiving nowness. And let go of each new eddy of experience as soon as it arises. Try the meditation in the box, and consider this teaching from Ajahn Chah:

If you let go a little, you will have a little peace.

If you let go a lot, you will have a lot of peace.

If you let go completely, you will be completely peaceful.

SWIRLING ALONG

Come to rest in your body ... here ... and now. Be aware of the breath continuing ... things going on being ...

Rest in fullness ... abiding with peace ... contentment ... love ...

(continued)

Be aware of sensations . . . sounds . . . thoughts . . . the reassuring coming of one experience after another . . .

Then focus on the going of experiences from one moment to the next . . . letting things change . . . Be aware of impermanence . . . Know that you continue to be all right even as every moment of consciousness dissolves into something else . . .

Be aware of different patterns of experience moving through awareness . . . eddies of sensation that may last a few seconds or longer . . . eddies of sounds that continue for a while . . . eddies of thoughts and emotional reactions . . . letting it all keep swirling along . . .

Be aware of the nature of these eddies of experience: changing, made of parts, interdependent with everything else, and empty of essence . . . Know that this is the nature of both mind and matter: impermanent . . . compounded . . . interdependent . . . empty . . .

Know that this is your nature . . . accepting that it is your nature to be changing . . . Accept that it is your nature to be made of many parts . . . that it is your nature to be the result in each moment of a vast web of causes . . . Accept that it is your nature to be an open process . . . It's all right . . . Resting in your own nature . . . Being your nature . . .

Rest in the nature of things even as things come apart and pass away . . . easing . . . letting go . . . Abiding as the nature of things . . . Being your own nature . . .

Good Practice

Recognize that whatever happened a few minutes ago is no longer here. It's gone. Its effects may linger, but what was reality a few years or days or even seconds ago is no longer reality now. You could explore your reactions to this recognition. Is it alarming? Sad? Freeing?

Also recognize that whatever might happen in a minute or in a year is not real now. Let this sink in as an experience, not just an idea. Open to feeling that whatever you fear or hope in the future does not exist now. How does this feel?

After something surprising has happened—it could be as simple as the doorbell ringing—rewind the "movie" of the first few seconds after it occurred. What happened in your mind during those seconds? Can you recognize alerting and orienting within the first second? Can you see evaluating and acting then coming online? These aspects of attention can happen so quickly that it feels like they overlap, but you can still tease them apart.

Deliberately rest in alerting and orienting... not needing to know or control anything... only receiving the freshness of the present moment.

Take refuge in one or more things. You could do this when you first wake up or when you go to bed, or make it part of your meditation.

See what happens when you regard a relationship, a situation, or yourself as more like a cloud than a brick. In other words, as an *eddy*: changing, made of parts, and swirling along based on the different currents moving through it. How does this feel?

8

OPENING INTO ALLNESS

> To learn the Buddha way is to learn about oneself.
> To learn about oneself is to forget oneself.
> To forget oneself is to perceive oneself as all things.
>
> Dōgen

n this chapter we'll explore how to release the sense of self and feel more connected with everything. These topics can seem merely intellectual on the one hand or very disturbing on the other. If you feel unsettled or unreal, slow down and focus on what is soothing and grounding: a fuller breath, something to eat, the feeling of being with someone you love. Take time for reflection and insight. Keep coming back to your own experience, to a simple sense of what it's like to be you in this moment.

The Person Process

Who am I?

This is one of the classic questions. How might we approach it?

The Buddha offered an answer to a man named Bahiya, who had

journeyed far to meet him. Bahiya said, "Please, sir, give me the teaching that will be for my long-term welfare and happiness!" But the Buddha replied, "This is not the time, Bahiya. I have entered the town for alms." After Bahiya implored him twice again, the Buddha said this (from Udana 1.10): "Bahiya, you should train yourself thus:

"In reference to seeing, there will be only seeing. In hearing, only hearing. In sensing, only sensing. In cognizing [for example, thinking, feeling, remembering], only cognizing. That is how you should train yourself.

"When for you there will be only seeing in seeing, only hearing in hearing, only sensing in sensing, only cognizing in cognizing, then, Bahiya, there is no you in connection with that.

"When there is no you in connection with that, there is no you there. When there is no you there, you are neither here nor yonder nor between the two.

"This, just this, is the end of suffering."

The passage concludes: "Through hearing this brief explanation of the Dharma, the mind of Bahiya was right then and there awakened."

DOES A PERSON EXIST?

I love this teaching for its drama, simplicity, and profundity. How can we make sense of it, and how can we practice with it?

Clearly, individual *persons* exist. The Buddha existed, and if we are to believe the sutta above, Bahiya also existed. (Alas, not long afterward, Bahiya was attacked and killed by a cow with a young calf—which existed as well.) As the Buddha did, we can use conventional language such as "I" or "you" to refer to persons, as when he said "I have entered the town" or "You should train yourself thus."

In my metaphor from the previous chapter, each person is a particular eddy rippling along. While persons interact, they are distinct from one another, like different waves in the ocean. Persons have rights and responsibilities, and we should treat them with decency and care. I am a person and you are a person, and we both exist.

> The abolition of the conceit I am—
> That is truly the supreme bliss.
>
> UDANA 2.1

DOES A SELF EXIST?

But what about the so-called *self*? Related terms include *ego, identity, I,* and *me.* The word *self* can be used for a person as a whole, but I mean it narrowly, as the supposed being inside who is looking out through your eyes. I'm focusing here on the purported *psychological* self rather than the possibility of something supernatural continuing from life to life, like a flame passing from candle to candle until there is no longer wick or wax.

I honestly don't know whether anything continues from life to life. I do have the sense of something deep within that is somehow both specific to me and beyond me. Perhaps this, too, is a conditioned eddy that will eventually disperse like all others, even the subtlest ones. Whether this happens or not, each step of the way seems worth taking, even if it culminates in a final last flickering of this flame.

On this path, it is not that we are *seeking* an eventual ending of existence. But it is helpful to be *disenchanted* with false promises, such as in advertising or in the expectation of lasting satisfaction in passing experiences. It is also helpful to wake up from the spells cast by Mother Nature to keep her children craving to increase their odds of survival—the spells that make us think things will be more painful or pleasurable than they will actually be. As we awaken, we take each step of practice for its own sake, not out of aversion toward life. In this process there is a natural letting go of all that fuels the fires of greed, hatred, and delusion, and an increasingly easy resting in wholeness, nowness, allness, and timelessness. And eventually, this resting is all there is.

Meanwhile, we can look into the apparent psychological self. This is an important topic, since the sense of being a self causes a lot of suffering, including taking things personally, becoming defensive, and getting possessive. When the sense of self decreases, well-being usually increases, with a feeling of ease and openness. As Anam Thubten put it: No self, no problem.

The psychological self is described in different ways in different cultures. In this book, the term *self* means a presumed "I" or "me" "who" is "inside" each person. In ordinary life, we tend to assume that such a self is indeed present in other people ... as well as inside ourselves. Conventionally, we think of this purported self as having three *defining* characteristics. It is supposed to be:

- *stable:* The self today is the same self as yesterday and a year ago.
- *unified:* There is only one "me" inside the mind.
- *independent:* Things may happen to the self, but it is not fundamentally altered by them.

These characteristics define the apparent self. They are necessary conditions for there actually to be a self. But are they all true?

> The self is not something in and of itself;
> rather we create the felt sense of it moment to moment.
>
> JOSEPH GOLDSTEIN

"SELF" IN THE MIND

When you observe your own experience, it's striking to find the *opposite* of the three defining characteristics of a supposed self:

1. *not stable* (that is, impermanent): The "I" or "me" in the moment keeps changing, and there are many times when there is little sense of self at all.

2. *not unified* (that is, compounded): If the self were unified, you could command every bit of yourself to stop liking sweets or start liking public speaking. There are multiple "I's" and "me's," including different sub-personalities and points of view.

3. *not independent* (that is, interdependent): The sense of self changes due to different influences, such as ebbs and flows in craving. The various "I's" and "me's" have also been shaped by internal and external factors, such as those in childhood.

Second, as you watch the mind, you can see many references to a presumed complete self that exists ... somewhere ... always out of sight. A complete "I" or "me" is routinely implied in experiences of planning, problem solving, daydreaming, and rumination. But try as you might, you will never find the presumed full self in your actual experience.

Third, the sense of self is often *added* to our experiences, and you can be mindful of this. For example, you could be walking down a street and just looking around with little sense of self—and then suddenly you see someone coming your way whom you don't particularly like; within a second or two, a much stronger sense of self could begin to develop in your awareness. It is perfectly possible for seeing to occur, and hearing and sensing and cognizing... without adding an "I" or a "me" to it. (We'll be exploring this experientially a little further on.)

Fourth, there is a quality of subjectivity in most experiences—an awareness *of*, a witnessing *of*. The brain "indexes" across moments of experience to find what is common to them, and there is an inference that all this witnessing must mean that there is a witness. But *subjectivity does not require a subject*. There is awareness, but that does not itself mean there is an unchanging "someone who" is aware. Look again and again, and you will not find that someone.

"SELF" IN THE BRAIN

Now let's shift from a subjective, *first person* perspective that looks at experiences from the inside out to an objective, *third person* perspective that looks at the brain from the outside in. When we do this, we can't find a stable, unified, and independent basis for a self in the brain, either. There are now many studies on how activity in your brain correlates with different experiences of "me, myself, and I," such as making a choice, recognizing your own face amidst others, deciding whether a word like "sensitive" describes you, or recalling something from childhood. What this research reveals is startling.

The neural activities that are the basis of self-related experiences are also:

1. *not stable* (that is, impermanent): They are transient and dynamic throughout the brain. If it were like a Christmas tree, the many lights indicating self-related activations would be continually flickering on and off.

2. *not unified* (that is, compounded): The neural correlates of the sense of self are scattered all over the brain. While activations in certain areas, such as the default mode network, tend to foster a sense of self, activations in other parts of the brain do this as well. Further, the many areas that underlie different aspects of the sense of self also perform other functions. There is no single place in the brain that "does" the self. We are all unique and in that sense special. But the self is not special in the brain.

3. *not independent* (that is, interdependent): These neural activations are the result of streams of internal and external stimuli, and they also depend upon underlying physical structures and processes.

A "SELF" IS LIKE A UNICORN

To sum up, our experiences of I, me, and mine—and their neural foundations—are impermanent, compounded, and interdependent. In a word, the apparent self is *empty* (in the sense discussed in chapter 7). This alone should encourage lightening up about it and not clinging to it. But I'd like to take this a step further.

We can have empty experiences of things that do actually exist, such as horses. Just because the *experience* of a horse is empty does not mean that the horse is not real. But we can also have empty experiences of things that do *not* exist, such as imagining a unicorn. If there is no creature with the defining characteristics of a unicorn—a horse with a long pointed horn—then unicorns are not real.

The presumed self is like a unicorn, a mythical beast that does not exist. Its necessary, defining characteristics—stability, unification, and independence—do not exist in either the mind or the brain. The complete self is never observed in experience. Subjectivity doesn't mean there is a stable subject, a one—and always the same one—to whom things happen. And the sense of being or having a self is not needed for consciousness—nor for opening a door or answering a question.

Realizing this often begins conceptually, and that's all right. These ideas highlight different aspects of your *experience*. Then you can observe the mind and practice with it much as the Buddha told Bahiya to do. And gradually there will be a felt knowing of what's true. There was a time this came home to me during a walk on a retreat. As I watched all the many thoughts, sensations, and feelings pop-pop-popping into awareness, it suddenly became overwhelmingly clear that this was all too complicated and too fast for any being to create or control. It was its own process, without an owner or director. I was flabbergasted, dismayed, relieved, and blown wide open.

> The profound realization that underlies the Buddha's awakening...[is] that neither a self nor something belonging to a self can be found at all, at any time, anywhere.
>
> BHIKKHU ANĀLAYO

PRACTICING WITH THE SENSE OF SELF

The Buddha encouraged practicing with the apparent self through insight into its empty nature and through gradually releasing *identification* ("that is me"), *possessiveness* ("that is mine"), and *conceit* ("I am better than you, I matter more than you"). As you explore these practices, it's normal to feel turned upside down and shaken. I first ran into these ideas—and it did feel like a collision—in Alan Watts's *The Book: On the Taboo Against Knowing Who You Are.* I was twenty-one and in my last quarter at UCLA, and on a whim thought it would be interesting to learn about Eastern spirituality. So I had a big pile of books, with his on the top. I remember sitting outside to read it and getting so frustrated that I threw it across the yard. It seemed unnerving and threatening. But after a while I picked it up again and slowly got more comfortable with what he was talking about.

When we face the fuzzy insubstantiality of the apparent "I," it's easy to slide into fears of annihilation, death, and nothing beyond it. Take your time with these practices. Stay mindful of the reassuring ongoingness of being a person: you're still breathing, still functioning, still here, still doing all right. Notice what a strong sense of me feels like—often tense, contracted, fearful—and what it feels like to open into simply abiding as a whole person. Recognizing the suffering in the one and the easing comfort in the other makes it clear why you are practicing with the sense of self.

As Jack Engler said, "You have to be somebody before you can be nobody." It's natural to want to feel appreciated, liked, and loved by other people. In both childhood and adulthood, taking in *healthy social supplies*—such as feeling seen, understood, and even cherished—can help you feel more secure and worthy inside. When you feel more valued as a *person,* it's easier to let go of trying to impress others or gain their approval. It's also easier to handle rejections or criticism without getting too upset about them.

Facing a challenge—such as feeling hurt by a family member—can stir up a strong sense of self. This could lead to some choppy back-and-forth between you and others in which their sense of self gets intensified as well. Then hopefully you have a growing sense of the bigger picture—and maybe they do, too—and eventually there's a good resolution. Afterward, the edges of me and I can soften and ease into the wholeness of all of you—perhaps with insight into how you could take things less personally the next time something similar happens.

Self-related thoughts, feelings, desires, et cetera, are not themselves a problem. They are experiences like any other. They come and they go. Problems begin if you *cling* to these parts of yourself: making them special, making them mean something, defending them, thinking that these empty ephemeral parts are the stable essence of yourself. I've found it really useful to recognize the apparent self and its many parts as processes that keep changing—in effect, a kind of *self-ing* rippling through awareness. Instead of trying to hold on to a presumed self, open into the "person process" you actually are, in which smaller eddies of self-ing can come... and go. And for a sustained practice of this, try the meditation in the box that starts on the next page.

RELAXING SELF-ING

Be mindful of the sense of self: its coming and going, and the causes of these changes. See what it's like to abide with little or no sense of self, yet still with awareness and ease. It helps to relax, and not tie yourself in knots trying to see the "one" who is observing the sense of self. Allow subjectivity to occur without presuming a subject. Be aware of being a person in which self-ing ebbs and flows.

Relax . . . find a stability of awareness . . . and be aware of your own mind . . . Be mindful of the sense of self increasing and decreasing . . . Be mindful of what happens in awareness just before an increase in the sense of self: perhaps some kind of desire, or a thought about a relationship.

Explore the difference between softly saying to yourself: "There is breathing" compared with "I am breathing" . . . "There is hearing" compared with "I am hearing" . . . "This foot is moving" compared with "I am moving my foot" . . . "There is thinking" or "I am thinking" . . . "There is knowing" . . . "I am knowing" . . . "There is awareness" . . . "I am aware" . . .

Relax increasingly into the sense of being a person in which the sense of self occasionally arises . . .

When a sense of I, me, or mine appears, be mindful of what it implies but never fully reveals . . . Is the full presumed self ever found?

Relax and let the person process unfold . . . opening wide into wholeness . . . being a person who is peaceful, contented,

(continued)

and warmhearted . . . in which a sense of I or me or mine can come and go . . . Breathing comfortably, still all right, a peaceful abiding . . . Breathing occurring on its own, no need for anyone to direct it.

Recognize the sense of I, me, or mine as simply an experience like any other . . . Recognize that these experiences of an apparent self are all empty . . . Breathing comfortably, awareness ongoing, abiding at ease . . .

Disengaging from I and me and mine . . . still going on as a person . . . being all right . . . being all right as a person without needing to be a self . . . Simply being what you are, a whole person in the present unfolding . . . in wholeness and nowness, a person happening without needing a self . . . at peace . . .

Allocentric Experiencing

In this section I'm drawing on the work of several scholars, particularly James Austin, a neurology professor and Zen practitioner. We'll explore the possible neural basis of awakenings in which the sense of self dissolves while the world shines forth in radiant perfection. And even without the fireworks of these peak, mystical, non-dual, or *self-transcendent* experiences, we can gradually soften the sense of self and open more into inter-being with all that is.

EGOCENTRIC AND ALLOCENTRIC PERSPECTIVES

One of the more remarkable features of your brain is that it routinely shifts back and forth between two different ways of experiencing the world:

- *egocentric:* things known from the personal, subjective perspective of "my body" or "my self"; what things have to do with *me*, a targeted, often narrow view.
- *allocentric:* things known from an impersonal, objective perspective; the whole setting or context in its own right; less sense of *I*; a wide view.

These perspectives draw on visual-spatial processing related to our physical environments. But they can be extended to our relationships, activities, the world as a whole—and in fact the entire universe. The terms that describe them are neutral. *Egocentric* does not mean selfish or arrogant, and *impersonal* does not mean cold or apathetic.

We don't usually notice the allocentric perspective because it operates mainly in the background. Still, in everyday life you can observe each of these perspectives coming and going in your mind. When you move into a new situation, your brain shifts into the allocentric perspective for a few moments to update your understanding of the total environment, and then it returns to an egocentric perspective about whatever you're doing at the time. If you look down at something that is close to you, the egocentric view comes online, since what's near to you tends to be most personally relevant. On the other hand, if you look out toward the horizon or up to the sky, the allocentric perspective gets active, since the focus has moved away from yourself toward the bigger picture.

Neurologically, the egocentric processing stream runs along the top of your brain, through the parietal lobes toward the prefrontal cortex. Not by accident, this stream draws on neural networks involved with the sense of "*I* am doing something to things that are separate from *me*," such as touch, manipulating objects that are close to you, and the somatic sense of being a particular body. Second, given its location and its function, the egocentric processing stream likely engages the focused attention network—discussed in chapter 7—that also runs along the top of the brain. Third, it probably also engages the midline cortical networks of "doing" covered in chapter 6: both the task-oriented part toward the front ("I am solving this problem") and the default mode part toward the rear ("I am ruminating about someone who hurt me").

Take a moment to reflect on these three aspects of egocentrism (in the sense meant here) and how they come together many times a day. For example, as you reach for something in the closet, your attention could be focused on a specific garment while you're thinking about what you'll be doing while wearing it. All very natural and helpful. Still, a *lot* of self-ing can happen in these interconnected networks.

On the other hand, the allocentric processing stream runs lower down and along the sides of your brain, through the temporal lobes toward the prefrontal cortex. Due to where it's located, it likely connects with the alerting-and-orienting attention network that runs along the lower right side of the brain. And it probably interacts with the lateral network of the "being" mode that is also right-sided.

To summarize a very key point: The "doing" mode, focused attention, and the egocentric perspective are connected with one another both experientially and neurologically. When one of these self-referential systems gets engaged, it tends to activate the other two. In much the same way, the "being" mode, alerting-and-orienting attention, and the allocentric perspective are also connected with one another both experientially and neurologically. *Wholeness, nowness, and allness thus support one another.* For example, coming into the now of this moment tends to bring with it a sense of wholeness and connection with the wider world. Practices that repeatedly stimulate and therefore strengthen the lateral networks of wholeness, the attention networks of nowness, and the allocentric networks of allness work synergistically together.

GRADUAL CULTIVATION, SUDDEN AWAKENING

If you do cultivate wholeness, nowness, and allness, what might emerge?

Around the world, many people say they've had intense, "nonordinary" experiences at one time or another. In particular, some people describe a powerful, extraordinary feeling of being immersed in reality with little or no sense of self. These self-transcendent experiences usually develop rapidly, and often suddenly. For example, James Austin has described how this happened for him. He was visiting England after eight years of Zen practice, and came up from the London Underground onto a railway platform:

> Instantly, the entire view acquires three qualities: Absolute Reality, Intrinsic Rightness, Ultimate Perfection.... Vanished in one split second is the familiar sensation that *this* person is viewing an ordinary city scene. The new viewing proceeds impersonally ... Three more indivisible themes penetrate ... at depths far beyond simple knowledge: This

is the eternal state of affairs.... There is nothing more to do.... There is nothing whatsoever to fear.

During this experience, what in the world was happening in his brain? Or in the brains of others during similar experiences?

It's as if the egocentric network just goes quiet. And with it, the networks of doing and focused attention disengage as well. Then only the allocentric perspective is present with its companions of wholeness and nowness. Previously, the egocentric and allocentric perspectives had exerted reciprocal inhibition over each other: like a seesaw, when one goes down, the other goes up. When the egocentric perspective drops out, that could release the allocentric perspective to surge forward. Then, according to Austin, "All root origins of selfhood and deep natural survival angsts seem to have dropped off. This acute, ineffable release from the deepest instincts of primal fear is especially liberating."

Austin points out a plausible way this could occur. The *thalamus* is a central switchboard in the subcortex, and all sensory inputs except smell pass through it. Ordinary consciousness depends on the information flowing back and forth between it and the cortex. Normally, the upper parts of the thalamus are continually "talking" with key regions in the cortex that help make the sense of self. If these signals between the thalamus and cortex were blocked, then the sense of self could stop as well. And as the Buddha said to Bahiya: "When there is no you there, you are neither here nor yonder nor between the two. This, just this, is the end of suffering."

How might this happen?

Several nearby tissues have GABA-releasing neurons that can suppress activity in the upper parts of the thalamus. If they suddenly discharged high levels of GABA into these parts of the thalamus, that could block major pathways through which the egocentric current in the stream of consciousness flows. For example, reduced activity in the parietal lobes is associated with less sense of self and a greater feeling of unity and related mystical experiences. It's as though a switch flips and then there's a non-dual experience of being one with everything, along with related insights and feelings.

In addition to Austin's story above, here are examples from three other people:

> One day I sat on top of a cliff overlooking a beach and gazed out into the blue abyss, and soon found myself completely consumed by the vast expanse of all that is. I felt oneness and timelessness with the universe profoundly. It felt as though a conscious energy outside of my mind was running through me, and although I could feel it transforming my very being, the experience seemed untouched by thought or judgment. Some of life's greatest mysteries were answered within this single experience and remain felt and known to this day.

> During one period of meditation [on retreat]...I gave everything I could to not missing a single breath.... [Then] servers brought us tea and a cookie. I received the tea and held the cup in my hands. As I lifted the cup to my lips and the tea went into my mouth, the world stopped!...In the experience, there was no self. Without any of my usual self-referencing, it was as if everything stood still.

> The instant I sat down [in meditation], the koan was there: "Who am I?" Then suddenly there was no boundary to me

at all. I was so shocked I actually got up....I was walking around, looking at things, and there was no border between me and anything else....There was a kind of intimacy between inside and outside....I was just walking around in this magic world of oneness.

LEANING INTO ALLNESS

These remarkable experiences must involve underlying neural processes. The rapid blockage of a key pathway in the thalamus may be just one of them. Or Austin's hypothesis could turn out not to be true. Still, *something* big must be happening in the brain, and it probably involves the neural networks of wholeness, nowness, and allness.

Dramatic awakenings come when they do, and we can't force them to happen. But we *can* cultivate their causes and conditions. Many of the people who report a profound self-transcendent experience had a foundation of significant personal practice, and often there was an intense period of focused practice, such as a meditation retreat soon before the experience. Further, this cultivation is worth doing in its own right. Wisdom and inner peace grow as boundaries soften between you and others, and you feel more connected with everything. Some people speak of feeling welcomed into nature and the entire universe. You can shift from seeing yourself as an isolated actor sometimes flailing against everything to feeling that everything is manifesting locally as *you*. In fact, there can be a profound sense of everything as a single whole, the totality of a single suchness.

> We live in illusion and the appearance of things.
> There is a reality. We are that reality.
> When you understand this,
>   you see that you are nothing.
> And being nothing, you are everything.
>
> KALU RINPOCHE

You can foster an opening into allness in a variety of ways:

- Practices of wholeness and nowness will tend to encourage the sense of being connected with the wider world.
- Resting in fullness is also a powerful support. Craving drives self-ing, so as you move into the Green Zone with its equanimity and well-being, the sense of self naturally decreases, and a feeling of openness and connection increases.
- Fullness, wholeness, and nowness foster tranquility, which engages GABA-releasing neurons. Repeated experiences of deep tranquility, such as in regular meditation, might increase GABA activity in the inhibitory nodes of the thalamus, perhaps priming them to "flip the switch" that could lead to an immersion in allness.
- A simpler life, with less self-referential task-doing, makes more room for an undefended, uncontracted receptivity to everything.
- Being in nature draws one out into the whole, and not coincidentally, most settings for deep contemplative practice are in forests, deserts, jungles, or mountains.

- Austin points out that some awakenings occur while looking up to the heavens, which naturally activates allocentric visual processing. Practices of sky gazing with the eyes open or having a sense of spaciousness with eyes closed might strengthen this circuitry.

FURTHER READING

The Book (Alan Watts)

"Dreaming Ourselves into Existence," *Buddhadharma* (Joseph Goldstein), fall 2018

No Self, No Problem (Anam Thubten)

Selfless Insight (James Austin)

Tao Te Ching (Lao-tzu, translated by Stephen Mitchell)

THE TIPPING POINT

We lean, and lean—and then may tip all the way over. In some cases, the transition into a sense of oneness seems unrelated to any external event. Much brain activity is organized around internally referenced processes, and perhaps somewhere a kind of neural domino just falls over and starts a transformational chain reaction. But many awakenings involve a surprise of some kind. For example, one moonlit evening in thirteenth-century Japan, the Zen nun Mugai Nyodai was carrying water in an old bucket made of bamboo strips. It suddenly broke and she had an awakening. I particularly like this version of her enlightenment poem from the writer Mary Swigonski:

> With this and that I tried to keep the bucket together
> and then the bottom fell out.
> Where water does not collect
> the moon does not dwell.

Experiences of surprise engage the wholeness networks of the brain, the alerting aspects of attention, and the allocentric perspective. While you can't train in surprise itself—then it wouldn't be surprising—you *can* develop related traits of playfulness, delight, humor, and not-knowing. And then you could become more prone to surprise—and to the doors it might open.

In the next section we'll explore expansive views that could also support your opening into allness. But first I suggest contemplating what we've covered already, with the practice in the box below.

ABIDING ALLOCENTRICALLY

Find a position that is relaxed and stable. Steady the mind and warm the heart . . . feeling peaceful, contented, and loving . . . needs met enough in the moment . . .

Feel tranquility spreading in your body . . . a deep calm spreading in your mind . . .

(continued)

Be aware of your body as a whole . . . Opening your eyes to be aware of the room or larger space you're in, getting a sense of it as a whole . . . your gaze moving out from your body, gently toward the horizon . . . looking above the horizon, opening to a sense of the larger whole . . . Then allow your gaze to relax and move where it will, being aware of your setting as it is . . . Feel a calm and objective knowing of the setting in its own right . . .

Let your eyes close, with a sense of spaciousness of awareness . . . a sky of mind through which experiences pass . . . Feel at ease and comfortable . . . alert and present . . . in the now . . . in the freshness of the moment . . . open and edgeless . . .

Be vast . . . be yourself . . . at the front edge of now, opening into everything . . .

Expansive Views

So far we've focused on what we are *subjectively* and *locally*, in terms of our moment-to-moment experiences. Now let's explore what we are *objectively* and *expansively*. As your view enlarges, your sense of being a person can reach beyond your skin into our common humanity, nature in its abundance, and the universe altogether.

I'll describe several views that build on one another. This might seem merely theoretical, but our views shape our experiences and actions. When you move out into everything to look back at yourself, you get a growing sense of being *all* of it—expressing itself through you. As John Muir wrote, "When we try to pick out anything by itself, we find it hitched to everything else in the Universe."

THE VIEW OF EMPTINESS

We've explored the empty nature of all our experiences, which lack any fundamental stability, unification, or independence. They are eddies in the stream of consciousness, swirling and dispersing.

We have also explored the empty nature of the neural processes that are the basis of our experiences. Just about everything in the physical universe is transient, made of parts, and conditioned. A proton, a leaf, a dinner party, and a storm on Jupiter that could swallow the earth are all eddies in the stream of materiality. Our Milky Way galaxy is a very big eddy, and still it will merge into an even larger eddy—the Andromeda galaxy—several billion years from now.

Empty mental processes and empty physical processes arise and eddy together, swirling along as two distinct aspects of one person-process patterning allness. As you watch waves on a beach, physical eddies in your brain are enabling the mental eddies of seeing the physical eddies in the sea. All of it existing, and all of it empty.

THE VIEW OF CULTURE

Each person's mind depends upon the minds of others. For example, without social experiences during childhood, none of us would have a normal personality. In daily life, the ideas and attitudes of other people swirl through your own consciousness. If we include information represented outside the nervous system as a kind of extended "mind," your mind is widely distributed, showing up in the

Facebook timelines of friends and stored in the cloud somewhere. Your feelings and my feelings, your mind and my mind: they eddy together and then stream out into the mind of the next person.

Thich Nhat Hanh writes:

> You are a flowing stream, the continuation of so many wonders. You are not a separate self. You are yourself, but you are also me. You cannot take the pink cloud out of my fragrant tea this morning. And I cannot drink my tea without drinking my cloud.
>
> I am in you and you are in me. If we take me out of you, then you would not be able to manifest as you are manifesting now. If we take you out of me, I would not be able to manifest as I am manifesting now. We cannot manifest without one another. We have to wait for each other in order to manifest together.

THE VIEW OF LIFE

It's so obvious that it's easy to overlook and not really feel it: each of us is a living animal, the result of nearly 4 billion years of biological evolution. Life expressing itself in a particular species; a species expressing itself in a particular body. Our parents had parents who had parents . . . reaching back eventually to hominid parents a million years ago . . . who had primate parents 10 million years ago . . . who had mammalian parents 100 million years ago . . . all the way back to the first life . . . from which we have descended in an unbroken line.

The human body contains about 40 trillion cells, each one guided by DNA molecules shaped over billions of years in the forge of evolution. It also contains about ten times as many microorganisms. To live, we harbor life and consume life. Life passing through us as we pass through life.

More from Thich Nhat Hanh:

> There is no phenomenon in the universe that does not intimately concern us, from a pebble resting at the bottom of the ocean, to the movement of a galaxy millions of light-years away....

> ...All phenomena are interdependent....

> Our Sangha aspires to live in harmony with the land, with all the vegetation and animals, and with all our brothers and sisters. When we are in harmony with each other, we are also in harmony with the land. We see our close relationship with every person and every species. The happiness and suffering of all humans and all other species is our own happiness and suffering. We inter-are. As practitioners we see that we are part of and not separate from the soil, the forests, the rivers, and the sky. We share the same destiny.

THE VIEW OF THE UNIVERSE

Every atom in your body that is heavier than helium was made inside a star, usually as it was exploding. Carbon, oxygen, iron: all of it. Take a breath—and breathe stardust with stardust. This body is billions of years old.

> We have come to realize in modern physics that the material world is not a collection of separate objects, but rather appears as a network of relations between the various parts of a unified whole.
>
> FRITJOF CAPRA

Imagine the causes swirling together to make this planet and this body and this brain. Early stars blowing up, new stars and solar systems forming, and eventually a big asteroidal bullet hitting the earth within a ten-minute window to clear out evolutionary niches that would be filled 65 million years later by many different creatures, including the smart primate who happens to be reading these words.

The stream of consciousness is eddies of mental and neural activity moving through a body. The body is itself a sluggish wave through quantum foam. The mind flows into the body, the body into the mind, and the two together flow out into the universe as it ripples back into you. As the writer and surfer Jaimal Yogis puts it, "All our waves are water."

Knowing this can be merely trippy. Or it can foster a felt sense of being an expression of a vast network of causes, a local rippling of uncountable threads in the tapestry of the universe. It's awe-inspiring and humbling to feel that what you are experiencing in each moment is being made by a brain while it is being made by a body, which is being made by the earth as it is being made by the entire universe.

THE VIEW OF ALLNESS

Going further, you can recognize reality as a whole—allness—much as you can recognize the mind as a whole. (For a practice of this, see the meditation in the box.)

Allness as allness is always allness. Try to get a sense of this as a mind-stopping experience, not just as an obvious truism.

Allness as allness is still, not moving. All changing phenomena are occurring in allness that is unchanging as allness.

Much as there is no problem in the mind as a whole, there is no problem in allness as a whole.

Allness as allness is a more reliable basis for lasting happiness than any changing phenomena within it.

Much as you can get a sense of mind as a whole, see if you can get a sense of allness as a whole.

ONLY ALLNESS

Relax . . . warmhearted and at ease . . . Feeling the whole body breathing . . . abiding as the mind as a whole . . . Resting in now . . . tranquil and present . . . Recognizing the empty nature of the sensations of breathing . . .

Know that your stream of consciousness is affected by other people . . . Simply feel this fact . . . knowing that what it feels like to be you is shaped by human culture . . .

Know that all experiences depend upon physical processes, that your mind depends on matter . . . Be aware of

(continued)

the physicalness of breathing . . . the hard parts and the soft parts of the body . . . Atoms flowing into the lungs with each breath, entering the blood and spreading through the body . . . atoms flowing out into the world . . . the feeling of breathing a result of these physical processes . . .

Receiving atoms of oxygen from countless plants . . . exhaling carbon dioxide for them to receive . . . breathing as part of a vast physical process . . .

Knowing that the exhalations of plants are powered by light from a ball of burning gas . . . receiving light into the body with every breath . . . Knowing that the atoms in your body are very old . . . that stars had to explode for you to be here today . . .

Knowing that your breathing and body blend into processes that extend outward into the universe . . . letting imagination and awareness open all the way outward, boundless . . . with awe and wonder . . . intuiting allness . . .

Relaxing into this knowing . . . that this moment of experience is the local patterning of the universe . . .

Intuiting allness . . . simply allness . . . always allness . . . allness abiding . . . only allness . . . being allness . . .

Good Practice

For an hour, observe the sense of possessing things ("I own that"), identifying with viewpoints or groups ("I am that"), and conceit ("I am better than you, I matter more than you"). Notice how these feel. And consider what was happening inside you or outside you to foster them.

For another hour, observe how you can do many things as a person without much if any sense of I, me, and mine.

In meditation, be attentive to the coming and going of the sense of I or me. Recognize how this sense of self has many aspects...that keep changing...due to many causes. Recognize how the apparent self is cloudlike, insubstantial, without a stable essence. You can also do this at various times throughout the day.

When you come very close to the present moment of experience, notice that nobody is running the show at the emergent edge of now. It's changing so fast that no one can possibly be in charge of it all.

If you have felt rejected or less than others, look for genuine experiences of feeling cared about or valued. Also look for opportunities to recognize your own worth and feel your natural goodness. When you are having these experiences, slow down to help them sink into you. Notice how growing your sense of being worthy as a person actually relaxes the sense of self.

In meditation, explore what it feels like to bring together a sense of wholeness, nowness, and allness. With practice, these can weave together in the background of awareness as you function in ordinary ways.

From time to time, recognize emptiness in everyday life. For example, a traffic jam is empty of (absolute self-causing) essence. Situations, tasks, and interactions are also empty—and so are any upsetting reactions to them.

Explore the feeling of being vulnerably dependent on many things, such as people, plants and animals, modern medicine, air and sunlight, and so on. Notice what may feel uneasy about this...and also what can feel very supportive. Get a sense of so many things rippling through you as you. See if you can be okay with this. Fundamentally, you *are* the many things manifesting as you.

9

FINDING TIMELESSNESS

Things appear and disappear
according to causes and conditions.
The true nature of things is not being born, and not dying.
Our true nature is the nature of no-birth and no-death,
and we must touch our true nature in order to be free.

THICH NHAT HANH

We have come to the last of our seven steps of awakening, both the most stable and the most slippery underfoot, always present and the farthest shore. Words can help us approach it, but they fall apart the closer we get.

Mind, Matter—and Mystery

The mind clearly exists: we are certainly having experiences, such as hearing, seeing, and feeling. From our experiences we infer matter, that we are perceiving something real, something that exists in its own right—whether anyone perceives it or not. Using the mind, we can study the physical world, and life and its evolution, and the nervous system and its brain. The mind can learn about the matter that is making the mind—which boggles my mind!

Mind and matter—so far, so good. These are the *natural* phenomena that include immaterial information and experiences, as well as material matter and energy. Within the natural frame are certainly many strange and wonderful things: joys and sorrows, gophers and galaxies, Beethoven and bumblebees.

And—is that all there is?

NIBBANA

As I understand it, the Buddha's quest was to find the most sublime happiness and the most radical liberation from suffering. A common belief of his time was that some aspect of an individual passed from life to life through rebirths; in that context, the aim of practice could be ending suffering in future lives as well as in this one. He tried one vehicle after another, beginning with a privileged life and its pleasures, and then leaving home to explore ascetic disciplines and increasingly subtle meditative practices. But he came to see that the experiences he had with each vehicle were unreliable because they were all *conditioned*—caused to come into being—and therefore subject to changing when their causes changed. (Besides "conditioned," we could say *fabricated*, *constructed*, or *inclined*, which add useful nuances.)

And so he kept looking until he found that which was *not* conditioned. Unchanging—not impermanent—and therefore a reliable basis for lasting happiness and peace. In a word: nibbana. As Bhikkhu Bodhi writes:

What lies beyond the round of rebirths is an unconditioned state called Nibbana. Nibbana transcends the conditioned world, yet it can be attained within conditioned existence, in this very life, and experienced as the extinction of suffering.... The realization of Nibbana comes with the blossoming of wisdom and brings perfect peace, untarnished happiness, and the stilling of the mind's compulsive drives. Nibbana is the destruction of thirst, the thirst of craving. It is also the island of safety amid the raging currents of old age, sickness, and death.

In Bhikkhu Bodhi's masterful anthology, *In the Buddha's Words*, he gathers these descriptions of nibbana from the Pali Canon. I like to let them all wash through my mind—and sometimes reflect on a specific word:

- the unborn, unaging, unailing, deathless, sorrowless, undefiled supreme security from bondage
- the destruction of lust, hatred, and delusion
- the unconditioned, uninclined, taintless, truth, far shore, subtle, very difficult to see, stable, undisintegrating, unmanifest, unproliferated, peaceful, sublime, auspicious, secure, destruction of craving, wonderful, amazing, unafflicted, dispassion, purity, freedom, nonattachment, island, shelter, asylum, refuge, the destination and the path leading to the destination

Nibbana is a fundamental aim of Buddhist practice:

O house-builder, you are seen!
You will not build this house again.

For your rafters are broken and your ridgepole shattered.
My mind has reached the unconditioned;
I have attained the destruction of craving.

DHAMMAPADA 154

This is peaceful, this is sublime, namely:
the stilling of all compounded things,
the extinction of craving,
cessation,
nibbana.

ANGUTTARA 10.60

The born, become, produced,
made, fabricated, impermanent,
composed of aging and death,
a nest of illnesses, perishing,
sprung from craving—
This is unfit for delight.
The escape from that,
calm, everlasting, beyond reasoning,
unborn, unproduced,
the sorrowless, stainless state,
the cessation of states of suffering,
the stilling of fabrications—bliss.

ITIVUTTAKA 43

OUTSIDE THE NATURAL FRAME

I think we can approach the unconditioned in three ways. First, we could practice "unconditioning" ourselves *from* reactions that lead to suffering while increasingly resting *in* undisturbed spacious awareness. Second, we could explore an extraordinary state of mind (usually the result of intensive meditative practice) *within ordinary reality* in which all conditioned experiences cease. Third, our practice might involve something that we believe could be truly transcendental, beyond ordinary conditioned reality and outside the "natural frame." (I'm using *transcendental* because that term is less specific and less burdened with the problematic associations some may have to words such as "God.")

The first two ways of approaching these matters don't seem very controversial. But the third one can be. So I'm going to slow down and try to walk carefully here.

> Precisely because there is an unborn, unbecome, unmade, unfabricated ... an escape from the born, become, made, fabricated is discerned.
>
> UDANA 8.3

In my experience, some people think there is no point in practicing with reference to anything transcendental. Their reasons include believing that nothing transcendental actually exists, or that there might be something transcendental but it's unknowable, or that there might be something both transcendental and knowable but it's irrelevant to practice. Other people think there is no point in practicing *without* reference to something transcendental. Their reasons include believing that there actually is a transcendental aspect to ultimate reality, or that even if this is unknowable, it serves them to practice in relationship to it. I've learned from teachers in both camps.

Scholars and teachers disagree about the proper translations and meanings of the passages above and similar ones from the Pali Canon. My own reading of these passages is that they do include references to something that is genuinely transcendental. But I could be wrong about that. And no matter what the texts "really" mean, the Buddha and their other authors could have been mistaken.

As a teacher, the Buddha encouraged people to come and see for themselves what they find to be true and useful. Well, for myself, both reason and experience say that ordinary reality is not all there is. So I approach the question "What does it mean to be unconditioned?" in all three ways noted above. Of course, you can explore this material in any way you like. In this chapter I'll be considering both natural and possibly transcendental aspects of practice.

POSSIBLE CHARACTERISTICS OF THE TRANSCENDENTAL

To begin with, it's important to distinguish between what may be *supernatural*—for example, rebirth, spirit beings, cosmological realms—and what may be *transcendental*: beyond whatever is supernatural and eternal and thus timeless. I'll be focusing on what could be transcendental here. People use different words for this, such as ultimate reality, infinite consciousnesses, Mystery, Ground, or God. There are many teachings and disagreements about these matters in Buddhism alone, and many more in other traditions and philosophies. I'm going to simplify and summarize, and emphasize the implications for practice.

Something transcendental might not exist. But if it *does* exist, hmmm, it would be useful to consider and perhaps even sense its possible characteristics.

First, the transcendental could be *unconditioned*, a timeless ground of possibility that enables time-bound conditioned actuality. What is always just before now is not yet conditioned. What becomes conditioned in both mind and matter is determined, set, actual, unfree. Whatever is transcendentally unconditioned is spacious and unbound. Things change, but it doesn't. For example:

> Move my mind now to that which holds
> Things as they change.
>
> WENDELL BERRY

There could be a stillness beyond all activity and noise:

> Who
> Are you? Whose
> Silence are you?
>
> THOMAS MERTON

Second, what may lie beyond ordinary reality could have a quality of *awareness*. As one way to approach this, consider recent experiments on quantum entanglement. A leading interpretation of their results is that an observing awareness is necessary for quantum possibility—a particle could somehow be both "up" and "down"—to become actuality (for instance, "up"). If this is true, perhaps some kind of awareness must be woven into the underlying fabric of the physical universe, everywhere and always, in order for what is possible to become what is actual, *now*.

Third, in their sense of the transcendental, people sometimes speak of a far-reaching *benevolence*. For example, I once saw the front door of a home painted with GOD IS LOVE.

Fourth, some describe a *sublime peace* in the transcendental, or related qualities of bliss or joy. Is this peace an attribute of the transcendental or what people experience when they recognize what is for them transcendental? Perhaps both, and perhaps it doesn't matter.

Last, some find a quality of *personhood*. A Being with whom one can have a relationship. A Being to love, perhaps worship.

These are some of the ways that people talk about and say they experience the transcendental. I will focus mainly on the first of them, the quality of being *unconditioned*.

> This holy life is not for the sake of gain, honor, and fame, or for the attainment of virtue, concentration, or knowledge and vision. Rather, it is this unshakable deliverance of mind that is the goal of this holy life, its heartwood, and its end.
>
> MAJJHIMA NIKAYA, 30

Turning to the Transcendental

Science cannot prove or disprove the existence of the transcendental. I love science, and believe that our world is much better because of it. But as powerful as it is, the scientific method has limitations. For example, it cannot prove that one person truly loves someone else. Some things are true that science cannot prove.

The practice of many people has been nourished by their sense of something transcendental. If there really is a transcendental aspect of ultimate reality, taking it into account could be important to you. It's been important to me, and I've practiced within the natural frame in part to become more open to what might lie beyond it.

Let's consider some ways of doing this.

CALMING THE CONDITIONED

We're drawn into what is conditioned when we feel distracted, rattled, or flooded. Consequently, the sense of what could be unconditioned is aided by steadying the mind, the first of the seven practices that we've explored.

We're also pulled into what is conditioned when we feel lonely, resentful, or inadequate. To address this, we engaged the second practice of awakening, warming the heart.

Feeling that something is missing, something is wrong, fuels the craving that drives much conditioned and stressful reactivity. So we've done the third practice, resting in fullness.

Dividing yourself internally leads to conditioned parts struggling with other parts. The fourth practice, being wholeness, reduces these inner conflicts and brings you into a stable spaciousness of mind.

When you're caught up in the past or the future, you're probably thinking about one conditioned thing after another. The fifth practice, receiving nowness, helps you move closer to the emergent edge of each moment, before many conditioned feelings and desires have had time to take hold.

Feeling separated from the world with a strong sense of self leads us to take the conditioned phenomena of life oh so personally. So we explored the sixth practice, opening into allness, softening the edges between the person you are and everything else.

While each of the first six practices of awakening has value in its own right, every one supports the others—and they have all led to the seventh practice, finding timelessness. For example, as you become more contented and peaceful, it's natural to open into the mind as a whole, and feel how it is fluttering in a thousand breezes within a vast undisturbable stillness.

> Indeed the sage who's fully quenched
> rests at ease in every way;
> no sense desire adheres to one
> whose fires have cooled, deprived of fuel.
> All attachments have been severed,
> the heart's been led away from pain;
> tranquil, one rests with utmost ease,
> the mind has found its way to peace.
>
> CULLAVAGGA 6.4.4

A SENSE OF POSSIBILITY

The quality of unconditionality—utter possibility—could be the primary necessary attribute of the transcendental, distinguishing it from ordinary conditioned reality. You can imagine and perhaps sense this possibility always just prior to the present moment. Personally, I have found this to be an amazing practice. It's like you're aware of what is just before now . . . a lot of the time.

You can also be aware of possibility within the natural frame. This is *like* transcendental unconditionality, and therefore a way to be reminded of it. For example, a blank piece of paper can represent infinite possibilities of images and words. The surface of a river can be patterned by an infinite variety of eddies.

In your mind, you can recognize that awareness is effectively unconditioned in a *mental* sense, able to represent an infinite variety of experiences. As your mind gets steadier, you can even recognize a kind of not-yet-conditioned space between the tiles—the sounds, thoughts, sensations, feelings, et cetera—of the mosaic of consciousness.

You can also imagine and perhaps sense the background hum of the nervous system, always on, always ready to respond to whatever might happen next. Much neural activity in the physical substrates of consciousness is not *in that moment* representing any information. These neurons keep firing so that they are prepared to represent new information, new signals, new conditionings. The neural substrates that are not in that moment representing information are effectively unconditioned in a *physical* sense, ready to be conditioned. They provide a field of fertile noise—a space of possibility—that is free to be patterned by any new signal.

Everyday life offers many opportunities for a feeling of possibility. As you approach tasks or situations, notice what it feels like to hold open options before constraining them. So many possible gestures of the hands, so many movements of the body, so many different words you could say. Also look for stillness, that which doesn't move and through which movement flows. For example, you might find stillness deep in your being, a kind of center point around which all mental motions come and go.

FURTHER READING

I Am That (Sri Nisargadatta Maharaj, edited by Sudhakar S. Dikshit)

The Island (Ajahn Passano and Ajahn Amaro)

The Perennial Philosophy (Aldous Huxley)

AN AWARENESS DEEPER THAN YOUR OWN

Your own awareness—and perhaps that of a squirrel or other animals—could be *like* potentially transcendental awareness. So the practice of abiding as awareness might deepen your intuition of a universal consciousness—and draw you into it as well. Once I was telling the teacher Shinzen Young about my sense of an awareness "deep down" that was very unlike my ordinary consciousness. He replied, "Yes—and as practice develops, there can be a shift, and instead of you observing it, you become this deeper awareness looking back at yourself." This deeper awareness might be simply an aspect of the natural, conditioned mind. Or it might transcend the ordinary mind. Personally, I experience this both ways, and am inspired by the Sanskrit saying *Tat tvam asi*: Thou art That.

However you interpret it, see if you can get a sense of this shift, if only for a moment. And then over time you can have a more consistent sense of an impersonal vast awareness as the backdrop or foundation of your personal particular experiences. To the extent that consciousness is necessary for quantum potentiality to become actuality, a sense of a transcendental awareness could be especially accessible as you come into the present moment, resting as close as possible to the emergent edge of now.

LIVED BY LOVE

As we've seen in previous chapters, love flowing in and flowing out can reduce craving and the sense of self, which in turn makes more room for a greater sense of what could be unconditioned. Additionally, if it is true that God is love, that love and possibility and consciousness are woven together in the transcendental, then your personal love could be *like* that vast transpersonal love and thus an entry into it.

You can explore the sense of your love opening out and becoming edgeless, boundless, unlimited, unconstrained, and unconditional. For example, a friend of mine was a monk in Southeast Asia for many years, and I asked him if he had met anyone who was enlightened. He laughed and said the standards are high there. They observe you for years, and it's not like having a white-light moment and getting a TV show. I persisted, and he said, sure, there were some people who were recognized as highly, highly developed, perhaps fully awakened. I asked, "What were they like?" He said, "Well, in a way, they were always the same. Yes, sometimes they were quiet and other times talkative, sometimes joking and sometimes serious. But in this way they were always the same: if you treated them well, they loved you, and if you treated them badly, they still loved you." That kind of love does not depend on conditions; in that way, it is unconditioned.

You can also intuit or imagine that "your" love is not just *like* transcendental love but is in some sense an aspect of it. People talk about a deep well of love that is bottomless, inexhaustible, forever flowing. You might have a sense of a love beyond yours living through you.

> Let go of the past, let go of the future,
>   let go of the present.
> Gone beyond becoming,
> with the mind released in every way,
> you do not again undergo birth and old age.
>
> DHAMMAPADA 348

MOMENTS OF AWAKENING

There's a saying: Moments of awakening—many times a day.

It's as if we spend our lives cloaked in black velvet surrounded by light. Each moment of awakening makes a little hole in the velvet that lets in a ray of light. Moment after moment, hole after hole, more and more light streams through. Eventually the cloak is so full of holes that it becomes transparent to the light that was always already there.

You can feel this around some beings. They live in this world while something unworldly shines through their eyes and words and actions.

I believe this is possible for all of us. We can cultivate a sense of the transcendental every day. It's like feeling that the "front" of you is living into conditioned reality while the "back" of you is resting in the unconditioned transcendental. A space of possibility, and perhaps profound awareness and love. The feeling of being an eddy in the stream of allness flowing along the banks of the unconditioned.

A FEELING OF FREEDOM

Establishing steadiness of mind . . . feeling loving . . . contented . . . and peaceful . . . Abiding as a whole . . . Tranquil and present . . . A sense of self may come and go . . . Opening into allness . . .

Intuiting or imagining a space of possibility in which all things occur . . . possibility always just before whatever happens . . . always not yet conditioned . . . Relaxing and opening into this possibility . . .

There could be a feeling of vast spaciousness . . . a sense of stillness . . . Resting in timelessness as time passes . . . Adding nothing, fabricating nothing . . . Nothing sticking, nothing landing . . . Abiding in this freedom . . .

If you like, explore other possible aspects of the transcendental . . . perhaps a sense of an awareness vaster than your own . . . boundless love . . . sublime peacefulness . . . benevolence toward you . . . Receiving and abiding . . .

A sense of abiding unconditioned . . . as conditioned phenomena appear and pass away . . . abiding unconditioned . . .

Eddies in the Stream

The process of moving toward what is unconditioned is itself conditioned. For example, we've explored a growing sense of steadiness, lovingness, fullness, wholeness, nowness, and allness, and with practice these become more deeply rooted, stable, and reliable. But they are still conditioned. Even the eternal now and the allness of everything are conditioned by the big bang and the underlying deep nature of the physical universe—whatever that is! And to the extent that what is unconditioned makes a difference for a person, those effects must involve conditioned changes in the person's body and mind.

How might we understand this meeting of conditioned and unconditioned? What could be happening as conditioned processes in the neural substrates of consciousness become extremely, perhaps utterly, quiet? And how might this quiet be an opening to what might lie beyond ordinary reality?

With respect for the mysteries these questions point to, I'd like to offer the reflections below. They summarize, pull together, and build on key themes we've been exploring.

———　∘　———

Rivers flow and eddies swirl along.

A river is made of molecules made of atoms made of quantum particles that are the substrate of the physical universe.

Scientists speak of a "quantum foam" through which eddies of matter and energy pass. Patterns of matter and energy change, but their substrate remains the same.

Eddies are patternings *of* a river. Similarly, all forms of matter and energy—from quarks to quasars, from microvolts to lightning bolts—are patternings *of* the substrate of the universe.

——— • ———

Twirling electrons, dancers in a club, freeway traffic, a person's life, moons and stars, clusters of galaxies, and our own blossoming universe surrounded by mystery—all eddies in the stream.

Every eddy is compounded of parts, dependent upon causes, and impermanent. All eddies disperse. All eddies are empty. Clinging to eddies is suffering.

——— • ———

The substrate of the universe enables an infinite variety of patterns, as a river enables an infinite variety of eddies. Eddies pattern a river momentarily without altering its capacity to be patterned. Just so, all eddies of matter and energy emerge, persist, and disperse without ever changing their substrate's capacity to birth, hold, and release them.

As soon as a pattern forms, its multiple possibilities have converged on a single actuality. Its substrate is a space of effectively infinite freedom in which actualities emerge into unfreedom and then pass away.

——— • ———

It is always now. The duration of now seems to be infinitesimally small. Yet somehow it contains the causes from the past that will create the future.

The quantum foam of the substrate of the universe is always rich with possibilities.

Just before the emergent edge of now, just before quantum potentiality coalesces into actuality, is always not yet conditioned.

———— · ————

Information is a reduction of uncertainty, a signal against a backdrop of noise.

Information is represented by patterning a suitable substrate. The information of Beethoven's "Ode to Joy" can be represented by a musical score on paper, pulsations in stereo speakers, and organized activations in neural networks.

The mind is the information and experiences represented by the nervous system.

The neural substrates of consciousness can represent an infinite variety of experiences.

Every experience depends on a brief dynamic coalition of many synapses.

An experience is an eddy of information mapped to an eddy of neural activity.

———— · ————

For any experience to emerge, there must be unused neural capacity to represent it. The substrate of noisy neural activity is fertile with potential.

It takes just milliseconds to form the coherent assembly of synapses that underlies an experience. Once a neural assembly eddies into existence, it is conditioned and unfree. The experience remains what it is until its synaptic pattern disperses, usually within a second or two. Then those synapses become available for representing new eddies of experiences.

Experiences rise out of and fall back into a field of infinite possibility.

———— · ————

There is always some unused neural capacity, firing noisily and quivering with possibility. Not yet patterned, conditioned, and unfree.

In meditation, we become increasingly intimate with this neural potentiality. As the signals moving through the neural substrates of consciousness quiet down, we become more aware of the effectively unconditioned capacity to represent the next experience, and less engaged with any particular experience arising and passing away.

In this way, a field of possibility for the mind can be observed directly. Similarly, a field of possibility for the brain and for all matter, at the quantum level, can be understood intellectually and intuited imaginatively—and perhaps known directly in some way as well.

As contemplative practice deepens—along with virtue and wisdom—we become increasingly aware of and centered in the freedom that exists prior to experiences.

We become aware of mental/neural eddies emerging and dispersing—none of them a reliable basis for lasting happiness.

We can abide in mental/neural possibility before patterns are pinned to it like notes to a bulletin board.

If there are indeed transcendental influences, the eternal space of possibility at the leading edge of now would be an opportune window for Grace.

———— · ————

Eddies of matter and eddies of mind have the same nature. They are impermanent and compounded, and they arise and pass away depending on their causes. They are patternings *of* their substrate that never change the substrate itself. At the front edge of now, they continually emerge from a field of effectively unconditioned possibility.

The whole universe and your own experiences have the same nature. The stars above, the grass and worms below, and your experiences of these are one in their nature.

Things change but their nature doesn't. Things are unreliable but their nature isn't.

In the nature of things, there is no problem. Nothing to grasp and no need for grasping. This is the nature of a cup, the hand that holds it, and the seeing of the hand.

Your nature already. My nature. The nature of everyone around you. Everyone in your life. The nature of the trees and the birds, every plant and every animal. The nature of every drop of water, every grain of sand. And the nature of every joy and every sorrow and the awareness through which these pass.

In everyday life, what would it be like to abide as the nature of mind and matter without clinging to any thought or thing?

———— • ————

Many people have a sense of something beyond this reality. Amidst ordinary activities or at particular times, there could be a feeling of vastness, mystery, presence, love. And this sense can be heightened through deep practices found in the world's spiritual traditions.

How might deep practice make a person more aware of what is transcendental?

As one example, if nibbana does have transcendental aspects, the path to and from it could teach us many things. In the Pali Canon, the steps toward it can progress through eight non-ordinary states of consciousness—the form and formless jhanas—along with radically penetrating insights. Understood within the natural frame, nibbana must have neural correlates. Even if nibbana includes transcendental aspects, the states of mind that precede and follow it must also have neural correlates.

To summarize and adapt descriptions of these steps, the first jhana is accompanied by applied and sustained attention, with bliss and happiness. In the second jhana, there is bliss and happiness as well as inner clarity and one-pointedness, and applied and sustained attention subside. In the third, there is happiness in the body and abiding in equanimity as bliss fades away. The fourth has neither elation nor distress, neither pain nor pleasure, and purity of mindfulness due to equanimity.

Then, with the passing away of perceptions of forms, the individual can enter upon the formless jhanas and dwell within "the base of the infinity of space"..."the base of the infinity of consciousness"..."the base of nothingness"..."the base of neither-perception-nor-nonperception"...and cessation...and nibbana...

———— • ————

In this movement through the form and formless jhanas, thought, focused attention, pleasure and pain, perception, and even non-perception—all gradually disperse.

The heart keeps beating and assemblies continue to form in the deep architecture of the nervous system. But in the brain's substrates of consciousness, eddies of information swirl apart, along with the neural assemblies that represent them. Signals drop out, stage by stage, leaving only fertile noise. Conditioned, unfree patterns disperse.

At the ultimate point, there is mostly if not entirely unconditioned mental and neural possibility. Other paths and practices in other traditions might also lead to this point. Profoundly open, continually in the emergence of the present moment before conditioning, immersed in what is unconditioned...this could be so *like* the transcendental that there is an opening into it. Freed from the ordinary mind, we could open into what is beyond ordinary reality.

For example, Bhikkhu Bodhi writes:

> Through the practice of the Buddha's path, the practitioner arrives at the true knowledge of conditioned phenomena, which disables the generation of active *sankharas* [compounded experiences], putting an end to the constructing of conditioned reality and opening the door to the Deathless, the *asankhata*, the unconditioned, which is Nibbana, the final liberation from impermanence and suffering.

——— · ———

While the transcendental may be timeless, time continues for the body. Eventually eddies of information begin to gather again in the neural streaming of consciousness. There can be profound insights into the nature of the mind, and perhaps reality itself.

For example, the words of Thich Nhat Hanh that opened this chapter are worth hearing again:

> Things appear and disappear according to causes and conditions. The true nature of things is not being born, and not

dying. Our true nature is the nature of no-birth and no-death, and we must touch our true nature in order to be free.

My own conviction is that the mind and the universe have the same deep nature, to be emergent, empty, and full of possibility. Within ordinary reality, this is our own nature, always. And our true nature opens into vast mystery.

An experience is an eddy through the mind, a body is an eddy through matter, and a person is an eddy through allness. Eddies in streams.

Things arise: snowflakes and stars, people and relationships, joys and sorrows. And always pass away. Yet the streams they pass through and the nature of these streams endure.

The streaming and its nature are our ground and refuge.

Abiding as the streaming, resting in the unconditioned.

As Zen master Hakuin wrote:

Pointing directly at the mind,
see your own nature
and become Buddha.

True Nature

May you enjoy the meditation that concludes this chapter.

Relaxing ... abiding now as a whole body breathing ... aware of the whole space around you ...

Steadily present while calming ... feeling compassion and kindness ... thankfulness and contentment ... resting at ease ...

Resting in the present as sensations pass through awareness . . . no work needs to be done . . . nothing to accomplish . . . no one you need to be . . .

As you abide, recognize the nature of the mind . . . with many parts . . . continually changing . . . affected by many things . . . without a fixed essence . . . empty . . . Letting yourself be the nature of the mind . . . in the nature of the mind, there is no problem . . . being your nature . . .

The mind occurring in unconditioned possibility . . . in a deep stillness . . . within a vast awareness . . .

Recognizing the nature of water: changing, many parts, affected by many things, without essence, empty . . . The same nature of your body . . . the earth . . . the universe . . . In the nature of things, there is no problem . . .

Resting in the nature of things . . . being the nature of things . . . All things happening in unconditioned possibility . . . a deep stillness . . . a vast awareness . . .

Resting in your nature . . . resting in timelessness . . .

Your true nature is the nature of all awakened beings . . .

Be at ease in true nature . . .

Good Practice

Take a little time to reflect on the universe. No need to be a scientist, just be aware of its vastness and some of the many things it holds, such as people you know, our earth and sun, atoms and galaxies. Then ask yourself: Is this all there is? Your answer might be "yes," "no," "I don't know," or "none of the above." No matter what your answer is, see what it's like to really own it. To stand in it and face the implications, whatever they are. How does or how could your answer affect your day-to-day practice?

In meditation, help your mind become very quiet. Then be aware of the process of making—fabricating, constructing, conditioning—experiences. Some of this is automatic (though this, too, can become very quiet with practice). But other "fabrications" are added more deliberately, such as reactions to sounds or thoughts. Be aware of this adding. And then explore what it is like to add as little as possible—even nothing at all. What does it feel like for fabricating, constructing, and conditioning to lessen? Can you have a sense of what not fabricating, constructing, or conditioning feels like? Could there be a sense of what is *not* fabricated, constructed, or conditioned in your mind... and perhaps more deeply and transcendentally?

Look at a blank sheet of paper. Recognize that you could draw or write an infinite variety of shapes upon it. Similarly, recognize that your awareness can hold an infinite variety of experiences. In these ways, get a sense of what is *effectively* unconditioned: a space of infinite possibility. Be aware of such spaces of possibility throughout your day. For example, the next time you talk with someone, recognize that an infinite number of things would be possible to say. Can you rest in this freedom? And then, within this freedom, make wise choices?

Be aware of stillness. It could be as simple as the space between inhaling and exhaling. Bring awareness to what is unchanging inside you, around you, and beyond you. Look up at the sky: clouds pass through its stillness. There could be a sense of stillness deep within you, even if there is activity around it. And when your whole being is quiet, it can feel still, like a tranquil pond.

If you like, explore an intuition of something beyond ordinary reality that is unconditioned... spacious... still... and timeless. Can you bring a sense of this into your experience, many times a day?

If you have a sense of supernatural or transcendental matters beyond ordinary reality, reflect on how you are engaging with these. Is there anything you would like to add or change?

If you have a sense of the transcendental, consider aspects of it that would serve you to focus on, such as a quality of possibility... awareness... love... peace... benevolence toward you personally...

If you do want to turn toward the transcendental, what would it feel like to become more available to it, more given over to it, more lived by it? What could you release in your mind or actions to become more transparent to it?

Part Four

ALWAYS ALREADY
HOME

10

THE FRUIT AS THE PATH

Things fall apart.
Tread the path with care.

Digha Nikaya 16

was once talking with the teacher Steve Armstrong, who had trained as a monk in Asia. I asked him if he could tell me about nibbana. He looked at me intently and then got a faraway look and said something I've thought about many times since: "It's as if you live in a deep valley surrounded by mountains. Then one day you're standing on top of the highest peak. The perspective is amazing. Still, you can't live there. And so you come back down to the valley. But what you've seen changes you forever."

We've been exploring seven steps on the path of awakening. Each of these practices is a kind of waking up, each one supports the others, and they all lead on to the highest happiness. And sometimes you may have had glimpses of the view from way high up. Now it's time to let things settle inside you and sink in. If reading this book were like being on a meditation retreat, it would also be natural to start thinking about going back home, and about what you might like to take back with you.

I hope you will bring along these seven ways of being and practicing. They are valuable in themselves. It feels good to be mindful and steady, with a kind heart, contented and peaceful, feeling whole in the present moment, connected with everything, and open to mystery. Growing these qualities in yourself will help others, too. And they are powerful practices that can continue to carry you to the heights. As you experience these ways of being, they will develop in you. They are *fruits* of practice as well as *paths* of practice. In what I heard was a Tibetan saying, we can take the fruit as the path.

In particular, it's useful to consider how to apply what we've explored to the relationships and tasks and pleasures of everyday life. We'll start with two meditations, one focused on gratitude and the other on softening the edges of things both inside you and between you and the wider world. Next, we'll see how you can make your own offering in life, and then we'll finish with practical suggestions for supporting your practice and continuing on your personal path of awakening in the days to come.

Giving Thanks for What You've Received

So much has already been offered to each one of us, including precious ideas and methods that have been developed by others, the gifts of land and life, and the sense of your deepest, truest nature. In effect, we have a simple job: to make room for what we've been given. This way of looking at things lowers any pressure to get it right or to hold on to anything. You've already received a lot and can simply let it sink into you in its own natural way.

A MEDITATION ON GRATITUDE

Come into the present, aware of your body, finding a posture that is comfortable and alert...

Bring to mind some simple things you are thankful for...such as food, flowers, fresh water...Let thankfulness be the focus of your meditation...becoming absorbed in thankfulness...and absorbing thankfulness into yourself...

Being aware of the land and plants and animals...offering thanks to them...aware of the earth as a whole, with gratitude...aware of the vastness of space...the amazingness of existing at all...resting in thankfulness...

Bring to mind people in your life, past and present, for whom you are thankful...feeling a warmhearted gratitude...

Bring to mind some of what you have received from your teachers...from their teachers...feeling thankful for your teachers, of all kinds...feeling grateful for the traditions of knowledge and wisdom that have helped you...

Being thankful for what has come to you from your practices over time...appreciating some of their benefits for you and others...feeling thankful for the fruits of practice...grateful for the chance to have a practice at all...

Being aware of what you've practiced in reading this book...appreciating your own efforts...appreciating steadying your mind...warming your heart...resting in fullness...being wholeness...receiving nowness...opening into allness...finding timelessness...

Be thankful for seeing clearly...for truth...

Thankful for the ultimate nature of things, whatever you sense that could be...

Thankful for this life...

Softening the Edges

To function, we need to make distinctions: between the tea and the cup, our feelings and theirs, sadness and happiness. But in these separations is a seed of suffering: setting one thought against another, one person against another. While there may be many edges, still we can soften them.

GENTLY SOFTENING

Relaxing... inhaling... exhaling... inhaling beginning and ending softly... exhaling beginning and ending softly... the edges of breathing softening...

Softening the edges of sensations in the skin as it touches clothing, earth, air...

The heart softening... sensations of the heart and chest softening together...

Breathing... being... edges softening... the world process and your person process softening together...

Letting life flow through you... your living flowing out into life... life flowing into your living... edges softening between your living and all life...

Air flowing in, air flowing out... the world flowing in... flowing out... edges softening between your body and the world...

Softening the edges inside the mind... everything blending together... still being fine... breathing and being...

The mind and body softening together... edges softening between you and all that is... all that is, flowing through you as you...

Edges softening between you and everything... between everything and you...

All edges softening...

Edges softening between conditioned and unconditioned... between time and timelessness...

Edges softening between individual awareness and a deeper awareness...

Love softening through you... softening into a knowing, a wisdom, coming through you...

All edges softening... flowing... softly... gently...

Making the Offering

There's a natural process in which you take what you've gained through practice and offer it out into the world. To do this, I've found it very useful to consider several themes.

COMPASSION AND EQUANIMITY

Compassion opens the heart and brings caring to the burdens and suffering of others and oneself. Equanimity is the experiencing of this with wisdom and inner peace. With equanimity, you can walk evenly over uneven ground and, as Howard Thurman put it, look out on life with quiet eyes.

We have explored many ways to strengthen compassion and equanimity, and sometimes it helps to focus on one in particular. For example, if you have a lot of emotional stability but also some cool detachment from others, you might want to bring more empathy and kindness into your meditations and daily actions. On the other hand, you might be very open to others but feel rocked by the waves of their emotions and other reactions. In this case, you could focus on calming and centering. You could also recognize the impermanent, interdependent, and empty nature of events and experiences, even the worst ones of all.

This balance of compassion and equanimity is important as we look beyond the local circle of friends and family. Being aware of so much suffering in the world and so much injustice, it is possible to be fiercely committed to the welfare of others while also being at peace about what is and what will be.

> Teach us to care and not to care
> Teach us to sit still.
>
> T. S. ELIOT

TENDING TO THE CAUSES

Let's say that you'd like to have some fruit. You could go get a seed and plant it carefully. As the seed becomes a sapling and then a tree, you could water and fertilize it, protecting it from pests and pruning it carefully. As the years go by, you can take good care of your fruit tree. But you cannot *make* it give you an apple.

We can tend to the causes. But we cannot control the results. Knowing this can bring a sense of peace, since so many of the factors that determine what happens are out of your hands. It also brings a sense of responsibility, since it is up to you to tend to the causes you can. We are interdependent, and still each of us must do our own practice—and tread our own path with care.

In this light, are there causes you could tend to more consistently in your relationships, health, or anything else that matters to you?

And could you help yourself be more at peace with whatever the results may be, including how others feel about you?

FURTHER READING

Being Peace (Thich Nhat Hanh)

Ecodharma (David Loy)

Radical Dharma (Rev. Angel Kyodo Williams and Lama Rod Owens, with Jasmine Syedullah)

Standing at the Edge (Roshi Joan Halifax)

For example, in the realm of work—including making a home and raising a family—it is interesting and very useful to practice being determined and enthusiastic—without getting stressed or driven about it. This sweet spot is *aspiration without attachment*. Dreaming big dreams, being "ardent, resolute, and diligent" as the Buddha said...while also feeling at ease inside, with a sense of passing through a larger space of being, and not trying to carry five quarts of tasks in a one-gallon bucket.

Can you find an example of what this feels like in your own life? Or can you see this in another person, and imagine how this would be for you to experience? Knowing what it feels like, consider how you could bring this attitude of easeful effort, pressureless determination, to your work. What would support this way of being? What would be the benefits?

Many years ago a friend told me about the first formal talk he was going to offer as an aspiring priest in a Zen temple. I had read in the newspaper that homeless people sought shelter in the temple, since it was warm, and I teased him that some in the audience might not be interested in his talk itself. He gestured as if placing something at my feet and said, "I just make the offering. I try to make it as good as I can, but after that it is out of my hands."

Can you be mindful of the inner and outer forces that draw you into drivenness, perhaps "shoulds" inside your mind or pressures coming from others? Consider how you could practice with these forces and gradually disengage from them.

In these ways we can bring our practice into the tasks and challenges of "real life"—which will bear fruit each step of the way.

OUR COLLECTIVE OFFERINGS

Moving from the level of the individual, we can see contributions made by larger groups of people. For example, in my home meditation center, Spirit Rock, there is a large stone statue of the Buddha behind the dining hall, and I like to imagine that it will still be there in five hundred years, simply more weathered and covered with lichen. His teachings and practices have endured because they are about the enduring essence of the mind and the universe. Still, over the years they have evolved into four major forms, in the Theravadan, Tibetan, Zen, and Pure Land traditions of Buddhism. From the perspective of people sitting with this statue many centuries from now, what might they see looking back upon our times? In addition to its troubles and strife, I believe they will recognize the emergence of a fifth major form of Buddhism in these recent developments:

- laypeople with a sustained and deep contemplative practice
- laypeople as teachers and leaders
- the growing inclusion of women, people of color, and other historically marginalized individuals as teachers and leaders
- science and related mental and physical health practices informing the dharma and being influenced by it, with a deepening understanding of the physical, embodied basis of suffering, its causes, and its end
- the eclectic application of Buddhist perspectives and practices in non-Buddhist settings

We can have different opinions about whether these developments are a good thing, but they are clearly a real thing. It feels inspiring and humbling to me to see how we are planting and tending to these seeds together, including in many ways that are not about Buddhism itself. We are co creating the future of practice, and more broadly, I hope we are planting seeds for greater wisdom and happiness in humanity as a whole, and in its relationship to all of life.

In ways seen and unseen, known and unknown, small and great, there is a larger offering moving through us all. To explore this further, you can try the meditation in the box on the next page.

OFFERING WITH PEACE

This meditation is about imagining your offerings in the days
to come, with a sense of an offering flowing through you
with ease, and with acceptance and peace about whatever
the results may be.

*Arriving here and now . . . aware of breathing . . . aware of
feelings of peacefulness . . . contentment . . . love . . . abiding
at ease . . .*

*Imagine offering a piece of fruit to someone and being at
peace with whether they want it or not . . . Get a sense of
what it is like to make an offering while accepting whatever
happens . . .*

*Be aware of some of what you offer already . . . what you
give in your home, in your work, to other people, to other
living things, and to the world . . . perhaps with a sense of life
moving through you to make these offerings . . . giving yourself
over to this powerful current and letting it carry you along . . .*

*Perhaps imagine new offerings . . . offering with kindness
and good intentions . . . offering with the knowing that you
cannot completely control the results . . . Let yourself care
about what will happen while letting go of attachment to the
results . . .*

*Know what it feels like to be speaking and acting while
being at peace in the core of your being . . . making your
offerings while already feeling contented, loving, and at
peace . . .*

*Letting life carry you along . . . letting life carry your
offerings naturally and easily outward to others and to the
world . . .*

Going Forth

The Buddha was said to have "gone forth" when he entered his path of awakening. One does not need to become a wandering monastic to appreciate the sense of aspiration, dignity, and opening into the world that is present in this phrase.

GRATITUDE FOR YOU

To begin with, I'd like to express my gratitude to you, the reader, for engaging this material with its demands and challenges. We probably do not know each other personally, yet I believe that each person's practice helps many others, in ways seen and unseen, known and unknown.

Thank you!

KEEP IT SIMPLE

We've explored a *lot* of ideas and methods. It's fine to let them settle inside and see how they affect you over time. We can recognize complexity while acting simply.

If you are not already doing this, consider committing to something contemplative—perhaps mindfulness of breathing, perhaps a prayer—for a minute or more each day. It may be the last thing you do before your head hits the pillow at night, but whenever you do it, make it one real minute—and perhaps many more.

Also, if you like, pick one simple change to make and to focus on, then stick with it. For example, if you get irritated, you could pause for one breath before speaking. Or light a candle before dinner. Or stop drinking alcohol. Or start each morning by recommitting to a purpose in life. Or bring a few minutes of compassion and kindness into your daily meditation.

In any moment, you can be aware of the suffering in it—your own and that of others. And aware of the happiness in it—both yours and theirs. With this simple awareness, there can be a natural letting go of the causes of suffering and a nourishing of the causes of happiness.

> I don't know so much if there are enlightened beings,
> but I know there are enlightened moments.
>
> SUZUKI ROSHI

DELIGHT IN PRACTICE

Whatever your practices are, you're more likely to keep doing them if you enjoy them. So look for what feels good and meaningful in what you are already doing, and perhaps find additional things that are naturally pleasurable for you. Ask yourself if you've been doing some things by rote, or if they've gotten dry for you; see if there are ways to help them be more rewarding. It's all right to let go of some things to make room for others that would be more fruitful for you.

It's good to bring playfulness, even delight, to your practices. See if you can be amused sometimes by your own mind, its zigging and zagging, the tricks it can play, the surprising sudden openings. I've gotten way too serious about my own practice in the past. Practice is less effective if it's heavy and somber most of the time. It's okay to have fun with it!

Try to practice for the sake of others as well as yourself. They can be in your heart as you meditate and as you act skillfully in different ways throughout your day.

HAVE PERSPECTIVE

You can trust that you will integrate your insights and practices into your everyday life. Give yourself time. Protect what is beneficial in what you've cultivated. Trust in your good nature. Trust in the deep nature we all share.

Ask yourself occasionally: Do I need to keep paying attention to this? Do I need to get driven about that? Do I need to be bothered by that person? Be mindful of accelerating, pressuring yourself and others, and turning fluid, cloudlike processes into static, brick-like things.

Imagine seeing a mountain pond. Breezes and storms can send waves moving across it, yet the pond as a pond is unmoving. The mind is like a pond, whose surface is awareness, and whose depths open into timelessness. Worldly winds blow and stir up thoughts and feelings that ripple across it, but eventually they settle down and it's quiet again—and all the while, the pond itself is still. As you go through your day, be aware of spaciousness, edgelessness, and still-ness. You can let go *of* any particular ripple and let go *into* being what you always are: whole, present, caring, peaceful, and full of possibility.

Be aware of your deepest longings and your highest purposes in this life. Let *them* live you and carry you along.

ENJOY THE RIDE

It's a wild life. Here we are on a small planet going around an ordinary star on the edge of one galaxy amidst a couple trillion others. Nearly 14 billion years have passed since our universe bubbled into being. And here we are now. Countless creatures have died so that tiny improvements in their capabilities could be stabilized through evolution in increasingly complex species, and eventually in us today. So many, many things have happened already. And here we are.

It's strange, isn't it, this life? You live and love and then you leave. My time will come, and yours, and everyone else's. Meanwhile, we can be gobsmacked with awe and gratitude, and committed to enjoying this life as best we can while learning as much as we can and contributing as much as we can each day.

Along the way, take in the good, helping your beneficial experiences sink in and become lasting strengths inside, woven into the fabric of your body. So many opportunities for this mindful cultivation occur in even the hardest life. Recognize what is wholesome, helpful, beautiful in yourself and in others and in everything. Let it land in you, becoming you.

I once asked the teacher Joseph Goldstein about an experience while wondering if I was on the right track. He listened and nodded and said, "Yes, that's it." And then he smiled and said, "Keep going."

ACKNOWLEDGMENTS

I'd like to thank the readers who gave me useful feedback, including James Austin, James Baraz, Leigh Brasington, Annette Brown, Alisa Dennis, Andrew Dreitcer, Peter Grossenbacher, Forrest Hanson, Jan Hanson, Kathy Kimber, John Kleiner, Edward Lewis, Richard Mendius, Venerable Sanda Mudita, Stephanie Noble, Sui Oakland, Lily O'Brien, Jan Ogren, John Prendergast, Tina Rasmussen, Ratnadevi, Jane Razavet, John Schorling, Michael Taft, Marina Van Walsum, Stephanie Veillon, Roger Walsh, and Jennifer Willis. Any errors that have survived their scrutiny are entirely my own.

I'm grateful to my teachers, some of whom are listed just above. Others include Ajahn Amaro, Guy Armstrong, Steve Armstrong, Tara Brach, Eugene Cash, Christina Feldman, Gil Fronsdal, Joseph Goldstein, Thich Nhat Hanh, Jack Kornfield, Kamala Masters, and Ajahn Succito. I've also learned greatly from Bhikkhu Anālayo, Stephen Batchelor, Thānissaro Bhikkhu, Bhikkhu Bodhi, Richard Gombrich, Mu Soeng, and Shinzen Young. And I'm thankful for the larger lineages and communities that have created, protected, and fostered wisdom around the world for thousands of years.

Scientists, scholars, clinicians, and teachers have developed useful understandings of the body and mind—including the neural basis of mindfulness, meditation, compassion, and kindness, and other aspects of awakening—as well as applications for practice. There are many more than I can name, but I'd like to pay my respects in particular to Bernard Baars, Richard Davidson, John Dunne, Bruce Ecker, Barbara Fredrickson, Chris Germer, Paul Gilbert, Timothea Goddard, Steve Hickman, Britta Holzel, Jon Kabat-Zinn, Dacher Keltner, Sara Lazar, Antoine Lutz, Jonathan Nash, Kristin Neff, Andrew Newberg, Stephen Porges, Jeffrey Schwartz, Shauna Shapiro, Dan Siegel, Ron Siegel, Evan Thompson, Fred Travis, David Vago, Cassandra Vieten, Alan Wallace, Mark Williams, Diana Winston, David Yaden—and to the memory of Francisco Varela.

Thank you both to the participants in the neurodharma retreats I've taught and to my co-teachers: Leslie Booker, Alisa Dennis, Peter Grossenbacher, Tara Mulay, Tina Rasmussen, and Terry Vandiver. I also have special gratitude for Sui Oakland, who organized and managed these retreats, and for Kaleigh Isaacs, who produced the online program based on them. Shambhala Mountain Center has been a beautiful and sacred home for these retreats. And from my heart, a deep thank-you to Judi Bell, Stuart Bell, Tom Bowlin, Daniel Ellenberg, Lee Freedman, Laurel Hanson, Marc Lesser, Crystal Lim-Lange, Greg Lim-Lange, Susan Pollak, Lenny Stein, Bob Truog, and Lienhard Valentin for your friendship and support of the neurodharma express!

I'm so grateful to the people who have come to our San Rafael Meditation Gathering over the years, and especially to our wonderful stewards, including Tom Brown, Nan Herron, Sundara Jordan, Lily O'Brien, Laurie Oman, Rob Paul, Christine Pollock, Gabriel Rabu, Tarane Sayler, Bill Schwarz, Trisha Schwarz, Donna Simonsen, Mark Stefanski, Shilpa Tilwalli, and Jerry White.

Truly, this book would not have been possible without my agent, Amy Rennert, and her support over the years. I'm also very thankful for my skillful and patient editor at Penguin Random House, Donna Loffredo, as well as for the whole team there. Additionally, the people who work with me at Being Well, Inc., have been absolutely instrumental in bringing this book to life; they include Forrest Hanson, Michelle Keane, Sui Oakland, Marion Reynolds, Andrew Schuman, Paul Van de Riet, and Stephanie Veillon.

Last and far from least, my precious, wonderful wife, Jan, has been endlessly encouraging and helpful with this book—and more profoundly, my whole life. She listened to me read it to her at night and gave me many useful suggestions—and, more fundamentally, her faith in its worth. With all my love: thank you.

NOTES

xv **Itivuttaka 1.22:** From *Gemstones of the Good Dhamma: Saddhamma-maniratana,* compiled and translated by Ven. S. Dhammika. Access to Insight (BCBS Edition), 30 November 2013, http://www.accesstoinsight.org/lib/authors/dhammika/wheel342.html.

CHAPTER 1: MIND IN LIFE

3 **Mind in Life:** This is also the title of Evan Thompson's excellent book on this subject, *Mind in Life: Biology, Phenomenology, and the Sciences of Mind.* It's a tour de force, and I recommend it highly. Also see F. J. Varela et al., *The Embodied Mind: Cognitive Science and Human Experience.*

3 **"If, by giving up":** Translation by Gil Fronsdal in *The Dhammapada: A New Translation of the Buddhist Classic, with Annotations.* Shambhala, 2006, p. 75.

4 **unattainable for the rest of us:** There may be very rare individuals who have an extraordinary and inexplicable transformation, and afterward they live on a plane of exalted realization. But these cases are so uncommon that they're hard to use as models of what we can become ourselves.

4 **seven practices of awakening:** This is my own model and not the only way to speak about awakening (or similar words) and its causes. And these seven practices—which are ways to organize and cluster together many ideas and methods—do not contain every possible aspect of awakening.

5 **enlightenment or full awakening:** While people may have "self-transcendent experiences" that propel them to the summit, they usually come back down, though they may be changed in some ways by what has happened for them. Full awakening means staying on the summit. See Yaden et al., "The Varieties of Self-Transcendent Experience."

I am drawing mainly on the account of awakening found in the Pali Canon and related Theravadan tradition. These descriptions of the stages and results of awakening are generally psychological and not mystical. For example, Bhikkhu Anālayo refers to awakening as "a condition of complete and permanent mental freedom." Anālayo, A *Meditator's Life of the Buddha*, p. 46.

AIMING HIGH

5   **Neuroscience is a young science:** For an exploration of issues in communicating brain science to a general audience, see the interview by Barry Boyce with the neuroscientists Amishi Jha and Clifford Saron here: https://www.mindful.org/the -magnificent-mysterious-wild-connected-and-interconnected-brain/.

5   **gone far up the mountain:** Numerous scholars have explored the intersection of brain science and deep contemplative practice. For example, see Gellhorn and Kiely, "Mystical States of Consciousness"; Davidson, "The Physiology of Meditation"; McMahan and Braun, eds., *Meditation, Buddhism, and Science*; Wallace, *Mind in the Balance*; and Wright, *Why Buddhism Is True*.

5   **definitive answers to these questions:** Since science keeps adding new information, there will never be neurologically definitive—in the sense of *final*—answers. But if we have to say everything about a topic before we can say something about it, we will never be able to say anything at all. We are inevitably left with questions of judgment: How much needs to be known about something before saying it? How much complexity needs to be added for an adequate account in the relevant context? Different people will answer these questions in different ways. In answering them here, I've tried to follow three principles: mention limitations to scientific knowledge; have many references; and focus on findings that highlight plausibly useful practices.

6   **mind offered by the Buddha:** This is the approach I know best, and of course not the only guide to the upper reaches of human potential.

6   **the Pali Canon:** The Buddha's teachings were handed down orally for several centuries before a written record survived. The primary source for what he taught is in the Pali Canon; Pali is an ancient language that is very close to the language used in northern India during the time of the Buddha. Related early versions of these texts have also been found in Chinese and Sanskrit. For a useful exploration of the Buddha's life and astute comparisons of the early surviving texts, see Anālayo, *A Meditator's Life of the Buddha*.

We will never know for sure what the Buddha actually said. This point also applies to some others quoted in this book, such as Milarepa, who lived a thousand years ago. Numerous scholars such as Bhikkhu Bodhi, Thānissaro Bhikkhu, Stephen Batchelor, Richard Gombrich, Leigh Brasington, and Bhikkhu Anālayo have sifted through the best available historical and textual records, but the picture they sketch is both illuminating and inexact.

We could preface statements attributed to these long-ago teachers with something like "it is said that they said" or "over centuries many people have shaped these teachings with their own historically contingent perspectives while errors also crept in," but this would be cumbersome. I simply write, "So-and-so said X," and hope the context will be understood and the words judged on their merits.

7   **applying key ideas and methods:** I've made selections from the extensive Pali Canon and occasionally other sources, chosen particular translations, and sometimes adapted them for the purposes of this book; please see these notes for the details. Scholars still disagree about the proper understanding of these ancient texts, plus this tradition has developed over more than 2,500 years. What we have around the world today are extractions from a large body of teachings and commentary, interpretations of these extractions, and applications in particular times and places. There is no single "right" Buddhism. I hope you will consider what I say on its own terms rather than whether it is "truly" Buddhist.

If you like, you can explore Buddhism with meditation centers, teachers, websites, and books. If I could recommend just one book as an introduction to Buddhism, it would be *Satipaṭṭhāna* by Bikkhu Anālayo, which is about the fundamental and far-reaching instructions for practice in the Foundations of Mindfulness Sutra.

7   *Come and see for yourself:* Ehipassiko, in Pali.

In *After Buddhism,* Stephen Batchelor explores the difference between dogmatic and pragmatic approaches to understanding truth claims.

A NEURODHARMA PERSPECTIVE

7   **The Buddha didn't use an MRI:** I believe he was in fact fully awakened; as usual, see for yourself what makes sense to you. I relate to him as a human teacher— someone who has done his own work and is pointing the way for others—not as a quasi divine figure. For me, it's his humanity that makes his teachings most credible and compelling. Attributing statements to him does give them authority, but I mean that here as the authority of expertise and personal example.

7   *neural* **basis of these mental factors:** There are many scholarly papers and books about the neuroscientific study of contemplative, spiritual, or religious experiences and practices—including critiques of doing such study at all. In addition to specific findings about neural correlates of experiences and practices, there are general considerations of definitions, research methodologies and technologies, use of psychoactive drugs, pathological experiences, clinical applications, and broader philosophical and theological issues. For example, see Newberg, "The Neuroscientific Study of Spiritual Practices," p. 215, and *Principles of Neurotheology,* Josipovic and Baars, "What Can Neuroscience Learn?" p. 1731; Dietrich, "Functional Neuroanatomy"; Walach et al., *Neuroscience, Consciousness and Spirituality;* Jastrzebski, "Neuroscience of Spirituality"; Dixon and Wilcox, "The Counseling Implications of Neurotheology"; Weker, "Searching for Neurobiological Foundations"; and Geertz, "When Cognitive Scientists Become Religious."

7   **"The dharma—understanding":** From "Your Liberation Is on the Line," *Buddhadharma,* spring 2019, p. 77.

7   **accurate descriptions of them:** The word *dharma* has multiple meanings in different contexts. See https://en.wikipedia.org/wiki/Dharma for more on this. Also

see Stephen Batchelor in *After Buddhism* (chapter 5, including p. 119) for how the word for truth in Pali, *sacca*, is not synonymous with *dharma*.

7   ***Neurodharma* is the term:** More broadly, one might say *biodharma*. Others besides me have explored what it could mean to nest Buddhist ideas and methods in a framework of natural causes and explanations. In a general sense, this could be called *naturalizing* the dharma. For example, see Flanagan, *The Bodhisattva's Brain*.

Other variants of –dharma include: Loy, *Ecodharma*; Unstated author(s), *Recovery Dharma*; Williams et al., *Radical Dharma*; and Gleig, *American Dharma*.

9   **avoid merely intellectual practice:** For a remarkable paper about the limitations of a scientific account of enlightenment as well as the importance of recognizing distinctions in how enlightenment is defined in different traditions, see Davis and Vago, "Can Enlightenment Be Traced?"

A PATH THAT PROGRESSES

10 **each person exists:** My view is that experiences, information, and matter (which includes energy; $E=mc^2$) do exist, and that the nature of this existence is impermanent, compounded, interdependent, and therefore "empty" of *inherent* existence. As we'll see in chapter 7, things (for example, experiences, information, and matter) exist... emptily. Just because things exist only in relation to other things does not mean that they do not exist at all.

GOING WHILE BEING

11 ***innate* perfection:** For an excellent discussion of key aspects of these two approaches, see Dunne, "Toward an Understanding of Non-dual Mindfulness."

11 **"Gradual cultivation ... sudden awakening":** Adapted from Zen master Chinul. Also listen to Joseph Goldstein's talk "Sudden Awakening, Gradual Cultivation" at www.dharmaseed.org.

11 ***In the beginning nothing came:*** Adapted from Ricard, *On the Path to Enlightenment*.

11 **"On the long, rough road":** From *Call Me by My True Names: The Collected Poems of Thich Nhat Hanh*, Parallax Press, 2001.

11 **settles into its innate resting state:** When undamaged by concussion or stroke, or not disturbed neurochemically.

LETTING BE, LETTING GO, LETTING IN

12 **awakening involves three kinds of practice:** Forrest Hanson and I have also written about these in our book *Resilient*.

HOW TO USE THIS BOOK

16 **"Allow the teachings to enter":** From the Introduction in *Understanding Our Mind: 50 Verses on Buddhist Psychology*, Parallax Press, 2002.

17 **exploration of what could be *unconditioned*:** My exploration of the seventh practice draws on but is not limited to Buddhist teachings in both the Pali Canon and the Mahayana tradition.

Unconditioned is a common rendering of the Pali *asankhata*, but its proper translation is in dispute, and it could also be translated as "unfabricated" (Thanissaro Bhikkhu; https://www.dhammatalks.org/suttas/KN/Ud/ud8_3.html) or "uninclined" (Stephen Batchelor, in *After Buddhism*).

When I write *unconditioned* (distinct from its appearance in some quotations), I mean it in the sense implied by its context in my text, *not* as a reference to a specific Pali word whose exact meaning and proper translation remain controversial.

18   **you'll see the path I've taken:** For example, I've chosen specific English renditions of key Pali terms such as *dukkha* ("suffering") and *piti* ("bliss"), summarized certain texts in adaptations of translations by others, and reordered some lists. I've tried to identify these choices, and you can judge them on their merits (or lack); please see other sources, including those I've referenced.

18   **many other ways to talk about:** For example, see Gross, *Buddhism After Patriarchy*, the fall 2019 issue of *Buddhadharma* magazine; and Weingast, *The First Free Women*.

18   **points I've written about elsewhere:** Some of the material in this chapter and the next one draws on these essays: "Positive Neuroplasticity," in *Advances in Contemplative Psychotherapy*, eds. Loizzo et al.; "Neurodharma: Practicing with the Brain in Mind," *Buddhist Meditative Praxis: Traditional Teachings and Modern Applications* (conference proceedings), ed. K. L. Dhammajoti (Hong Kong: University of Hong Kong, 2015), 227–44; "Mind Changing Brain Changing Mind: The Dharma and Neuroscience," *Exploring Buddhism and Science*, ed. C. Sheng and K. S. San; and "Seven Facts About the Brain That Incline the Mind to Joy," *Measuring the Immeasurable: The Scientific Case for Spirituality* (Sounds True, 2008).

20   **grounded and resourced internally:** For example, in some paths of intensive contemplative practice—such as the "Stages of Insight" laid out in the Visuddhimagga, written in the fifth century CE by Buddhaghosa (see Buddhaghosa, *Path of Purification*)—periods of fear, misery, disgust, and desires to stop practicing are to be expected as necessary preludes to deeper awakening.

So it is important to be prepared for these experiences through external resources, such as skilled teachers and supportive communities, as well as internal resources, such as steadiness of mind, equanimity, insight into the "empty" nature of painful experiences, and an understanding of their place in the larger journey (see A. Grabovac, "The Stages of Insight").

While reading this book does not involve intensive contemplative training, any process of personal development carries risks, particularly for more vulnerable individuals. (Of course, *not* developing oneself also carries risks, such as not acquiring capabilities that could improve coping, though these risks are not commonly talked about.) A risk is not a certainty, but to manage the challenges that do actually arise in practice, we draw on inner and outer resources, and the development of inner resources is a major focus here. As your practice deepens, if you do encounter disturbing experiences, reach out to a knowledgeable teacher and perhaps a therapist. There are also good books with useful suggestions, such as Culadasa et al., *The Mind Illuminated*.

20 **depression, trauma, dissociation, or psychotic processes:** Lindahl et al., "The Varieties of Contemplative Experience." Willoughby Britton has been a pioneering researcher on this topic: see https://vivo.brown.edu/display/wbritton#.

CHAPTER 2: THE ENCHANTED LOOM

23 **"Think not lightly of good":** Adapted from a translation by Acharya Buddharakkhita, https://www.accesstoinsight.org/tipitaka/kn/dhp/dhp.09.budd.html.

23 **network with several hundred trillion nodes:** Amidst another hundred billion or so support cells.

24 **being woven by an enchanted loom:** Hansotia, "A Neurologist Looks at Mind."

Suffering and Happiness

24 **there is suffering:** This is the common translation of the Pali word *dukkha*; other translations include "stress," "dissatisfaction," and "unsatisfactoriness."

25 **"Pain is inevitable, suffering is optional":** I can't find a specific source for this saying. See https://fakebuddhaquotes.com/pain-is-inevitable-suffering-is-optional/.

25 **It has a source: "craving":** This is the usual translation of the Pali *tanha*; other translations are "clinging" and "attachment." See Stephen Batchelor's approach to these topics in "Turning the Wheel of Dhamma," beginning p. 18, at https://www.stephenbatchelor.org/media/Stephen/PDF/Stephen_Batchelor-Pali_Canon-Website-02-2012.pdf. This collection of key texts from the Pali Canon is also valuable in general.

25 **Fourth Noble Truth describes a path:** This is the Eightfold Path of wise (sometimes translated as "right") view, intention, speech, livelihood, action, effort, mindfulness, and concentration.

25 **fulfills this promise:** As a related way to think about the Four Noble Truths, the Buddha has been described as a kind of physician who (1) recognized our malady, suffering; (2) diagnosed its cause, craving; (3) identified the cure, the cessation of craving; and (4) prescribed a course of treatment, the Eightfold Path. See Anālayo, *Mindfully Facing Disease and Death*, pp. 9–10.

25 **These four truths:** There are a variety of approaches to these topics, including whether they are best framed as "truths" at all. For provocative and diverging perspectives, see https://tricycle.org/magazine/the-far-shore/ and https://tricycle.org/magazine/understand-realize-give-develop/. In particular, see Stephen Batchelor's *After Buddhism*, an extraordinary book.

It's useful to ask ourselves whether statements such as "craving leads to suffering" are best approached as truth claims to be scrutinized abstractly or as invitations for experiential investigation. Whether something is actually the case (that is, true) is of course often relevant to practice; the truth of an oasis in the desert is relevant to seeking it if you're thirsty. Still, the emphasis here is on practice itself. To avoid repetition, I won't preface most of my statements with an encouragement to explore them experientially, but that opportunity is always implicit.

26 **"the happy one":** Digha Nikaya 16, in multiple places.

The Natural Mind

26 **several billion years of biological evolution:** Current estimates are that life has been present on earth for at least 3.5 billion years. See https://en.wikipedia.org/wiki/Earliest_known_life_forms.

27 **"Brain cells have particular ways":** Kandel, *In Search of Memory*, p. 59. Also see Grossenbacher, "Buddhism and the Brain," 2006, p. 10: "A brain functions by virtue of communication between neurons and the dynamic information processing within this intercellular communication. The principle [*sic*] function of a neuron is to produce signals that influence the activity of other cells."

27 **"...Electrical signaling represents":** Kandel, *In Search of Memory*, p. 74.

27 **"...All animals have some":** Ibid., p. 108.

27 **its headquarters, the brain:** My focus on the nervous system and in particular the brain is not meant to minimize or dismiss the role of other aspects of the body, or life in general. Many systems in the body affect the nervous system. For example, the microbiome in the gut and other gastrointestinal factors can affect mood and other aspects of consciousness. Some inflammatory processes (for example, involving certain kinds of cytokines) can also affect mood. Exactly how the body, notably its brain, makes the experiences of a human being—or a cat—is not clear. Difficult and unanswered questions remain. See Thompson, *Waking, Dreaming, Being.*

Scientists describe neural *correlates* of our experiences, but even these are not precisely understood. For example, the structures and processes of the brain are extremely complicated, so the localization of function found in studies is a fuzzy first approximation. It's like seeing a picture of fractals: the closer you look, the more complex it gets. For examples of this, see Christoff, "Specifying the Self."

Also, much of the information processing in the nervous system is occurring without our being directly aware of it.

27 **representing patterns of information:** Tononi et al., "Integrated Information Theory," p. 450.

27 **an open question:** Koch et al., "Neural Correlates of Consciousness," p. 307.

27 **what the brain is doing:** For a sampling, see Panksepp, *Affective Neuroscience*; Porges, *The Polyvagal Theory*; and Decety and Svetlova, "Putting Together Phylogenetic and Ontogenetic Perspectives."

27 **depend upon neural activity:** To be sure, the connections between neural activity and mental activity are complex and difficult to study. For an exploration of some key issues, see Fazelpour and Thompson, "The Kantian Brain." From two pioneers in these investigations, Francisco Varela and Evan Thompson, see Varela, "Neuro-phenomenology: A Methodological Remedy"; and Thompson, "Neurophenomenology and Contemplative Experience."

Drawing on quantum physics may be necessary for a full account of the relationship between mind and brain, including the possibility that consciousness may have effects at the quantum level on interactions among neurons. See Schwartz et al., "Quantum Physics in Neuroscience and Psychology"; and Tarlaci, "Why We Need Quantum Physics."

27 **three pounds of tofu-like tissue:** Credit to the neurologist Richard Mendius for this metaphor.

28 **in a stream of neural activity:** Tononi et. al., "Integrated Information Theory," p. 450.

MIND CHANGING BRAIN CHANGING MIND

28 *states* **can be gradually hardwired:** For example, see Ott et al., "Brain Structure and Meditation."

MECHANISMS OF NEUROPLASTICITY

29 **existing synaptic connections:** Clopath, "Synaptic Consolidation"; and Whitlock et al., "Learning Induces Long-Term Potentiation."

29 **excitability of individual neurons:** Oh et al., "Watermaze Learning Enhances Excitability."

29 (*epigenetic* **effects):** Day and Sweatt, "Epigenetic Mechanisms in Cognition"; Szyf et al., "Social Environment and the Epigenome."

29 **making new connections:** Matsuo et al., "Spine-Type-Specific Recruitment"; and Löwel and Singer, "Selection of Intrinsic Horizontal Connections."

29 **birthing new neurons:** Spalding et al., "Dynamics of Hippocampal Neurogenesis"; Kempermann, "Youth Culture in the Adult Brain"; and Eriksson et al., "Neurogenesis in the Adult Human Hippocampus."

29 **activity in specific regions:** Davidson, "Well-Being and Affective Style."

29 **reshaping particular neural networks:** Martin and Schuman, "Opting In or Out."

29 **changing the** *glial cells*: Underwood, "Lifelong Memories May Reside."

29 **neurochemicals such as serotonin:** Hyman et al., "Neural Mechanisms of Addiction."

29 **increasing** *neurotrophic* **factors:** Bramham and Messaoudi, "BDNF Function."

29 *hippocampus* **and** *parietal* **cortex:** Brodt et al., "Fast Track to the Neocortex."

30 **"replay events":** Grosmark and Buzsáki, "Diversity in Neural Firing Dynamics"; and Karlsson and Frank, "Awake Replay of Remote Experiences."

30 **long-term storage in the** *cortex*: Nadel et al., "Memory Formation, Consolidation."

30 **coordination of the hippocampus and cortex:** Sneve et al., "Mechanisms Underlying Encoding."

30 *consolidation* **of learning in the cortex:** Paller, "Memory Consolidation: Systems."

30 **slow-wave and rapid eye movement:** Hu et al., "Unlearning Implicit Social Biases"; and Cellini et al., "Sleep Before and After Learning."

30 **a concept as simple as 2 + 2 = 4:** Some of these neurons may be the same, but many will be different.

30 **The mind has causal power:** Tononi et al., "Integrated Information Theory," p. 450.

31 **the mind uses the brain:** See Siegel, *The Mindful Brain*. Dan is a brilliant and prolific author and teacher. Also see his recent books, including *Aware*.

CHANGING THE BRAIN WITH MEDITATION

31 **brain-changing effects of mindfulness:** For a recent review, see Brandmeyer et al., "The Neuroscience of Meditation."

31 *posterior* (**rearward**) *cingulate cortex:* Creswell et al., "Alterations in Resting-State Functional Connectivity."

31 *default mode network:* Also see chapter 6 about the default mode network.

32 **greater top-down control over the *amygdala*:** As with most parts of the brain above the brain stem, there are actually two amygdalae, as well as two hippocampi, cingulate cortices, et cetera. But the (confusing) convention is to speak of them in the singular, which I'll do here.

32 **triggers the neural/hormonal stress response:** Kral et al., "Impact of Short- and Long-Term Mindfulness Meditation."

32 **grow more tissue in their hippocampus:** Hölzel et al., "Investigation of Mindfulness Meditation Practitioners."

32 **less of the stress hormone *cortisol*:** Tang et al., "Short-Term Meditation Training."

32 **thicker layers of neural tissue:** Lazar et al., "Meditation Experience Is Associated."

32 **more tissue in their *insula*:** Ibid.

32 **right and left hemispheres:** Technically, the left and right hemispheres of the cortex.

32 **words and images, logic and intuition:** Fox et al., "Is Meditation Associated with Altered Brain Structure?"

33 **unusually rapid recovery:** Lutz et al., "Altered Anterior Insula Activation."

33 **gamma-range brain wave activity:** Lutz et al., "Long-Term Meditators Self-Induce." Heightened gamma wave activity is even found during sleep: see Ferrarelli et al., "Experienced Mindfulness Meditators."

33 **large areas of cortical real estate:** I believe the phrase "cortical real estate" comes from Sharon Begley's excellent book *Train Your Mind, Change Your Brain*.

33 **associated with enhanced learning:** Uhlhaas et al., "Neural Synchrony."

33 **shift from deliberate self-regulation:** Josipovic and Baars, "What Can Neuroscience Learn?"

33 **people who do Transcendental Meditation:** Mahone et al., "fMRI During Transcendental Meditation."

33 **Christian:** Newberg et al., "Cerebral Blood Flow."

33 **Islamic:** Newberg et al., "A Case Series Study."

33 **compassion and kindness meditations:** Hofmann et al., "Loving-kindness and Compassion Meditation."

33 **other practices:** Cahn and Polich, "Meditation States and Traits."

33 **research will improve over time:** There are many kinds of meditation and even more kinds of mental training, and we will undoubtedly find nuanced differences in their effects on the brain. Other factors must play a role as well, such as

individual temperament—perhaps those who are naturally calmer are drawn to meditation in the first place—community, associated religious aspects, culture, and moral purpose.

33 **emotional regulation, and sense of self:** Hölzel et al., "How Does Mindfulness Meditation Work?"

33 **Sustained long-term practice can alter:** Goleman and Davidson, *Altered Traits.*

33 **gratitude, relaxation, kindness:** For example, see Baxter et al., "Caudate Glucose Metabolic Rate Changes"; Nechvatal and Lyons, "Coping Changes the Brain"; Tabibnia and Radecki, "Resilience Training That Can Change the Brain"; Lazar et al., "Functional Brain Mapping"; and Dusek et al., "Genomic Counter-Stress Changes."

33 **your mind takes its shape:** I heard this from the teacher James Baraz, who adapted it from Majjhima Nikaya 19: "Whatever one frequently thinks and ponders upon, that will become the inclination of their mind."

33 **your brain takes *its* shape:** Including in the connections among neurons and in the ebbs and flows of neurochemicals.

33 **what you rest your attention on:** McGaugh, "Memory."

CHAPTER 3: STEADYING THE MIND

43 **Going down to a river:** Adapted from translations by John Ireland (https://www.accesstoinsight.org/tipitaka/kn/snp/snp.2.08.irel.html) and Thānissaro Bhikkhu (https://www.dhammatalks.org/suttas/KN/StNp/StNp2_8.html).

43 **Sutta Nipāta 2.8:** *Sutta* in Pali is the equivalent of *sutra* in Sanskrit: a text, often with religious significance.

CONCENTRATION POWER

44 **virtue:** Sometimes translated as morality or restraint.

44 **virtue, wisdom—and concentration:** In Pali: *sila, panna, samadhi.* We draw on these pillars of practice in the moment as we need them, and we also develop them over time.

44 **focus that fosters liberating insight:** I'm focusing here on one aspect of samadhi; other aspects include the purification of problematic tendencies, the intensification of beneficial qualities of mind in increasingly distilled forms, and non-ordinary states of consciousness.

44 **sharpness of the razor is insight:** *Vipassana,* in Pali.

44 **power of the stick is concentration:** Also referred to as *samatha,* in Pali, which means the calm abiding that steadies, unifies, and concentrates the mind.

44 **called the *jhanas*:** This summary description is adapted from translations by Andrew Olendzki, http://nebula.wsimg.com/bb54f2da6f46e24d191532b9ca8d1ea1?AccessKeyId=EE605ED40426C654A8C4&disposition=0&alloworigin=1), Bhikkhu Bodhi, *In the Buddha's Words,* and H. Gunaratana, "A Critical Analysis of the Jhānas in Theravāda Buddhist Meditation," PhD diss., American University, 1980 (http://www.buddhanet.net/pdf_file/scrnguna.pdf).

There are some controversies over the proper translations of key words, and it's useful to consider other translations, such as from Leigh Brasington (http://www.leighb.com/jhana_4factors.htm), Shaila Catherine (http://www.imsb.org/wp-content/uploads/2014/09/FiveJhanaFactors.pdf), and Bhikkhu Anālayo (Anālayo, *A Meditator's Life of the Buddha*).

In particular, Brasington and others argue that the term "applied and sustained attention" (for *vitakka* and *vicara*, in Pali) could be better rendered as "thought and examination."

45 **jhanas are described in psychological:** As psychological phenomena, presumably they have neural correlates. For example, Leigh Brasington offers his hypotheses here: http://www.leighb.com/jhananeuro.htm.

45 **into the "cessation":** Leigh Brasington (personal communication) has helpfully pointed out that the same English word, cessation, is used for multiple meanings and applications in the Pali Canon. My meaning for it here is the ending, the ceasing, of ordinary consciousness, which enables a kind of transition into nibbana.

46 **guidance from knowledgeable teachers:** For more on the jhanas, I recommend the retreats and books of Leigh Brasington, Tina Rasmussen and Stephen Snyder, Shaila Catherine, and Richard Shankman.

46 **many days on retreat:** Typically also on a strong foundation of meditative practice.

Skittery Attention

47 **"We live in forgetfulness":** Thich Nhat Hanh, *Understanding Our Mind: 50 Verses on Buddhist Psychology*. Parallax Press, 2002, ch. 42, p. 208.

47 **"monkey mind":** A traditional metaphor.

Cultivation

47 **Cultivation:** This section is a summary of material discussed at length in my book *Hardwiring Happiness*.

48 **what endures within you:** From ancient teaching stories to current psychological research, the cultivation of inner resources such as patience and secure attachment has been highly valued. For example, the Buddha encouraged the development of these *factors of awakening*: mindfulness, investigation, energy, bliss, tranquility, concentration, and equanimity. None of these is airy-fairy or metaphysical, and each one is something you can grow over time.

48 **The systematic training:** Dalai Lama and Cutler, *The Art of Happiness*, p. 44.

Learning in the Brain

49 **Experience what you'd like to develop:** Most learning begins with an experience, such as a thought, perception (including sensations), emotion, desire, or sense of an action.

49 **turning passing states into lasting *traits*:** For an example of this process in training mindfulness, see Kiken et al., "From a State to a Trait."

49 **little or no lasting gain:** In a study, the *average* response to an intervention may be

significantly greater than the average change in the control group, while still many people in the intervention group did not gain in any measurable way. Or the conversion rate from states to traits may stay flat even as experiential states are getting better. For example, the past few decades have seen many new ideas and methods in psychotherapy, but there is no clear trend of improved therapeutic outcomes and in fact some signs of decline. See Johnsen and Friborg, "The Effects of Cognitive Behavioral Therapy"; and Carey et al., "Improving Professional Psychological Practice."

THE NEGATIVITY BIAS

50　**product of evolution in harsh conditions:** Rozin and Royzman, "Negativity Bias, Negativity Dominance"; Vaish et al., "Not All Emotions"; Hamlin et al., "Three-Month-Olds Show."

50　**emotional and somatic residues:** Baumeister et al., "Bad Is Stronger Than Good."

50　**sensitizes the amygdala and weakens the hippocampus:** Harkness et al., "Stress Sensitivity and Stress Sensitization"; and Load, "Beyond the Stress Concept."

51　**once you reach the farther shore:** This is a central metaphor in Buddhism; see Majjhima Nikaya 22.

HEALING YOURSELF

51　**"incidental learning":** Such as referred to in the work of Barbara Fredrickson and others in her broaden-and-build theory of positive emotions. See Fredrickson, "The Broaden-and-Build Theory"; and Kok and Fredrickson, "Upward Spirals of the Heart."

　　This body of work is groundbreaking and very useful. I'm just pointing out that the build effect is usually described as (1) an upward spiral of beneficial *states* leading to other beneficial states, rather than the development of durable psychological traits, or (2) the acquisition of traits through non-deliberate, incidental processes.

52　**negative material can feel overwhelming:** It might be necessary to engage negative material in versions of the Link step for a full healing from trauma. This is often best done while working with a licensed professional.

52　**conversion into long-term memory:** Ranganath et al., "Working Memory Maintenance Contributes."

52　**increases its signals to the hippocampus:** Packard and Cahill, "Affective Modulation."

52　**lasting change in neural structure or function:** Talmi, "Enhanced Emotional Memory"; and Cahill and McGaugh, "Modulation of Memory Storage."

52　*pleasurable or meaningful about it:* As perspective, consider this from Bhikkhu Anālayo: "Wholesome types of happiness need not be shunned, as they can support progress to awakening.... Some types of pleasure are obstructive, but others are not. The decisive criterion is not the affective nature of a particular experience, but its wholesome or unwholesome repercussions." (Anālayo, *A Meditator's Life of the Buddha*, p. 83).

52   **moves into long-term storage:** Madan, "Toward a Common Theory for Learning"; Sara and Segal, "Plasticity of Sensory Responses"; McDonald and Hong, "How Does a Specific Learning?"; Takeuchi et al., "The Synaptic Plasticity and Memory Hypothesis"; and Tully and Bolshakov, "Emotional Enhancement of Memory."

52   **sensitive to what's beneficial:** For example, some people are particularly affected by positive environmental influences. These individual differences might be partially *acquired*—rather than due only to heritable, innate, genetic factors—through mental training or other experiences. For a recent review, see Moore and Depue, "Neurobehavioral Foundation of Environmental Reactivity."

52   **"Keep a green bough":** This is attributed to Lao-tzu or simply described as a Chinese proverb, but I can't find specific sourcing.

53   **Bhikkhu:** a Pali term for a monk.

53   **Anālayo:** Anālayo, *A Meditator's Life of the Buddha*, p. 29.

FINDING YOUR PLACE

53   **that could create *place memory*:** Quiroga, "Neural Representations Across Species."

53   **move out into life from this secure base:** The term "secure base" has specific meanings in attachment theory; I'm using it more broadly here.

FIVE FACTORS TO STEADY THE MIND

FOUNDATIONS OF PRACTICE

57   **for the sake of others as well as yourself:** More formally, there could be a "dedication of merit" from one's practice. For example, see https://www.lionsroar.com/how-to-practice-dedicating-merit/.

57   **specific object of attention:** Sometimes called an "anchor" of attention.

57   ***open awareness:*** Sometimes called "open monitoring."

57   **experiencing awareness itself:** The teacher Diana Winston calls this "natural awareness." See Winston, *The Little Book of Being*.

59   **neural activity in these areas will decrease:** Also mentioned in chapter 1.

ESTABLISHING INTENTION

59   **breathing out when you are breathing out:** This and some of my other suggestions are adapted from the Anapanasati (Mindfulness of Breathing) Sutta.

60   **vulnerable to *willpower fatigue*:** Gailliot et al., "Self-Control Relies on Glucose."

EASING YOUR BODY

61   **cortisol and *adrenaline*:** Benson and Klipper, *The Relaxation Response*.

ABIDING WHOLEHEARTED

62   **neurochemical *oxytocin*:** Termed a hormone when it has effects outside the nervous system.

62 **feeling loving or close to others:** As I mention in the next chapter, increased oxytocin activity can also foster protective feelings and actions toward "us" that can fuel dismissiveness or aggression toward "them."

62 **amygdala can have an inhibitory effect:** The effects of oxytocin activity in the amygdala are complex. On the one hand, see Meyer-Lindenberg, "Impact of Pro-social Neuropeptides"; Huber et al., "Vasopressin and Oxytocin Excite"; and Liu et al., "Oxytocin Modulates Social Value Representations." On the other hand, note a potential distinction between the effects in children compared with adults: Kritman et al., "Oxytocin in the Amygdala."

62 **oxytocin increase in the prefrontal cortex:** Kritman et al., "Oxytocin in the Amygdala."

62 **sense of anxiety usually decreases:** Sobota et al., "Oxytocin Reduces Amygdala Activity"; and Radke et al., "Oxytocin Reduces Amygdala Responses."

62 **part of the *tend-and-befriend*:** Taylor, "Tend and Befriend Theory."

FEELING GRATEFUL AND GLAD

64 **upper-outer regions of the prefrontal cortex:** D'Esposito and Postle, "The Cognitive Neuroscience of Working Memory."

64 **They have a kind of gate:** Braver and Cohen, "On the Control of Control"; and Braver et al., "The Role of Prefrontal Cortex."

65 **a gate-opening surge is less possible:** This neurological mechanism could be a reason why happiness and bliss are listed as elements of the first and second jhanas, with happiness continuing in the third jhana. The jhanas involve great steadiness of mind. In fact, happiness and bliss are considered to be *factors* of the jhanas, helping you to gain access to them. Applied and sustained attention are also jhana factors, as well as singleness of mind. In a regular meditation practice, you can certainly cultivate happiness and applied and sustained attention, and with practice you can potentially experience bliss and singleness of mind. These factors are not themselves the jhanas, but from experience I can say that they feel good and help to steady the mind.

CHAPTER 4: WARMING THE HEART

67 **"With good will":** This is a differently phrased portion of the Metta Sutta (Sutta Nipata 1.8) that is presented more fully below.

68 **"One is not wise":** Adapted from translations by Acharya Buddharakkhita https://www.accesstoinsight.org/tipitaka/kn/dhp/dhp.19.budd.html and Thanissaro Bhikkhu https://www.dhammatalks.org/suttas/KN/Ud/ud8_3.html.

68 **compassion, kindness, and happiness:** Along with equanimity, these are the four *Brahmaviharas* (sometimes called Immeasurables) that are the dwelling places of exalted beings as well as available to all of us, with practice.

69 **develop compassion and kindness:** Birnie et al., "Exploring Self-Compassion"; Boellinghaus et al., "The Role of Mindfulness"; and Fredrickson et al., "Positive Emotion Correlates."

69   **Related but distinct networks:** Mascaro et al., "The Neural Mediators of Kindness-Based Meditation"; and Engen and Singer, "Affect and Motivation Are Critical."

69   **brain regions that produce experiences of physical pleasure:** Lieberman and Eisenberger, "Pains and Pleasures of Social Life"; and Eisenberger, "The Neural Bases of Social Pain."

69   **stimulate neural reward centers:** Including the *caudate nucleus* and *ventral striatum,* in the *basal ganglia* in the subcortex. For a good review of this topic, see Tabibnia and Lieberman, "Fairness and Cooperation Are Rewarding." More generally, see Decety and Yoder, "The Emerging Social Neuroscience."

69   **networks that underlie physical pain:** Lieberman and Eisenberger, "Pains and Pleasures of Social Life"; and Eisenberger, "The Neural Bases of Social Pain."

69   **developed in the nervous system:** Lippelt et al., "Focused Attention, Open Monitoring"; and Lee et al., "Distinct Neural Activity."

69   *orbitofrontal cortex*: Other areas include the ventral striatum. See Engen and Singer, "Compassion-Based Emotion Regulation."

69   **faces of strangers and their own faces:** Trautwein et al., "Decentering the Self?"

69   **support feelings of empathy toward others:** Leung et al., "Increased Gray Matter Volume."

Compassion and Kindness

70   **compassion is wishing that beings not suffer:** To give a fuller definition of compassion as I mean it here, it involves empathy for suffering, benevolence toward that suffering, and a desire to relieve it if one can. For background, see Gilbert, "The Origins and Nature of Compassion Focused Therapy."

70   **wishing that they be happy:** Salzberg, *Lovingkindness.*

GOOD WILL

70   **healthy desire:** *Chandha,* in Pali.

70   **parts of the brain handle *liking*:** Berridge and Kringelbach, "Pleasure Systems in the Brain."

A SWEET COMMITMENT

71   *metta* **as kindness:** Often rendered as "lovingkindness." For a full translation of this important sutta, Sutta Nipata 1.8, from nineteen (!) sources that have been curated by Leigh Brasington, please see http://www.leighb.com/mettasuttas.htm. This section of the sutta is adapted from translations at this website, particularly by Bhikkhu Bodhi and Thanissaro Bhikkhu.

AN ENNOBLING DEVELOPMENT

72   **Truths of the Noble Ones:** "Understand, Realize, Give Up, Develop: A Conversation with Stephen Batchelor, Christina Feldman, and Akincano M. Weber," Tricycle, fall 2017, https://tricycle.org/magazine/understand-realize-give-develop/.

72   **intentional actions of thought, word, and deed:** Gombrich, *What the Buddha Thought.*

72 **Four *Ennobling* Truths:** Bhikkhu Anālayo makes a similar point about the "ennobling" potential of these truths. See Anālayo, *A Meditator's Life of the Buddha*, p. 143.

73 **resilience, healthy relationships, and spiritual practice:** For example, see Sin and Lyubomirsky, "Enhancing Well-Being." Of course, nudging the mind—letting go of what is painful and harmful, and letting in what is enjoyable and beneficial—is just part of practice. Much of the time, we're simply letting be.

GOOD WISHES FOR EVERYONE

74 *someone who is challenging for you:* Sometimes called the "difficult" person. A friend pointed out that this term could imply that someone is *inherently* difficult, and she encouraged me to use this other terminology, which I've adopted.

74 **"Happy indeed we live":** Adapted from a translation by Acharya Buddharakkhita, https://www.accesstoinsight.org/tiptaka/KN/dhp.15.budd.html.

THE BLISS OF BLAMELESSNESS

76 **his son, Rahula, came to practice:** There is a significant backstory. As best we know, the man who became the Buddha grew up in northern India roughly 2,500 years ago. When he was twenty-nine or so, his wife, Yasodhara, gave birth to their first child, and about this time he left to become a wandering ascetic. No way around it: the Buddha's path of practice began with leaving his family. We can consider this in terms of both our modern standards and the norms of his own time. I see him as someone who struggled and made choices, and this humanizes and enriches my sense of his teachings.

76 **As the sutta explains:** Majjhima Nikaya, 61.

77 **"To attain.... deep insight":** Palmo, *Reflections on a Mountain Lake*, p. 45.

77 **"May I be loving":** Larry Yang, from "In the Moments of Non-Awakening," *Buddhadharma*, spring 2019, p. 95. I've changed some punctuation and formatting for emphasis.

78 *vagus nerve complex:* Porges and Carter, "Polyvagal Theory and the Social Engagement System."

78 **originate in the *brain stem:*** Specifically, in the medulla.

78 **in better control of yourself:** And as we saw in the previous chapter, warmheartedness also increases oxytocin activity, which helps calm fear-based reactions.

79 **"There are those who do not realize":** From a translation by Acharya Buddharakkhita, https://www.accesstoinsight.org/tipitaka/kn/dhp/dhp.01.budd.html.

NOT HARMING OTHERS—AND YOURSELF

79 **practical guidelines from the Eightfold Path:** I've adapted and summarized these from various passages in the Pali Canon. They're framed as trainings we undertake rather than commandments from on high that it would be a sin to violate.

HOW WE HURT OURSELVES

80 **ask yourself the first question below:** These questions are organized around wise action, with the additional admonition against lying in the five precepts.

A GIVING HEART

81 **how to replace a harsh tone:** Thich Nhat Hanh has developed this approach in beautiful, powerful ways with his Five Mindfulness Trainings. See https://www .learnreligions.com/thich-nhat-hanhs-five-mindfulness-trainings-449601.

81 **traces are now woven into our DNA:** For example, see Trivers, "Evolution of Reciprocal Altruism"; and Bowles, "Group Competition, Reproductive Leveling."

82 **"If people knew":** Translation by John Ireland, https://www.accesstoinsight.org /tipitaka/kn/iti/iti.1.024-027.irel.html.

82 **be a little more generous:** Of course, this does not mean tipping into *pathological altruism*, giving in ways that are damaging to yourself or foster inappropriate dependencies in others. For example, see Oakley et al., *Pathological Altruism*.

SELF-COMPASSION

83 **try new things and to be ambitious:** For reviews and practical suggestions, see Bluth and Neff, "New Frontiers"; Neff and Dahm," Self-Compassion: What It Is"; Neff, *Self-Compassion: The Proven Power*; Germer, *The Mindful Path to Self-Compassion*; Allen and Leary, "Self-Compassion, Stress, and Coping"; and Germer and Neff, "Self-Compassion in Clinical Practice."

83 **taking things very personally:** See the remarkable work of Professor Paul Gilbert, originator of Compassion-Focused Therapy, including "Introducing Compassion-Focused Therapy" and *Compassion Focused Therapy: Distinctive Features*.

83 **sense of *common humanity*:** Which has been emphasized by Chris Germer and Kristin Neff.

83 **"There is a crack":** Leonard Cohen, "Anthem," *The Future*, Columbia Records, 1992.

A PRACTICE OF SELF-COMPASSION

84 **Mindful Self-Compassion program:** See https://centerformsc.org/.

OMITTING NONE

86 **typically with several dozen members:** Hill et al., "Co-residence Patterns in Hunter-Gatherer Societies"; and Boyd et al., "Hunter-Gatherer Population Structure."

86 **more able to pass on their genes:** For a discussion of how natural selection in evolution could operate at the level of social groups, see Wilson and Wilson, "Rethinking the Theoretical Foundation of Sociobiology."

86 **over the past few million years:** Dunbar, "The Social Brain Hypothesis"; and Lieberman, *Social*.

TWO WOLVES

87 **paraphrase a parable:** For a source, see https://www.firstpeople.us/FP-Html -Legends/TwoWolves-Cherokee.html. On the other hand, see https://crossing enres.com/you-know-that-charming-story-about-the-two-wolves-its-a-lie -d0d93ea4ebff. Since I've been unable to establish clear sourcing, I've presented this parable in a simplified form and without specific attribution.

87 **characteristics that are sometimes useful:** For example, see the Dalai Lama's essay "Don't Let Hatred Destroy Your Practice," in *Buddhadharma*, spring 2019, pp. 58–71, excerpted from Dalai Lama, *Perfecting Patience: Buddhist Techniques to Overcome Anger,* trans. Thubten Jinpa. Shambhala, 2018.

87 **including by systemic social forces:** See Owens and Syedullah, *Radical Dharma.*

87 **norepinephrine to feel rewarding:** Angus et al., "Anger Is Associated"; and Bersani and Pasquini, "The 'Outer Dimensions.'"

87 **both people get burnt:** Drawn from Buddhaghosa, Path of Purification, IX 21.

87 **I-Thou and I-It:** Martin Buber, *I and Thou.*

EXPANDING THE CIRCLE OF "US"

88 **foster suspicion and hostility toward "them":** De Dreu et al., "The Neuropeptide Oxytocin Regulates Parochial Altruism"; De Dreu et al., "Oxytocin Motivates Non-cooperation"; and De Dreu, "Oxytocin Modulates Cooperation."

88 **"As the earth gives us food":** "Journeys: What About My Retreat?" Buddhadharma, winter 2013. Also see https://www.lionsroar.com/journeys-what-about -my-retreat/.

89 **more rewarding, we treat others better:** See Preston, "The Rewarding Nature of Social Contact"; and Hung et al., "Gating of Social Reward."

CHAPTER 5: RESTING IN FULLNESS

93 **"When touched by the ways":** Adapted from translations by Thānissaro Bhikkhu (https://www.dhammatalks.org/suttas/KN/StNp/StNp2_4.html) and Piyadassi Thera (https://www.accesstoinsight.org/tipitaka/KN/snp/snp.2.04.piya.html). The "ways of the world" refers to gain and loss, praise and criticism, pleasure and pain, and status and loss of status (also called the "eight worldly winds," sometimes with other words).

93 **deep source of so much of our suffering:** Stephen Batchelor has pointed out that suffering can cause craving. (See *After Buddhism.*) For example, if I'm suffering the hurt of rejection, I might understandably crave comfort and love. Mindful awareness of how experiences of stress or emotional upset foster craving is very useful. Craving and suffering promote each other in circular ways. This chapter will focus on how craving leads to suffering.

93 **four *tasks*:** I am drawing on and adapting portions of the Samyutta Nikaya 56.11, as well as perspectives from Thānissaro Bhikkhu, https://www.accesstoinsight .org/lib/study/truths.html; and *After Buddhism* by Stephen Batchelor.

IN THE BASEMENT OF THE MIND

WHEN YOU WERE YOUNG

94 **fully formed before most babies are born:** The amygdala (technically, the two amygdalae) is anatomically mature by the eighth month of development of a fetus. See Ulfig et al., "Ontogeny of the Human Amygdala."

94   **around the third birthday:** For a thorough review, see Semple et al., "Brain Development in Rodents and Humans."

94   *episodic memories:* Also termed autobiographical memories.

95   *avoidance behaviors* **such as withdrawing or freezing:** This developmental feature is reversed in the brain for many left-handed people, but the effects are the same. See Schore, *Affect Regulation and the Origin of the Self.*

95   **nervous system was especially vulnerable:** Semple et al., "Brain Development in Rodents and Humans."

95   **the body remembers:** See Rothschild, *The Body Remembers.*

95   *spiritual bypass:* Welwood, "Principles of Inner Work."

95   **psychotherapy and self-help practices:** Clinical approaches for addressing psychological pain include Eye Movement Desensitization and Reprocessing (EMDR), developed by Francine Shapiro, and other forms of *bilateral stimulation,* Compassion-Focused Therapy from Paul Gilbert, Somatic Experiencing from Peter Levine, and Coherence Therapy from Bruce Ecker. The American Psychological Association has developed "clinical practice guidelines" for the treatment of post-traumatic stress disorder (PTSD); you can see them here—https://www.apa.org/ptsd-guideline/—along with links to resources for individuals and families. Personal practices (sometimes adapted for clinical work) include Focusing from Eugene Gendlin, trauma-sensitive mindfulness from David Treleaven, and TIMBo yoga created by Sue Jones.

SOOTHING AND REPLACING SUFFERING

96   **Link step in the HEAL process:** The general method summarized in the Link step is used in clinical settings and in personal development practices, and it can be adapted for different needs and situations.

96   *window of reconsolidation:* The duration of the window of reconsolidation is not exact, but it appears to be less than six hours. See Nader et al., "Fear Memories"; and Alberini and LeDoux, "Memory Reconsolidation." For clinical applications, see this excellent review: Ecker, "Memory Reconsolidation Understood."

96   **refocusing occasionally on only the positive:** I'm summarizing here; for the details, see the references just above and the material on linking in my book *Hardwiring Happiness.*

IS LIFE SUFFERING?

99   *All conditioned things are suffering:* In Pali: *Sabbe sankhara dukkha.*

100   **"All human experiences are suffering":** We might generalize this to include any animal with a nervous system.

102   **the gain of each new moment that arises:** Bhikkhu Anālayo has also offered a critique of broad-brush statements that all elements of consciousness are always suffering. See Anālayo, *A Meditator's Life of the Buddha,* chap. 16.

The Causes of Craving

104 **"Just as a felled tree grows again"**: Translation by Gil Fronsdal in *The Dhamma-pada: A New Translation of the Buddhist Classic, with Annotations*. Shambhala, 2006, p. 88.

THREE CAUSES OF CRAVING

104 **insecure attachment:** See https://en.wikipedia.org/wiki/Attachment_theory.

104 **language of early Buddhism:** For details, see https://en.wikipedia.org/wiki/Pali.

THREE KINDS OF PRACTICE

106 **including gender, class, and history:** I am *not* trying to criticize the role of monasticism per se in Buddhism. I am deeply grateful to the monastic lineages that have kept Buddhism alive for twenty-five centuries, and to the monks and nuns who have been my teachers.

106 **Leave nothing out of your practice:** I heard it described as a Zen saying but can't find a source.

106 **"Any sensual bliss in the world":** Translation by Thānissaro Bhikkhu, https://www.dhammatalks.org/suttas/KN/Ud/ud2_2.html.

Embodied Craving

106 **monkeys, mice, and lizards:** I am summarizing a great deal of material here. For useful background, I recommend the papers of Kent Berridge, Terry Robinson, and Morten Kringelbach. For example, see Berridge and Robinson, "What Is the Role of Dopamine?"; Berridge et al., "Dissecting Components of Reward"; and Kringelbach and Berridge, "Neuroscience of Reward, Motivation, and Drive."

107 **The most fundamental causes of craving:** Of course, practices of recognition are extremely useful, and we will draw on them a lot in later chapters.

107 *avoid* **harms,** *approach* **rewards, and** *attach*: These three ways of meeting our needs—avoid, approach, attach—could also be framed as withdraw, enter, stay; prevent, promote, persist; and destroy, create, preserve.

107 *reptilian brain stem, mammalian subcortex*: The anatomical and functional boundaries between these three parts of the brain are inherently fuzzy, and where they are marked can be somewhat arbitrary and in dispute. The subcortex, as I am using this term, includes the amygdala, hippocampus, basal ganglia, thalamus, and hypothalamus. Besides the hypothalamus, the other parts of the subcortex come in pairs, one on either side of the brain. Related parts of the brain include the pons, in the upper part of the brain stem, and the ventral tegmental area at the top of the pons. Other terms are sometimes used besides subcortex, but this word is still used widely; for example, see Keuken et al., "Large Scale Structure-Function Mappings."

107 *primate/human neocortex*: For context and details, please see chapter 3 in my book *Hardwiring Happiness*.

A HEALTHY EQUILIBRIUM

107 *salience network*: The major elements of the salience network include the anterior insula and dorsal anterior cingulate cortex in the neocortex; the amygdala and *nucleus accumbens* in the subcortex; and the ventral tegmental area at the top of the brain stem. For the locations: *anterior* = front; *posterior* = rear; *dorsal* = upper; *ventral* = lower; *medial* = middle; and *lateral* = side. See Seeley et al., "Dissociable Intrinsic Connectivity Networks"; and Menon, "Salience Network."

108 *default mode network*: The major elements of the default mode network are centered in the medial prefrontal cortex, posterior cingulate cortex, precuneus, and hippocampus. See Raichle et al., "Default Mode of Brain Function"; and Vago and Zeidan, "The Brain on Silent." Note that this network is sometimes referred to as the "resting state network" or the "intrinsic network."

108 *executive control network*: The major elements of the executive control network include the dorsolateral prefrontal cortex and the lateral posterior parietal cortex. See Habas et al., "Distinct Cerebellar Contributions."

HEDONIC TONES

108 *hedonic tones*: In Pali, these are the *vedana* of experiences, commonly translated as "feeling tones," though they are not about emotion per se.

108 **in modern psychology:** For example, see Laricchiuta and Petrosini, "Individual Differences in Response to Positive and Negative Stimuli."

108 **neural basis of pain and pleasure:** Boll et al., "Oxytocin and Pain Perception"; and Shiota et al., "Beyond Happiness."

MANAGING NEEDS BY CRAVING

110 *reactive* **mode, or the Red Zone:** Stephen Batchelor refers to "reactivity" as synonymous with craving in *After Buddhism* (p. 121).

110 **one way or another:** Robert Sapolsky used this turn of phrase in his classic book about stress, *Why Zebras Don't Get Ulcers.*

110 **worry about the future:** See the next chapter about the midline cortices and "doing" mode.

110 **depletes and rattles body and mind:** And can gradually impair judgment and self-regulation by weakening connections in the prefrontal cortex. See Datta and Arnsten, "Loss of Prefrontal Cortical Higher Cognition."

MANAGING NEEDS BY *NOT* CRAVING

111 **his own preparation for awakening:** For a great summary of the Buddha's life based on well-translated selections from the Pali Canon, including the reference to experiences not invading the mind and remaining (in the Majjhima Nikaya 36), see https://www.accesstoinsight.org/ptf/buddha.html.

111 **suffering in the Third Noble Truth:** See https://www.stephenbatchelor.org /media/Stephen/PDF/Stephen_Batchelor-Pali_Canon-Website-02-2012.pdf, p. 18.

112 **"Whose mind, standing like rock"**: Translation by Thānissaro Bhikkhu, https://www.dhammatalks.org/suttas/KN/Ud/ud4_4.html.

LIVING IN THE GREEN ZONE

112 **praise and blame, fame and slander:** From Anguttara Nikaya 8.6.

112 **"first darts":** Sometimes translated as "arrows"; Samyutta Nikaya 36.6.

GROWING GENERAL STRENGTHS

113 **freedom to *choose* your response:** This phrasing is loosely related to a saying attributed to Viktor Frankl: "Between stimulus and response there is a space. In that space is our power to choose our response. In our response lies our growth and our freedom." But actually it comes from Stephen Covey, who thought he had read it in a book by Frankl. See https://quoteinvestigator.com/2018/02/18/response/#note-17978-8.

113 **Foundations of Mindfulness:** The Satipatthana Sutta, Majjhima Nikaya 10, which could also be translated as where mindfulness is to be "established."

113 **observe the pain mindfully:** Mindfulness of physical pain is not a miracle cure, but it can often help, especially with the emotional side effects. See Hilton et al., "Mindfulness Meditation for Chronic Pain." For practical tools, see the work of Vidyamala Burch and Toni Bernhard.

113 **labeling experiences to yourself:** Also called "noting."

113 **calming down the amygdala:** Creswell et al., "Neural Correlates of Dispositional Mindfulness"; Burklund et al., "The Common and Distinct Neural Bases"; and Torrisi et al., "Advancing Understanding of Affect Labeling."

GROWING STRENGTHS MATCHED TO NEEDS

114 **resources for particular needs:** This is a brief summary. For a systematic approach, applied to different situations, see *Hardwiring Happiness* and *Resilient.*

FEELING ALREADY FULL

116 **reptilian:** I'm using *reptilian* loosely. The brain stem began to evolve before the first reptiles.

116 **mammalian:** Also using *mammalian* loosely. Some reptiles have neural structures that are similar to those in the mammalian subcortex. See Naumann et al., "The Reptilian Brain"; and Pritz, "Crocodilian Forebrain."

117 **"There is no greater woe":** Translated by Xiankuan (Donald Sloane), personal communication. See his excellent book *Six Pathways to Happiness: Mindfulness and Psychology in Chinese Buddhism*, vol. 1, Outskirts Press, 2019.

117 **very positive effects:** For a foundational review, see Fredrickson, "What Good Are Positive Emotions?"

117 **fight-or-flight sympathetic nervous system:** For a review of benefits for the autonomic nervous system, including management of stress, see Kreibig, "Autonomic Nervous System."

117 *natural opioids:* Shiota et al., "Beyond Happiness."

117 **can reduce pain:** Sneddon, "Evolution of Nociception in Vertebrates."

117 **craving a future pleasure:** Berridge and Kringelbach, "Pleasure Stems in the Brain."

117 **weather separations from them:** Burkett et al., "Activation of μ-Opioid Receptors"; Schweiger et al., "Opioid Receptor Blockade"; and Eisenberger, "Attachment Figures Activate."

117 **well-known benefits for bonding with others:** Shiota et al., "Beyond Happiness."

117 **calming and reassuring, lowering anxiety:** See the discussion of oxytocin in chapter 3, "Five Factors to Steady the Mind." And see Sobota et al., "Oxytocin Reduces Amygdala Activity"; and Radke et al., "Oxytocin Reduces Amygdala Responses."

117 **pursuit of opportunities:** De Dreu et al., "Oxytocin Enables Novelty Seeking."

CHAPTER 6: BEING WHOLENESS

123 **"Flowers in springtime":** Wumen Huikai, in Judy Roitman, "Six Facts About Kong-ans," *Buddhadharma*, fall 2018, p. 85.

THE INNER THEATER
MIDLINE CORTICAL NETWORKS

124 **loosely divided into two sections:** These two networks are distinct, and they are inversely correlated with each other: when activity in one increases, activity in the other decreases. See Josipovic, "Neural Correlates of Nondual Awareness."

124 **solving problems, performing tasks, and making plans:** Mullette-Gillman and Huettel, "Neural Substrates of Contingency Learning"; and Corbetta et al., "The Reorienting System of the Human Brain." The front portion of the midline network also draws on aspects of the "executive control network" (discussed in the previous chapter) that are off to the sides of the prefrontal cortex.

125 **strong sense of self:** Farb et al., "The Mindful Brain and Emotion Regulation"; Northoff and Bermpohl, "Cortical Midline Structures and the Self"; Brewer et al., "What About the 'Self' Is Processed?"

  In addition to its activations in the rearward "default mode" portions of the midline cortex, the sense of self also arises when the frontal, task-oriented portions of this cortex are active. See Christoff et al., "Specifying the Self."

125 **"relating to moods, feelings, and attitudes":** https://www.lexico.com/en/definition/affective.

125 **help it organize itself:** Raichle, "The Restless Brain."

125 **creative connections and hopeful possibilities:** Smallwood and Andrews-Hanna, "Not All Minds That Wander Are Lost."

125 **they've come with a price:** For example, the "frenetic restlessness of mental time travel that is characteristic of daily activity in the postmodern setting." (In the first paragraph of the Discussion section, Vago and Zeidan, "The Brain on Silent.")

125 **"Why am I so stupid/ugly/unlovable?":** Farb et al., "Minding One's Emotions"; and Cooney et al., "Neural Correlates of Rumination."

125 **your mind can roam all over the place:** Christoff et al., "Experience Sampling During fMRI."

125 **wandering mind about half the time:** Killingsworth and Gilbert, "A Wandering Mind."

126 **more it tends to tilt negatively:** Ibid.; and Vago and Zeidan, "The Brain on Silent."

LATERAL CORTICAL NETWORKS

126 **activity in *lateral* networks on the sides of your head increases:** Farb et al., "Attending to the Present"; and Brewer et al., "Meditation Experience Is Associated."

126 **internal body sensations and "gut feelings":** Craig, "How Do You Feel?"

FEELING DIVIDED

128 *radical acceptance:* Brach, *Radical Acceptance.*

DOING AND BEING

130 **medial networks are for "doing":** The term *doing* is particularly apt when the frontal midline networks are active, since they're called upon when we are working on tasks. See Josipovic, "Neural Correlates of Nondual Awareness." "Doing" is looser when applied to the rearward networks of the default mode, though we're still busy in daydreams or ruminations.

130 **midline or to the side of the brain:** For example, the mental activities in the "doing" column do not entirely correlate with neural activations close to the midline. See Christoff et al., "Specifying the Self."

130 **two groups that are quite distinct:** Many others have also distinguished between being and doing, from ancient teachers such as Lao-tzu (see Xiankuan, *Six Pathways to Happiness*) to present-day scholars and therapists, such as John Teasdale and Zindel Segal (*The Mindful Way Through Depression*); Marsha Linehan (*Cognitive-Behavioral Treatment of Borderline Personality Disorder*); and Stephen Hayes (*The Act in Context*).

130 **prominent self-as-object:** We'll be exploring the apparent self in depth in chapter 8.

THE SENSE OF WHOLENESS

SENSORY FOCUS

132 *left* **side of your brain:** This is reversed for many left-handed people.

132 **Focusing on internal sensations:** Farb et al., "The Mindful Brain."

132 **reducing emotional reactivity and depressive mood:** Farb et al.," Minding One's Emotions."

NOT KNOWING

132 **rest in the seeing alone?:** This echoes the Bahiya Sutta, which includes the instruction "You should train yourself thus: in the seen will be merely what is seen."

(Udana 1.10; trans. John Ireland, https://www.accesstoinsight.org/tipitaka/kn/ud/ud.1.10.irel.html). We'll explore this sutta in chapter 8.

133 **"don't know mind"**: Emphasized in the Korean Zen tradition. See Sahn and Sŏnsa, *Only Don't Know*, and Shrobe, *Don't-Know Mind.*

LET YOUR MIND BE

134 **glue them to each other:** I heard this from a friend who heard it from Tsoknyi Rinpoche, but alas I can't recall the details.

134 **"leave your mind alone":** When I heard this instruction, it was loosely attributed to Tibetan sources.

GESTALT AWARENESS

134 **this awareness shifts your state of mind:** For example, in the Mindfulness of Breathing Sutra (Majjhima Nikaya 118), there are references to "mindfully experiencing the whole body when breathing in... mindfully experiencing the whole body when breathing out" (adapted from a translation in Anālayo, *Meditator's Life of the Buddha*, p. 64). I got the "left... right... both together" instruction from Richard Miller.

135 **"You are the sky":** This saying is widely attributed to the teacher Pema Chödrön, but I've been unable to find specific sourcing of it.

TRANQUILITY

135 **one of the seven factors of awakening:** The others are mindfulness, investigation, energy, bliss, concentration, and equanimity. For a great summary of core Buddhist teachings, including the factors of awakening, see B. Thānissaro, *The Wings to Awakening.*

135 **"breathe in, tranquilizing the body":** Majjhima Nikaya, adapted from Bodhi and Nanamoli, *The Middle Length Discourses.*

Unhindered

THE FIVE HINDRANCES

138 *Fatigue and laziness:* This is my adaptation of the common translations of the Pali terms as "torpor and sloth."

RESOURCES FOR SPECIFIC HINDRANCES

139 **key resources:** With gratitude to Leigh Brasington for some excellent suggestions here.

140 **be enlivened by fresh air:** For a thorough (and to me, charming) list of suggestions from the Buddha for dealing with drowsiness while meditating, see the "Nodding Sutra," Anguttara Nikaya 7.58 (https://www.accesstoinsight.org/tipitaka/an/an07/an07.058.than.html).

140 **reflection from the Tibetan tradition:** I don't know the exact source.

141 **help you form new good habits:** You could also take a look at the "Motivation" and "Aspiration" chapters in *Resilient.*

141 **"what is it you plan to do":** From "The Summer Day," in M. Oliver, *Devotions: The Selected Poems of Mary Oliver*. Penguin Press, 2017, p. 316.

142 **These are big topics:** With Forrest Hanson, I've written about them in *Resilient*; also see other books such as Tara Brach's gem *Radical Acceptance*.

142 *mental proliferation:* Papanca, in Pali.

BEING THE MIND AS A WHOLE

144 **be present as the mind as a whole:** I usually use the term *mind* to mean all of the information in the nervous system, most of which is unconscious. But for the phrase "experience mind as a whole," I'm focusing on that portion of the mind that is consciously accessible.

AWARENESS AND THE BRAIN

144 **open awareness:** Sometimes called *open monitoring*.

144 **aware of awareness:** Dan Siegel has a lovely practice of this in his Wheel of Awareness meditation, which includes all four kinds of awareness. See Siegel, *Aware*.

145 **abide as awareness:** As mentioned in chapter 3, Diana Winston calls this "natural awareness."

145 **simply being awareness:** Abiding as awareness can be described in various ways, including with references to "nondual awareness." For an academic account, see Josipovic, "Neural Correlates of Nondual Awareness." For a description aimed at personal practice, see John Prendergast's masterpiece *The Deep Heart*.

145 **abiding as awareness:** Diana Winston describes this process very clearly in *The Little Book of Being: Practices and Guidance for Uncovering Your Natural Awareness*.

145 **those with simple nervous systems:** For a consideration of the functions of awareness in even simple animals, see Earl, "The Biological Function of Consciousness."

145 **the fly is aware:** Since flies can't report on their experiences, it's conceivable that what appears to be a primitive awareness of their surroundings is entirely reflexive and unconscious. For diverging perspectives on this topic, see Barron and Klein, "What Insects Can Tell Us"; and Key et al., "Insects Cannot Tell Us."

But frogs? Alligators? Squirrels? Dogs? Gorillas? On the evolutionary ladder, we can recognize a continuity extending from humans to cats to frogs to, potentially, flies with regard both to the neural basis of awareness and to the behavioral demonstrations of awareness. For an interesting review of research on human and non-human animals, see Boly et al., "Consciousness in Humans and Non-human Animals." For an exploration of awareness in cephalopods (octopi), see Mather, "Cephalopod Consciousness."

145 *global workspace of consciousness:* Baars, "Global Workspace Theory." Coincidentally, and happily for me, Dr. Baars was a key advisor on my dissertation committee.

For a general account of the neural architecture of consciousness, see Damasio, *The Feeling of What Happens*. For a discussion of "higher order" theories of consciousness, see Wikipedia, https://en.wikipedia.org/wiki/Higher-order_theories

_of_consciousness. For an elegantly written overview of challenges in developing a scientific theory of consciousness, see Harris, *Conscious.*

146 *neural correlates of consciousness:* Koch et al., "Neural Correlates of Consciousness."

146 **enable eddies of experiences:** We'll explore this metaphor of eddies further in chapters 8 and 9.

146 **absolute unconditioned existence of its own:** John Prendergast pointed out (personal communication) that in some traditions, such as Advaita Vedanta and Tantric Shaivism, awareness (certainly of humans) is considered to have unconditioned aspects that extend beyond ordinary reality. We'll explore this possibility in chapter 9.

146 **"An attitude of open receptivity":** Adapted from *True Meditation,* https://www .adyashanti.org/teachings/library/writing/subject/16#true-meditation.

ABIDING AS AWARENESS

147 **transpersonal:** Beyond personal identity; see https://en.wikipedia.org/wiki/ Transpersonal.

CHAPTER 7: RECEIVING NOWNESS

151 **"What can anyone give you":** William Stafford, from "You Reading This, Be Ready," in Stafford, *The Way It Is.*

151 **"learn to let thoughts arise":** https://www.theatlantic.com/international/archive /2017/12/buddhism-and-neuroscience/548120/, about a quarter of the way through the article. This article was adapted from M. Ricard and W. Singer, *Beyond the Self: Conversations Between Buddhism and Neuroscience.* MIT Press, 2017. Also see Ricard, *Happiness.*

THE MAKING OF THIS MOMENT

152 **your nervous system at that moment:** Which is affected by other factors, including different systems in your body as well as the influences of relationships, events, culture, nature, and so on.

THE PHYSICS OF NOW

152 **"The Big Bang":** Muller, *Now,* pp. 293, 294, and 304.

153 **the creation of new space:** For example, by astronomers measuring the speed at which distant galaxies are all moving away from one another.

153 **"For the time being":** The great Zen master Dōgen lived in Japan during the first half of the thirteenth century. This passage is adapted from his essay "The Time Being," based on a rendition from Norman Fischer, "For the Time Being," *New York Times,* August 7, 2009, https://opinionator.blogs.nytimes.com/2009/08/07 /for-the-time-being/. For another translation, see https://www.thezensite.com /ZenTeachings/Dogen_Teachings/Uji_Welch.htm.

WAKEFULNESS

153 **establishing a state of *vigilance*:** Langner and Eickhoff, "Sustaining Attention to Simple Tasks."

154 **norepinephrine throughout your brain:** See Posner and Petersen, "The Attention System of the Human Brain"; and Petersen and Posner, "The Attention System of the Human Brain: 20 Years After." They use the term *alerting* for what I am calling "vigilance." Also note that findings about the right hemisphere are reversed for many left-handed people.

154 ***upper attention network:*** Whose elements include the frontal eye fields and intraparietal sulcus.

154 **on both sides of the brain:** Corbetta et al., "The Reorienting System."

ORIENTING

155 **developing knowledge of *what*:** As a simplification, I am placing two separate functions—locating and identifying—under the heading of "orienting."

155 **a *lower attention network:*** In the prefrontal cortex, insula, and temporoparietal junction.

155 **quiets the default mode network:** Austin, "Zen and the Brain."

155 **"They do not grieve over the past":** Adapted from a translation by Andrew Olendzki (https://www.accesstoinsight.org/tipitaka/sn/sn01/sn01.010.olen.html).

BEING HERE NOW

WAKEFULNESS

158 **networks on the right side of the brain:** This is on the left side for many left-handed people. From now on, I won't repeat this point when referring to the right side of the brain.

158 **"If we don't have now":** This was my wife's comment while reading this chapter, which pretty much sums it up.

ALERTING

159 **receptive global awareness:** Austin, "Zen and the Brain."

159 **two major meditation centers:** The Insight Meditation Society and the Barre Center for Buddhist Studies.

ORIENTING

160 **Sometimes we do need:** Corbetta et al., "The Reorienting System."

THE PARTS OF EXPERIENCE

162 **framework in the Pali Canon:** For example, see Majjhima Nikaya 18, the Honeyball Sutta (https://www.accesstoinsight.org/tipitaka/mn/mn.018.than.html). This framework is often termed the five "aggregates," a translation of the Pali *khandas*, which can also mean "piles" or "heaps." In my model, you'll see parallels to that framework and also some departures. For example, I'm listing forms and perceptions in the plural, since I think that reads better.

162 **1. forms:** Some descriptions of the form aggregate include *both* the physical universe and sensory experiences of it. My model here is entirely about our experiences.

162 **2. hedonic tones:** As mentioned in chapter 5, these are often termed *feeling tones,* though they are not about emotions per se.

162 **3. perceptions:** In early drafts of this book, I placed perceptions second in this list because the hedonic tone of a stimulus is often shaped by the perception of what it is (which could be semiconscious and automatic). Is it a snake on the path...or a vine? There are many studies on how priming and otherwise influencing people's perceptions can affect their hedonic reactions to a stimulus. Also, in the initial moment of perception, there is less hedonic—and emotional—charge, so locating perceptions right after forms would be consistent with the practice we're moving toward, of focusing mainly on forms and perceptions, at the front end of the neuro-psychological processing stream before a lot of suffering has had time to take hold.

On the other hand, sometimes a hedonic tone that is painful or pleasurable clearly and immediately follows contact with a new stimulus *before* perceptions have come into play, such as the first instant of pain on touching a hot stove. Additionally, the Buddha taught that hedonic tones come before perceptions, and teachers such as Leigh Brasington make strong arguments that it is both true that this is the case and useful to practice with this orientation. Taking all this into account, I've maintained the sequence that one finds in the Pali Canon.

162 **5. awareness:** Often translated as "consciousness" (*vinnana* in Pali). I prefer the term *awareness,* since consciousness has two different meanings. First, it can refer simply to awareness; for example, "What are you conscious of?" has the same meaning as "What are you aware of?" Second, consciousness can refer to *both* awareness and its contents (for example, the stream of consciousness). Since the previous four parts of experience are distinct from the "field" in which they occur, "awareness" seems clearer and more appropriate. Plus, consciousness can have metaphysical connotations as an aspect of an eternal "cosmic consciousness," and as mentioned in the previous chapter, the Buddha referred to *vinnana* as arising dependently, not outside the frame of conditioned phenomena. Last, "consciousness" can seem special and reserved only for human beings, but awareness is a natural process that we share with other animals. When I use the term *consciousness,* I'm referring to its second meaning, as awareness and its contents together.

PARTS AND MORE PARTS

163 **"All conditioned things are impermanent":** Translation by Gil Fronsdal in *The Dhammapada: A New Translation of the Buddhist Classic with Annotations.* Shambhala, 2006, p. 72.

BEFORE SUFFERING

163 *craving, sense of self, or suffering:* There could be pain and other aspects of the unpleasant hedonic tone, but there are not yet the complex emotional and self-referential dimensions of experience that are the main elements of suffering.

164 **"craving for becoming"**: Itivuttaka 58.

164 **The neurological basis for this**: Bar, "The Proactive Brain"; Manuello et al., "Mindfulness Meditation and Consciousness"; and Friston, "The History of the Future of the Bayesian Brain."

164 **including in the *cerebellum***: Sokolov et al., "The Cerebellum."

164 **process of antici . . . pation**: With a tip of the hat to *The Rocky Horror Picture Show.*

164 **constructing/imagining a sense of self**: Seth et al., "An Interoceptive Predictive Coding Model."

165 **"There is no past"**: Roshi Hogen Bays said this in a group I was in, July 2019.

165 *motor planning*: This is the process of the brain preparing for movement.

Resting in Refuges

166 **everything turns to dust**: Grabovac, "The Stages of Insight."

167 **"going on being"**: Winnicott, "Primary Maternal Preoccupation." For more on Winnicott, see http://www.mythosandlogos.com/Winnicott.html.

167 **earth for comfort and strength**: For example, see B. O'Brien, "The Enlightenment of the Buddha: The Great Awakening," https://www.learnreligions.com/the-enlightenment-of-the-buddha-449789.

167 **body's stress response systems**: Esch and Stefano, "The Neurobiology of Stress Management."

168 **"In truth we are always present"**: This quote is attributed to the teacher Howard Cohn, but I cannot find a specific source. See http://www.missiondharma.org/our-teacher---howard-cohn.html for more about him.

168 **wholesome qualities you've cultivated**: For example, in one of his final teachings, the Buddha encouraged people to become a refuge for themselves through developing the four foundations of mindfulness. See Anālayo, *A Meditator's Life of the Buddha*, pp. 168–69.

168 **consider these key refuges**: I'm drawing on the Buddhist framework of the Three Jewels: Buddha, dharma, sangha.

169 *The Taught:* In a touching sutta passage (Samyutta Nikaya 45.2), the Buddha's primary attendant, Ananda, refers to the monks nearby and exclaims that practicing together is "half the holy life." The Buddha replies, "Not so, Ananda, not so: it is actually the whole of the holy life."

The Nature of Mind and Matter

172 **"In the deepest forms of insight"**: From https://tricycle.org/magazine/perfect-balance/. For more on Gil Fronsdal, see https://en.wikipedia.org/wiki/Gil_Fronsdal. For a beautiful remembrance of U Pandita, see https://www.spiritrock.org/the-teachings/article-archive/article-sayadaw-u-pandita.

172 **"In Buddhist practice"**: This point extends to many paths and practices outside the Buddhist tradition.

WHAT IS THE NATURE OF THE MIND?

173 **information about other things:** For example, information about the heart must be separated from information about the ears; otherwise, chaos would reign.

173 **a mosquito just landed:** This happened to me while I was meditating on retreat.

173 **permanent, unified, self-causing essence:** See https://en.wikipedia.org/wiki/Śūnyatā for a rich exploration of this important idea.

173 **Thoughts, joys, and sorrows:** Just because something is made of parts within parts, and so on, does not mean it doesn't exist. For example, the sight of a meadow exists, even if it lacks an essence. Similarly, the physical meadow itself is still there even while it is made of molecules made of atoms made of protons, and so on. See the same point in the notes for chapter 1.

173 **it is the nature of any experience:** From the perspective of *4E cognition*, the mind is embodied, embedded, extended, and enacted. See A. Newen, L. De Bruin, and S. Gallagher eds., *The Oxford Handbook of 4E Cognition*. Oxford University Press. An embodied, embedded, extended, and enacted mind is also impermanent, compounded, interdependent, and empty.

WHAT IS THE NATURE OF THE BRAIN?

174 *neurogenesis:* Kempermann et al., "Human Adult Neurogenesis."

174 **other brain cells die naturally:** Yuan et al., "Diversity in the Mechanisms of Neuronal Cell Death."

174 **New synapses form:** Shors, "Memory Traces of Trace Memories."

174 **less used ones wither away:** Paolicelli et al., "Synaptic Pruning."

174 **Individual neurons routinely fire:** Roxin et al., "On the Distribution of Firing Rates."

174 **100 billion supporting glial cells:** These estimates are still developing. See Herculano-Houzel, "The Remarkable, Yet Not Extraordinary"; and Lent et al., "How Many Neurons."

174 **"Interdependence means":** *Buddhadharma*, Summer 2019, p. 52; from Thich Nhat Hanh, *Understanding Our Mind*. ReadHowYouWant.com, 2008.

174 **Neuronal activity interacts with:** Dzyubenko et al., "Neuron-Glia Interactions in Neural Plasticity."

THE MIND-BODY PROCESS

175 **"Everything is connected":** Lew Richmond, *Tricycle*, fall 2018, p. 10.

SWIRLING STREAMING

177 **"If you let go a little":** From *No Ajahn Chah—Reflections, Dhamma Garden, #101*. See http://ajahnchah.org/pdf/no_ajahn_chah.pdf and https://www.abhayagiri.org/reflections/83-quotes-from-no-ajahn-chah.

CHAPTER 8: OPENING INTO ALLNESS

181 **"To learn the Buddha way":** This is adapted from a famous passage, which has multiple translations into English. I used the translation from Kosen Nishiyama and John Stevens (K. Nishiyama and J. Stevens, 1975. *Dogen Zenji's Shobogenzo: The Eye and Treasury of the True Law*) at www.thezensite.com, and changed their phrase "the Buddhist way" to "the Buddha way," an expression used by other translators that seems more general. Also see https://buddhismnow.com/2015/02/15/study-the-self-by-maezumi-roshi/ and http://www.thezensite.com/ZenTeachings/Dogen_Teachings/GenjoKoan8.htm#mas4. As to the proper translation of the last line, instead of "perceive oneself as," other common translations are "be actualized by" or "be enlightened by" all (or "myriad") things. Personally, I would like: "To forget oneself is to be lived by all things."

THE PERSON PROCESS

182 **"Bahiya, you should":** Udana 1.10, adapted from translations by Thānissaro Bhikkhu—https://www.dhammatalks.org/suttas/KN/Ud/ud1_10.html—and John Ireland (www.leighb.com/ud1_10.htm), with additional input from Leigh Brasington. He pointed out that Pali does not use articles such as *the.* Consequently, a precise translation would be: "in reference to seen, there will be only seen," and so on. But this is awkward in English. He suggested using gerunds such as *seeing,* which also has the advantage of bringing us into the experiential flow of this practice, and I've adopted his suggestion.

DOES A PERSON EXIST?

182 **individual *persons* exist:** As discussed in chapters 2 and 7, I believe we do exist... emptily. There are important distinctions and subtleties about this point, and I am not presenting it as orthodox Buddhism. See http://leighb.com/sn12_15.htm for a sutta in which the Buddha seems to say we should disengage from notions of existence or nonexistence.

183 **"The abolition of the conceit":** From translation by John Ireland (https://www.accesstoinsight.org/tipitaka/kn/ud/ud.2.01.irel.html).

DOES A SELF EXIST?

183 *disenchanted:* In Pali, *nibbida.*

184 **spells cast by Mother Nature:** In terms of biological evolution.

184 **the apparent psychological self:** Many other teachers and traditions have made similar recommendations. For example, see Dahl et al., "Reconstructing and Deconstructing the Self," particularly the section on the "deconstructive family" of meditation practices.

184 **being a self causes a lot of suffering:** Leary, *The Curse of the Self.*

184 **becoming defensive, and getting possessive:** Dambrun and Ricard, "Self-Centeredness and Selflessness."

184 **No self, no problem:** Thubten, *No Self, No Problem*. I've heard this saying from others as well.

184 **different ways in different cultures:** Baumeister, *Meanings of Life*; and Mosig, "Conceptions of the Self."

185 **"The self is not something":** J. Goldstein: "Dreaming Ourselves into Existence," *Buddhadharma*, fall 2018, p. 69.

"SELF" IN THE MIND
186 **full self in your actual experience:** In *Beyond Buddhism* (p. 95), Stephen Batchelor referred to "the unfindability of a core self within."

"SELF" IN THE BRAIN
187 **basis of self-related experiences are also:** Gillihan and Farah, "Is Self Special?"; and Legrand and Ruby, "What Is Self-Specific?"

A "SELF" IS LIKE A UNICORN
188 **"The profound realization":** Anālayo, *A Meditator's Life of the Buddha*, p. 50.

PRACTICING WITH THE SENSE OF SELF
189 *Taboo Against Knowing Who You Are*: Watts, *The Book*.

189 **fears of annihilation, death, and nothing:** An excellent resource for helping others with these issues—and perhaps finding insights for oneself—is Vieten and Scammell, *Spiritual and Religious Competencies*.

189 **"You have to be somebody":** Engler, "Being Somebody and Being Nobody." Also see http://blogs.warwick.ac.uk/zoebrigley/entry/being_somebody_and/.

190 **easier to handle rejections:** In this limited space we can't address some important topics, including how to develop secure attachment and healthy self-worth ("person-worth"?!) in childhood, how to heal feelings of inadequacy, and how to stand up for yourself and others as *persons* without being self-righteous or mean.

ALLOCENTRIC EXPERIENCING
192 **James Austin:** See Austin, *Selfless Insight* and "Zen and the Brain." Professor Austin kindly reviewed my account here and offered a few suggestions that I've implemented.

192 **world shines forth in radiant perfection:** While these "oneness" or "non-dual" experiences may occur within a religious or spiritual framework, such as *kensho* or *satori* in Zen, I'm exploring aspects of them here without reference to that context.

192 **without the fireworks of these peak:** Maslow, *Religions, Values, and Peak-Experiences*.

192 **mystical, non-dual, or *self-transcendent*:** For an excellent review, see Yaden et al., "The Varieties of Self-Transcendent Experience."

192 **open more into inter-being:** This is Thich Nhat Hanh's beautiful term.

EGOCENTRIC AND ALLOCENTRIC PERSPECTIVES

193 **related to our physical environments:** Zaehle et al., "The Neural Basis of the Egocentric and Allocentric."

193 **understanding of the total environment:** Galati et al., "Multiple Reference Frames."

194 **egocentric processing stream runs along the top:** *Dorsal* is the technical term for the top of the brain, like the dorsal fin of a shark that is on the top of its body.

194 **parietal lobes toward the prefrontal cortex:** I'm simplifying; see Austin's account for the details.

194 **somatic sense of being a particular body:** Austin, "Zen and the Brain."

194 **allocentric processing stream runs lower:** *Ventral* is the term for being lower in the brain.

194 **alerting-and-orienting attention network that runs:** Discussed in chapter 7. See ibid.

194 **"being" mode that is also right-sided:** Discussed in chapter 6.

GRADUAL CULTIVATION, SUDDEN AWAKENING

195 **immersed in reality with little or no sense of self:** Hood et al., *The Psychology of Religion*, p. 4. Also see Kornfield, *After the Ecstasy, the Laundry*; Boyle, *Realizing Awakened Consciousness*; and Vieten et al., "Future Directions in Meditation Research."

196 **"There is nothing whatsoever to fear":** From https://en.wikipedia.org/wiki/James_H._Austin. The original source is J. H. Austin, *Zen and the Brain: Toward an Understanding of Meditation and Consciousness.* MIT Press, 1999, p. 537.

196 **in the brains of others during similar experiences:** Yaden et al., "The Varieties of Self-Transcendent Experience." The nuances of these experiences can vary from person to person, and their characteristics and the interpretations of them can be shaped as well by cultural and religious contexts. There is a *lot* of philosophy and theology about non-dualism, including many details and controversies summarized here: https://en.wikipedia.org/wiki/Nondualism.

196 **allocentric perspective to surge forward:** Austin, *Zen-Brain Reflections*.

196 **"All root origins":** Austin, "Zen and the Brain," p. 7.

196 **Austin points out a plausible:** Ibid., especially pp. 4–5.

196 *thalamus***:** There are two thalami, one on each side of the brain.

196 **cortex that help make the sense of self:** Notably the medial and dorsolateral prefrontal cortex, the posterior cingulate cortex, and the retrosplenial cortex.

196 **nearby tissues:** The reticular nucleus, zona incerta, and anterior pretectal nucleus.

196 **GABA:** GABA stands for gamma-aminobutyric acid. It is a key inhibitory neurotransmitter. See https://en.wikipedia.org/wiki/Gamma-Aminobutyric_acid.

196 **upper parts of the thalamus:** Austin, "How Does Meditation Train Attention?"

197 **egocentric current in the stream:** Related points have been made in Newberg and Iversen, "Neural Basis"; and Newberg et al., "The Measurement of Regional Cerebral Blood Flow."

197 **unity and related mystical experiences:** This refers to parts of the parietal lobes.
For the details, see Newberg et al., "The Measurement of Regional Cerebral Blood
Flow"; Farrer and Frith, "Experiencing Oneself Versus Another Person"; Azari et
al., "Neural Correlates of Religious Experience"; Beauregard and Paquette, "Neu-
ral Correlates of a Mystical Experience"; and Johnstone et al., "Right Parietal
Lobe-Related 'Selflessness.'"

197 **"One day I sat":** From A.B., personal communication.

197 **"During one period of meditation":** Gil Fronsdal, in *Realizing Awakened Consciousness*, ed. Boyle, p. 124.

197 **"The instant I sat down":** Shinzen Young, in ibid., p. 25. Shinzen is a deeply practiced teacher who has developed numerous innovative and effective approaches to
learning and practicing mindfulness. See https://www.shinzen.org/ as well as his
various books, including S. Young, *The Science of Enlightenment: How Meditation
Works*. Sounds True, 2016.

197 **koan:** From the Zen tradition, a question or story with a teaching purpose, often
provocative and paradoxical.

LEANING INTO ALLNESS

198 **underlying neural processes:** Which does not rule out the possibility of additional factors outside of ordinary reality. This said, I am focusing in this chapter on
neuropsychological factors within the "natural frame."

198 **networks of wholeness, nowness, and allness:** For related possible neuropsychological explanations, not mutually exclusive with the one I'm offering and overlap-
ping it to some extent, see Boyle, "Cracking the Buddhist Code." Also consider
possible interruptions of "narrative self" activations centered in medial prefrontal
cortex and posterior cingulate cortex (elements of the default mode network). See
Denny et al., "A Meta-analysis of Functional Neuroimaging Studies." This might
enable the "minimal phenomenal self" to be what is most present, experientially,
based on activations in the anterior insula, temporo-parietal junction, and hypothalamus (and other regions that maintain basic homeostatic functioning). See
Gallagher, "Philosophical Conceptions of the Self"; and Damasio, *Self Comes to
Mind.*

My own hunch is that prototypical nondual or "self-transcendent" experiences
probably involve all of these systems. Yet what remains unclear is how a dramatic
neurological change that correlates with such a dramatic psychological change is
triggered.

198 **retreat soon before the experience:** Other precipitating conditions include psychedelics, vision quests, rituals, and intensive physical practices such as yoga. For
example, see Pollan, *How to Change Your Mind.*

198 **Some people speak of feeling welcomed:** Thanks to Jan Ogren for this point.

199 **"We live in illusion":** I saw a version of this quoted in the Gratitude Hut at Spirit
Rock Meditation Center. The teacher James Baraz pointed me to the somewhat
different and widely accepted form of this quotation online—which is what is

used here—but I've been unable to find the original source. Lama Palden (personal communication) suggested that this could be a paraphrase of texts in Kalu Rinpoche and the Dalai Lama, *Luminous Mind.*

199 **inhibitory nodes of the thalamus:** As well as in other parts of the nervous system, with related beneficial experiences of calming and soothing.

200 **which naturally activates allocentric visual processing:** Austin, *Selfless Insight.*

THE TIPPING POINT

200 **internally referenced processes:** Fazelpour and Thompson, "The Kantian Brain."

200 **surprise of some kind:** Austin, *Selfless Insight.*

200 **Zen nun Mugai Nyodai:** Also known as Chiyono; see https://en.wikipedia.org /wiki/Mugai_Nyodai. For a lovely collection of other stories of awakened women, see Caplow and Moon, *The Hidden Lamp.*

201 **"With this and that I tried":** Mary Swigonski. See "Chiyone and the Bottomless Bucket," https://justalchemy.com/2014/03/17/chiyono-and-the-bottomless -bucket/.

201 **wholeness networks of the brain:** Neuroscientist Wil Cunningham, personal communication.

202 **awareness . . . a sky of mind:** I first heard this phrase from the teacher Adi Da and have enjoyed Ray Lynch's music album with the same title. You can also listen to Jack Kornfield's guided meditation about this: https://jackkornfield.com/a-mind -like-sky/.

EXPANSIVE VIEWS

202 **nature in its abundance, and the universe altogether:** Leary et al., "Allo-inclusive Identity."

202 **"When we try to pick out":** Muir, *My First Summer in the Sierra,* p. 110. For some background, including misquotations of Muir, see https://vault.sierraclub.org /john_muir_exhibit/writings/misquotes.aspx#1.

THE VIEW OF EMPTINESS

203 **Just about everything:** I'm qualifying this a bit since certain aspects of our universe seem enduring, such as Planck's constant. But at a minimum, everything is conditioned by the big bang.

203 **a storm on Jupiter:** See https://en.wikipedia.org/wiki/Great_Red_Spot.

THE VIEW OF CULTURE

204 **"You are a flowing stream":** Hanh, *Inside the Now.*

THE VIEW OF LIFE

205 **"There is no phenomenon":** Hanh, *The World We Have.*

205 **Sangha:** Community.

THE VIEW OF THE UNIVERSE

206 **"We have come to realize":** http://www.fritjofcapra.net/werner-heisenberg
-explorer-of-the-limits-of-human-imagination/.

206 **asteroidal bullet hitting the earth:** For a remarkable description of this event, see
D. Preston, "The Day the Dinosaurs Died," *New Yorker*, April 8, 2019, https://www
.newyorker.com/magazine/2019/04/08/the-day-the-dinosaurs-died.

206 **"All our waves are water":** See Yogis, *All Our Waves Are Water.*

CHAPTER 9: FINDING TIMELESSNESS

211 **"Things appear and disappear":** Adapted from Thich Nhat Hanh, "Becoming
Truly Alive," *Buddhadharma*, winter 2009. In his article, Thich Nhat Hanh was referring to a passage in the Pali Canon (Majjhima Nikaya 143) in which a teaching
was offered to a man who was dying. I'm presenting Thich Nhat Hanh's words at
face value, to be considered as they stand, not as a representation of what is said in
Majjhima Nikaya 143.

MIND, MATTER—AND MYSTERY

NIBBANA

212 **the Buddha's quest:** There are many accounts of the Buddha's life and his motiv-
ations. A key summary is found in Majjhima Nikaya 26, the Noble Search.
See https://www.accesstoinsight.org/tipitaka/mn/mn.026.than.html.

213 **"What lies beyond":** Bodhi, *In the Buddha's Words*, p. 183.

213 *In the Buddha's Words:* Bodhi, *In the Buddha's Words.*

213 **reflect on a specific word:** For another summary, see https://www.accesstoin
sight.org/ptf/dhamma/sacca/sacca3/nibbana.html. How key Pali terms are translated can *really* shape their apparent meaning. See Batchelor, *After Buddhism*, chapter 5, for many examples of this.

213 **"supreme security from bondage":** Bodhi, *In the Buddha's Words*, p. 55.

213 **"lust, hatred, and delusion":** Ibid., p. 364.

213 **"path leading to the destination":** Ibid., p. 365.

213 **"O house-builder":** From a translation by Acharya Buddharakkhita. There are
alternative translations of this important passage that do not use the term *the unconditioned.* See this one from Thānissaro Bhikkhu (https://www.accesstoinsight.org
/lib/authors/Thānissaro/dhammapada.pdf): "House-builder, you're seen! You will
not build a house again. All your rafters broken, the ridgepole dismantled, immersed in dismantling, the mind has attained to the end of craving."

  Also see this one from Gil Fronsdal: "House-builder, you are seen! You will not
build a house again! All the rafters are broken, The ridgepole destroyed; The mind,
gone to the Unconstructed, Has reached the end of craving!"

214 **"This is peaceful":** Adapted from a translation by Piyadassi Thera at: https://
www.accesstoinsight.org/tipitaka/an/an10/an10.060.piya.html.

214 **"The born, become, produced":** Adapted from translations by Thānissaro Bhikkhu and John Ireland, https://www.accesstoinsight.org/tipitaka/kn/iti/iti.2.028

-049.than.html#iti-043 and https://www.accesstoinsight.org/tipitaka/kn/iti/iti
.2.042-049x.irel.html.

OUTSIDE THE NATURAL FRAME

215 **"Precisely because"**: Adapted from Thānissaro Bhikkhu's translation here: https://www.dhammatalks.org/suttas/KN/Ud/ud8_3.html.

215 **some people think there is no point**: For example, see Stephen Batchelor's books, including *After Buddhism, Buddhism Without Beliefs,* and *Confession of a Buddhist Atheist.* Also see the work of Sam Harris, such as *Waking Up.*

215 ***without* reference to something**: I mean "something" in the widest and vaguest ways possible, and am not trying to imply that whatever might be beyond ordinary reality is thing-like, or noun-like, or anything-in-particular-like.

216 **to practice in relationship to it**: A version of this latter approach is "Pascal's wager"; see https://en.wikipedia.org/wiki/Pascal%27s_wager.

216 **teachers in both camps**: And if there is one topic that inspires, ah, vigorous debate in Buddhist circles, it is this one—a discussion echoed in other disagreements between atheists and believers in something transcendental. For example, see Dawkins, *The God Delusion;* and Crean, *God Is No Delusion.*

POSSIBLE CHARACTERISTICS OF THE TRANSCENDENTAL

216 **distinguish between what may be *supernatural***: References to supernatural matters such as spirits (for example, *devas*) or past lives run throughout the Pali Canon. They're also present in religious texts and spiritual practices around the world. And many people report uncanny experiences that seem to them evidence of the supernatural. For example, Meg Madden (personal communication) writes: "A non-local intelligence [is] resident in all nature. It can be experienced directly in meditation. It is loving and conscious, and resides in all sentient beings, including rocks, trees, anything we can imagine. I have experienced that some animals, plants and even mountains are actually superior to some people in connecting to this wisdom. They might be called awake." Also see Vieten et al., "Future Directions in Meditation Research."

Nonetheless, we can ask whether anything supernatural actually exists, and whether presuming the existence of the supernatural is useful for practice. Reasonable people can disagree about these matters. I've thought many times about this discussion between Stephen Batchelor and Robert Thurman: Batchelor and Thurman, "Reincarnation: A Debate."

217 **First, the transcendental**: This is a note on *the*. Pali does not contain definite or indefinite articles, so *the* or *a/an* are suggested at most. (For complications, see https://palistudies.blogspot.com/2018/05/pali-pronouns.html.) Using definite articles in phrases such as "the unconditioned" in translations is inexact though widely done. Further, saying "*the* unconditioned" or "*the* transcendental" risks implying that these are thing-like. But leaving out *the* in some sentences is awkward. So I use *the* as little as possible with these terms, acknowledging the (!) issues with this pesky little word.

217 *unconditioned*, **a timeless:** For a very cool idea, neurologist and author Richard Mendius pointed out to me that as one approaches the speed of light, time slows down. Consequently, for a photon traveling at the speed of light, there could be literally no time. In some sense, therefore, light could be timeless...so that timelessness could be full of light!

217 **Whatever is transcendentally:** Distinct from extraordinarily unconditioned—unfabricated, unconstructed, uninclined—states of mind within *ordinary* reality. This is the second way to approach what could be "unconditioned."

217 **"Move my mind":** Berry, "Sabbaths—1982," *A Timbered Choir.* See https://www .goodreads.com/work/quotes/141101-a-timbered-choir-the-sabbath-poems -1979-1997.

217 **"Who are you?":** Thomas Merton was a Trappist monk with a deep interest in Buddhism (https://en.wikipedia.org/wiki/Thomas_Merton). These lines are from "In Silence," Merton and Szabo, *In the Dark Before Dawn.* For the full poem and a touching picture of him, see https://www.innerdirections.org/the-poetry-of -thomas-merton/.

218 **become actuality:** Muller, *Now;* also see Schwartz et al., "Quantum Physics in Neuroscience and Psychology."

218 **"This holy life":** Adapted from translations by Bikkhu Bodhi, https://suttacentral .net/mn29/en/bodhi; Bikkhu Sujato, https://suttacentral.net/mn29/en/sujato; Thānissaro Bhikkhu, https://www.dhammatalks.org/suttas/MN/MN30.html; and I. B. Horner, https://suttacentral.net/mn30/en/horner. The simile of heartwood is found in more than one sutta.

TURNING TO THE TRANSCENDENTAL
CALMING THE CONDITIONED

220 **"Indeed the sage who's fully quenched":** There are references in this passage to metaphors of fire and fuel, which were often used in the religious ceremonies of his time as well as in daily life. The Buddha also frequently used a related metaphor, to "nutriments" (common translation of the Pali *ahara*, also meaning "food"), which evokes the agricultural and pastoral society in which he lived. A root meaning of the word nibbana is to be "blown out," such as the flame of a lamp; thus "quenched." For a discussion of the Buddha in his own time and the roots of his teachings and the deep meanings of many words he used, see Gombrich, *What the Buddha Thought.*

220 **"the mind has found its way to peace":** Translated by Andrew Olendzki, https:// tricycle.org/magazine/modest-awakening/.

AN AWARENESS DEEPER THAN YOUR OWN

222 **abiding as awareness:** Mentioned in chapters 3 and 6.

223 *Tat tvam asi:* See https://en.wikipedia.org/wiki/Tat_Tvam_Asi.

LIVED BY LOVE

224 **"Let go of the past:"** Translation by Gil Fronsdal in *The Dhammapada: A New Translation of the Buddhist Classic with Annotations.* Shambhala, 2006, p. 90.

MOMENTS OF AWAKENING

224 **Moments of awakening**—: The teacher Mark Coleman attributes this saying to Tulku Urgyen Rinpoche.

EDDIES IN THE STREAM

226 **"quantum foam"**: See Wikipedia, https://en.wikipedia.org/wiki/Quantum_foam.

231 **along with radically penetrating insights**: For example, see Kraft, *Buddha's Map*.

231 **must also have neural correlates**: Though their neural correlates are uncertain. For example: "The formless states ... have [not] yet been clearly distinguished in cognitive neuroscience." Vago and Zeidan, "The Brain on Silent."

231 **descriptions of these steps**: Adapted from Bodhi, *In the Buddha's Words*, pp. 397–98. See the full description in chapter 2.

231 **...and cessation**: For example, see Anguttara Nikaya 9.34, the Unbinding Sutta (https://www.accesstoinsight.org/tipitaka/an/an09/an09.034.than.html). For a far-reaching exploration, also see http://leighb.com/epractices.htm.

232 **"Through the practice of the Buddha's path"**: From the introduction to his translation of the Samyutta Nikaya, in Bodhi, *Connected Discourses of the Buddha*.

232 **and perhaps reality itself**: For example, "The moment of fruition, subsequent to the path moment [that is, nibbana], is the understood experience and results in a turned-around vision of existence." A. Khema (1994), in section 12, Path and Fruit, in "All of Us: Beset by Birth, Decay, and Death," 1994, https://www.accesstoin sight.org/lib/authors/khema/allofus.html. This whole essay is excellent, including the many comments about nibbana in section 12.

233 **"Pointing directly at the mind"**: This comes from a scroll inscribed by Hakuin with the Japanese words *Jikishi ninshin, Kensho jobutsu*. On the Wikipedia page for Hakuin (https://en.wikipedia.org/wiki/Hakuin_Ekaku), these are translated as "Direct pointing at the mind of man, seeing one's nature and becoming Buddha."

CHAPTER 10: THE FRUIT AS THE PATH

239 **"Things fall apart"**: These were reportedly the Buddha's last words. This translation comes from Stephen Batchelor, in *After Buddhism*, p.102. Also see https://www.buddhistinquiry.org/article/the-buddhas-last-word-care/. There are other translations, such as this one from Bhikkhu Bodhi (personal communication): "Conditioned things are subject to vanish. Achieve the goal by means of heedfulness."

239 **"what you've seen changes you forever"**: For more about Steve Armstrong, see http://vipassanametta.org/.

240 **we can take the fruit as the path**: I believe this is a Tibetan saying but haven't found a specific source.

MAKING THE OFFERING

COMPASSION AND EQUANIMITY

243 **walk evenly over uneven ground**: For example, see Samyutta Nikaya 1.7: "Those to whom the Dhamma is clear ... walk evenly over the uneven."

243 **Howard Thurman put it:** Schaper, *40-Day Journey with Howard Thurman.*

244 **what is and what will be:** This could be called *engaged practice* (for example, "engaged Buddhism"). Many people and organizations around the world are doing this, from simple acts at the individual level up to large-scale social movements.

244 **"Teach us to care":** From "Ash Wednesday," Eliot, *Collected Poems 1909–1962.*

TENDING TO THE CAUSES

244 **like to have some fruit:** This example is adapted from the teachings of Ajahn Chah and also mentioned in *Resilient.*

245 **"diligent" as the Buddha said:** Udana 3.2.

246 **"out of my hands":** Also told in *Resilient.*

OUR COLLECTIVE OFFERINGS

246 **Theravaden, Tibetan, Zen, and Pure Land:** With different schools in each of these. Also, arguably there are more than four major forms, particularly regarding Chan Buddhism (see Wikipedia, https://en.wikipedia.org/wiki/Chan_Buddhism).

247 **science and related mental and physical:** For example, see Wallace and Shapiro, "Mental Balance and Well-Being."

247 **practices in non-Buddhist settings:** Such as mindfulness-based cognitive therapy for depression. See Segal et al., *Mindfulness-Based Cognitive Therapy.*

GOING FORTH

249 **"gone forth":** See Sutta Nipata 3.1; this term is also used for people entering monastic life.

KEEP IT SIMPLE

250 **"I don't know so much":** Quoted in D. Penick, "Love Passing Beneath Shadows," *Tricycle,* Spring 2019. Note that this article refers to *Letters from Max: A Book of Friendship by Sarah Ruhl and Max Ritvo.* Milkweed Editions, 2018. The quotation itself is said to have come by way of the poet and Zen priest Philip Whalen.

HAVE PERSPECTIVE

251 **Worldly winds:** Praise and blame, pleasure and pain, gain and loss, fame and ill repute.

ENJOY THE RIDE

252 **amidst a couple trillion others:** See E. Siegel, "This Is How We Know There Are Two Trillion Galaxies in the Universe," Forbes.com, Oct. 18, 2018, https://www.forbes.com/sites/startswithabang/2018/10/18/this-is-how-we-know-there-are-two-trillion-galaxies-in-the-universe/#f512d625a67b.

252 **"Keep going":** I also told this story in *Resilient.*

BIBLIOGRAPHY

Adyashanti, *The Deep Heart: Our Portal to Presence*, J. J. Prendergast, Boulder, CO: Sounds True, 2019.

Alberini, C. M., and J. E. LeDoux. "Memory Reconsolidation." *Current Biology* 23, no. 17 (2013): R746–50.

Allen, A. B., and M. R. Leary. "Self-Compassion, Stress, and Coping." *Social and Personality Psychology Compass* 4, no. 2 (2010): 107–18.

Anālayo. *A Meditator's Life of the Buddha: Based on the Early Discourses.* Cambridge, UK: Windhorse Publications, 2017.

———. *Mindfully Facing Disease and Death: Compassionate Advice from Early Buddhist Texts.* Cambridge, UK: Windhorse Publications, 2016.

———. *Satipaṭṭhāna: The Direct Path to Realization.* Cambridge, UK: Windhorse Publications, 2004.

Angus, D. J., et al. "Anger Is Associated with Reward-Related Electrocortical Activity: Evidence from the Reward Positivity." *Psychophysiology* 52, no. 10 (2015): 1271–80.

Armstrong, G. *Emptiness: A Practical Guide for Meditators.* New York: Simon & Schuster, 2017.

Austin, J. H. "How Does Meditation Train Attention?" *Insight Journal* 32 (2009): 16–22.

———. *Selfless Insight: Zen and the Meditative Transformations of Consciousness.* Cambridge, MA: MIT Press, 2011.

———. "Zen and the Brain: Mutually Illuminating Topics." *Frontiers in Psychology* 4 (2013): 784.

———. *Zen-Brain Reflections: Reviewing Recent Developments in Meditation and States of Consciousness.* Cambridge, MA: MIT Press, 2006.

Azari, N. P., et al. "Neural Correlates of Religious Experience." *European Journal of Neuroscience* 13, no. 8 (2001): 1649–52.

Baars, B. J. "Global Workspace Theory of Consciousness: Toward a Cognitive Neuroscience of Human Experience." *Progress in Brain Research* 150 (2005): 45–53.

Bar, M. "The Proactive Brain: Using Analogies and Associations to Generate Predictions." *Trends in Cognitive Sciences* 11, no. 7 (2007): 280–9.

Baraz, J. *Awakening Joy: 10 Steps That Will Put You on the Road to Real Happiness.* New York: Bantam, 2010.

Barron, A. B., and C. Klein. "What Insects Can Tell Us About the Origins of Consciousness." *Proceedings of the National Academy of Sciences* 113, no. 18 (2016): 4900–08.

Batchelor, S. *After Buddhism: Rethinking the Dharma for a Secular Age.* New Haven, CT: Yale University Press, 2015.

———. *Buddhism Without Beliefs: A Contemporary Guide to Awakening.* New York: Penguin, 1998.

———. *Confession of a Buddhist Atheist.* New York: Random House, 2010.

———, and R. Thurman. "Reincarnation: A Debate." *Tricycle: The Buddhist Review,* summer 1997: http://www. tricycle. com/feature/reincarnation-debate.

Baumeister, R. F. *Meanings of Life.* New York: Guilford Press, 1991.

———, et al. "Bad Is Stronger Than Good." *Review of General Psychology* 5, no. 4 (2001): 323–70.

Baxter, L. R., et al. "Caudate Glucose Metabolic Rate Changes with Both Drug and Behavior Therapy for Obsessive-Compulsive Disorder." *Archives of General Psychiatry* 49, no. 9 (1992): 681–9.

Beauregard, M., and V. Paquette. "Neural Correlates of a Mystical Experience in Carmelite Nuns." *Neuroscience Letters* 405, no. 3 (2006): 186–90.

Begley, S. *Train Your Mind, Change Your Brain: How a New Science Reveals Our Extraordinary Potential to Transform Ourselves.* New York: Random House, 2007.

Benson, H., and M. Z. Klipper. *The Relaxation Response.* New York: William Morrow, 1975.

Berridge, K. C., et al. "Dissecting Components of Reward: 'Liking,' 'Wanting,' and 'Learning.'" *Current Opinion in Pharmacology* 9, no. 1 (2009): 65–73.

Berridge, K. C., and M. L. Kringelbach. "Pleasure Systems in the Brain." *Neuron* 86, no. 3 (2015): 646–4.

Berridge, K. C., and T. E. Robinson. "What Is the Role of Dopamine in Reward: Hedonic Impact, Reward Learning, or Incentive Salience?" *Brain Research Reviews* 28, no. 3 (1998): 309–69.

Berry, W. *A Timbered Choir: The Sabbath Poems, 1979–1997.* Washington, DC: Counterpoint, 1998.

Bersani, F. S., and M. Pasquini. "The 'Outer Dimensions': Impulsivity, Anger/Aggressiveness, Activation." In *Dimensional Psychopathology,* edited by M. Biondi et al., Basel: Springer, 2018, pp. 211–32.

Birnie, K., et al. "Exploring Self-Compassion and Empathy in the Context of Mindfulness-Based Stress Reduction (MBSR)." *Stress and Health* 26, no. 5 (2010): 359–71.

Bluth, K., and K. D. Neff. "New Frontiers in Understanding the Benefits of Self-Compassion." *Self and Identity* 17, no. 6 (2018): 605–8.

Bodhi, B. *In the Buddha's Words: An Anthology of Discourses from the Pali Canon.* New York: Simon & Schuster, 2005.

————, and B. Nanamoli. *The Middle Length Discourses of the Buddha: A Translation of the Majjhima Nikaya.* Sommerville, MA: Wisdom Publications, 2009.

Boellinghaus, I. F., et al. "The Role of Mindfulness and Loving-Kindness Meditation in Cultivating Self-Compassion and Other-Focused Concern in Health Care Professionals." *Mindfulness* 5, no. 2 (2014): 129–38.

Boll, S., et al. "Oxytocin and Pain Perception: From Animal Models to Human Research." *Neuroscience* 387 (2018): 149–61.

Boly, M., et al. "Consciousness in Humans and Non-human Animals: Recent Advances and Future Directions." *Frontiers in Psychology* 4 (2013): 625.

Bowles, S. "Group Competition, Reproductive Leveling, and the Evolution of Human Altruism." *Science* 314, no. 5805 (2006): 1569–72.

Boyd, R., et al. "Hunter-Gatherer Population Structure and the Evolution of Contingent Cooperation." *Evolution and Human Behavior* 35, no. 3 (2014): 219–27.

Boyle, R. P. "Cracking the Buddhist Code: A Contemporary Theory of First-Stage Awakening." *Journal of Consciousness Studies* 24, no. 9–10 (2017): 156–80.

————. *Realizing Awakened Consciousness: Interviews with Buddhist Teachers and a New Perspective on the Mind.* New York: Columbia University Press, 2015.

Brach, T. *Radical Acceptance: Embracing Your Life with the Heart of a Buddha.* New York: Bantam, 2004.

————. *Radical Compassion: Learning to Love Yourself and the World with the Practice of RAIN.* New York: Viking Press, 2019.

————. *True Refuge: Finding Peace and Freedom in Your Own Awakened Heart.* New York: Bantam, 2012.

Brahm, A. *Mindfulness, Bliss, and Beyond: A Meditator's Handbook.* New York: Simon & Schuster, 2006.

Bramham, C. R., and E. Messaoudi. "BDNF Function in Adult Synaptic Plasticity: The Synaptic Consolidation Hypothesis." *Progress in Neurobiology* 76, no. 2 (2005): 99–125.

Brandmeyer, T., et al. "The Neuroscience of Meditation: Classification, Phenomenology, Correlates, and Mechanisms." *Progress in Brain Research* 244 (2019), 1–29.

Braver, T., and J. Cohen. "On the Control of Control: The Role of Dopamine in Regulating Prefrontal Function and Working Memory." In *Control of Cognitive Processes: Attention and Performance* 18, edited by S. Monsel and J. Driver. Cambridge, MA: MIT Press, 2000.

Braver, T., et al. "The Role of Prefrontal Cortex in Normal and Disordered Cognitive Control: A Cognitive Neuroscience Perspective." In *Principles of Frontal Lobe Function*, edited by D. T. Stuss and R. T. Knight. New York: Oxford University Press, 2002.

Brewer, J. *The Craving Mind: From Cigarettes to Smartphones to Love? Why We Get Hooked and How We Can Break Bad Habits.* New Haven, CT: Yale University Press, 2017.

Brewer, J. et al. "Meditation Experience Is Associated with Differences in Default Mode Network Activity and Connectivity." *Proceedings of the National Academy of Sciences* 108, no. 50 (2011): 20254–59.

————, et al. "What About the 'Self' Is Processed in the Posterior Cingulate Cortex?" *Frontiers in Human Neuroscience* 7 (2013): 647.

Brodt, et al. "Fast Track to the Neocortex: A Memory Engram in the Posterior Parietal Cortex." *Science* 362, no. 6418 (2018): 1045–48.

Buddharakkhita, A., trans. *The Dhammapada: The Buddha's Path of Wisdom.* Kandy, Sri Lanka: Buddhist Publication Society, 1985.

Burkett, J. P., et al. "Activation of μ-Opioid Receptors in the Dorsal Striatum Is Necessary for Adult Social Attachment in Monogamous Prairie Voles." *Neuropsychopharmacology* 36, no. 11 (2011): 2200.

Burklund, L. J., et al. "The Common and Distinct Neural Bases of Affect Labeling and Reappraisal in Healthy Adults." *Frontiers in Psychology* 5 (2014): 221.

Cahill, L., and J. L. McGaugh. "Modulation of Memory Storage." *Current Opinion in Neurobiology* 6, no. 2 (1996): 237–42.

Cahn, B. R., and J. Polich. "Meditation States and Traits: EEG, ERP, and Neuroimaging Studies." *Psychological Bulletin* 132, no. 2 (2006): 180.

Caplow, F., and S. Moon, eds. *The Hidden Lamp: Stories from Twenty-Five Centuries of Awakened Women.* Somerville, MA: Wisdom Publications, 2013.

Carey, T. A., et al. "Improving Professional Psychological Practice Through an Increased Repertoire of Research Methodologies: Illustrated by the Development of MOL." *Professional Psychology: Research and Practice* 48, no. 3 (2017): 175.

Cellini, N., et al. "Sleep Before and After Learning Promotes the Consolidation of Both Neutral and Emotional Information Regardless of REM Presence." *Neurobiology of Learning and Memory* 133 (2016): 136–44.

Chödrön, P. *When Things Fall Apart: Heart Advice for Difficult Times.* Boulder, CO: Shambhala Publications, 2000.

Christoff, K., et al. "Experience Sampling During fMRI Reveals Default Network and Executive System Contributions to Mind Wandering." *Proceedings of the National Academy of Sciences* 106, no. 21 (2009): 8719–24.

————, et al. "Specifying the Self for Cognitive Neuroscience." *Trends in Cognitive Sciences* 15, no. 3 (2011): 104–12.

Clopath, C. "Synaptic Consolidation: An Approach to Long-Term Learning." *Cognitive Neurodynamics* 6, no. 3 (2011): 251–7.

Cooney, R. E., et al. "Neural Correlates of Rumination in Depression." *Cognitive, Affective, & Behavioral Neuroscience* 10, no. 4 (2010): 470–8.

Corbetta, et al. "The Reorienting System of the Human Brain: From Environment to Theory of Mind." *Neuron* 58, no. 3 (2008): 306–24.

Craig, A. D. "How Do You Feel? Interoception: The Sense of the Physiological Condition of the Body." *Nature Reviews Neuroscience* 3, no. 8 (2002): 655.

Crean, T. *God Is No Delusion: A Refutation of Richard Dawkins.* San Francisco: Ignatius Press, 2007.

Creswell, J. D., et al. "Alterations in Resting-State Functional Connectivity Link Mindfulness Meditation with Reduced Interleukin-6: A Randomized Controlled Trial." *Biological Psychiatry* 80, no. 1, (2016): 53–61.

————, et al. "Neural Correlates of Dispositional Mindfulness During Affect Labeling." *Psychosomatic Medicine* 69, no. 6 (2007): 560–65.

Culadasa, et al. *The Mind Illuminated: A Complete Meditation Guide Integrating Buddhist Wisdom and Brain Science for Greater Mindfulness*. New York: Atria Books, 2017.

Dahl, C. J., et al. "Reconstructing and Deconstructing the Self: Cognitive Mechanisms in Meditation Practice." *Trends in Cognitive Sciences* 19, no. 9 (2015): 515–23.

Dalai Lama and H. Cutler. *The Art of Happiness: A Handbook for Living*. New York: Riverhead Books, 2009.

Damasio, A. R. *The Feeling of What Happens: Body and Emotion in the Making of Consciousness*. Boston: Houghton Mifflin Harcourt, 1999.

————. *Self Comes to Mind: Constructing the Conscious Brain*. New York: Vintage Books, 2012.

Dambrun, M., and M. Ricard. "Self-Centeredness and Selflessness: A Theory of Self-Based Psychological Functioning and Its Consequences for Happiness." *Review of General Psychology* 15, no. 2 (2011): 138–57.

Dass, R. *Be Here Now*. New York: Harmony Books, 2010.

Datta, D., and A. F. Arnsten. "Loss of Prefrontal Cortical Higher Cognition with Uncontrollable Stress: Molecular Mechanisms, Changes with Age, and Relevance to Treatment." *Brain Sciences* 9, no. 5 (2019): 113.

Davidson, J. M. "The Physiology of Meditation and Mystical States of Consciousness." *Perspectives in Biology and Medicine* 19, no. 3 (1976): 345–80.

Davidson, R. J. "Well-Being and Affective Style: Neural Substrates and Biobehavioural Correlates." *Philosophical Transactions: Biological Sciences* 359, no. 1449 (2004): 1395–1411.

Davis, J. H., and D. R. Vago. "Can Enlightenment Be Traced to Specific Neural Correlates, Cognition, or Behavior? No, and (a Qualified) Yes." *Frontiers in Psychology* 4 (2013): 870.

Dawkins, R. *The God Delusion*. New York: Random House, 2016.

Day, J. J., and J. D. Sweatt. "Epigenetic Mechanisms in Cognition." *Neuron* 70, no. 5 (2015): 813–29.

Decety, J., and M. Svetlova. "Putting Together Phylogenetic and Ontogenetic Perspectives on Empathy." *Developmental Cognitive Neuroscience* 2, no. 1 (2011): 1–24.

Decety, J., and K. J. Yoder. "The Emerging Social Neuroscience of Justice Motivation." *Trends in Cognitive Sciences* 21, no. 1 (2017): 6–14.

De Dreu, C. K. "Oxytocin Modulates Cooperation Within and Competition Between Groups: An Integrative Review and Research Agenda." *Hormones and Behavior* 61, no. 3 (2012): 419–28.

————, et al. "The Neuropeptide Oxytocin Regulates Parochial Altruism in Intergroup Conflict Among Humans." *Science* 328, no. 5984 (2010): 1408–11.

————, et al. "Oxytocin Enables Novelty Seeking and Creative Performance Through Upregulated Approach: Evidence and Avenues for Future Research." *Wiley Interdisciplinary Reviews: Cognitive Science* 6, no. 5 (2015): 409–17.

————, et al. "Oxytocin Motivates Non-cooperation in Intergroup Conflict to Protect Vulnerable In-Group Members." *PLoS One* 7, no. 11 (2012): e46751.

Denny, B. T., et al. "A Meta-analysis of Functional Neuroimaging Studies of Self- and Other Judgments Reveals a Spatial Gradient for Mentalizing in Medial Prefrontal Cortex." *Journal of Cognitive Neuroscience* 24, no. 8 (2012): 1742–52.

D'Esposito, M., and B. R. Postle. "The Cognitive Neuroscience of Working Memory." *Annual Review of Psychology* 66 (2015): 115–42.

Dietrich, A. "Functional Neuroanatomy of Altered States of Consciousness: The Transient Hypofrontality Hypothesis." *Consciousness and Cognition* 12, no. 2 (2004): 231–56.

Dixon, S., and G. Wilcox. "The Counseling Implications of Neurotheology: A Critical Review." *Journal of Spirituality in Mental Health* 18, no. 2 (2016): 91–107.

Dunbar, R. I. "The Social Brain Hypothesis." *Evolutionary Anthropology: Issues, News, and Reviews* 6, no. 5 (1998): 178–90.

Dunne, J. "Toward an Understanding of Non-dual Mindfulness." *Contemporary Buddhism* 12, no. 1 (2011): 71–88.

Dusek, J. A., et al. "Genomic Counter-Stress Changes Induced by the Relaxation Response." *PLoS One* 3, no. 7 (2008): e2576.

Dzyubenko, E., et al. "Neuron-Glia Interactions in Neural Plasticity: Contributions of Neural Extracellular Matrix and Perineuronal Nets." *Neural Plasticity* (2016): 5214961.

Earl, B. "The Biological Function of Consciousness." *Frontiers in Psychology* 5, (2014): 697.

Ecker, B. "Memory Reconsolidation Understood and Misunderstood." *International Journal of Neuropsychotherapy* 3, no. 1 (2015): 2–46.

———, et al. *Unlocking the Emotional Brain: Eliminating Symptoms at Their Roots Using Memory Reconsolidation.* London: Routledge, 2012.

Eisenberger, N. I. "The Neural Bases of Social Pain: Evidence for Shared Representations with Physical Pain." *Psychosomatic Medicine* 74, no. 2 (2012): 126.

———, et al., "Attachment Figures Activate a Safety Signal-Related Neural Region and Reduce Pain Experience." *Proceedings of the National Academy of Sciences* 108, no. 28 (2011): 11721–26.

Eliot, T. S. *Collected Poems 1909–1962.* London: Faber & Faber, 2009.

Engen, H. G., and T. Singer. "Affect and Motivation Are Critical in Constructive Meditation." *Trends in Cognitive Sciences* 20, no. 3 (2016): 159–60.

———. "Compassion-Based Emotion Regulation Up-regulates Experienced Positive Affect and Associated Neural Networks." *Social Cognitive and Affective Neuroscience* 10, no. 9 (2015): 1291–301.

Engler, J. "Being Somebody and Being Nobody: A Re-examination of the Understanding of Self in Psychoanalysis and Buddhism." In *Psychoanalysis and Buddhism: An Unfolding Dialogue*, edited by J. D. Safran. Boston: Wisdom Publications, 2003, pp. 35–79.

Eriksson, P. S., et al. "Neurogenesis in the Adult Human Hippocampus." *Nature Medicine* 4, no. 11 (1998): 1313–17.

Esch, T., and G. B. Stefano. "The Neurobiology of Stress Management." *Neuroendocrinology Letters* 31, no. 1 (2010): 19–39.

Farb, N. A., et al. "Attending to the Present: Mindfulness Meditation Reveals Distinct Neural Modes of Self-reference." *Social Cognitive and Affective Neuroscience* 2, no. 4 (2007): 313–22.

———, et al. "The Mindful Brain and Emotion Regulation in Mood Disorders." *Canadian Journal of Psychiatry* 57, no. 2 (2012): 70–77.

———, et al. "Minding One's Emotions: Mindfulness Training Alters the Neural Expression of Sadness." *Emotion* 10, no. 1 (2010): 25.

Farrer, C., and C. D. Frith. "Experiencing Oneself Versus Another Person as Being the Cause of an Action: The Neural Correlates of the Experience of Agency." *NeuroImage* 15, no. 3 (2002): 596–603.

Fazelpour, S., and E. Thompson. "The Kantian Brain: Brain Dynamics from a Neurophenomenological Perspective." *Current Opinion in Neurobiology* 31 (2014): 223–29.

Ferrarelli, F., et al. "Experienced Mindfulness Meditators Exhibit Higher Parietal-Occipital EEG Gamma Activity During NREM Sleep." *PLoS One*, no. 8 (2013): e73417.

Flanagan, O. *The Bodhisattva's Brain: Buddhism Naturalized.* Cambridge, MA: MIT Press, 2011.

Fox, K. C., et al. "Is Meditation Associated with Altered Brain Structure? A Systematic Review and Meta-analysis of Morphometric Neuroimaging in Meditation Practitioners." *Neuroscience & Biobehavioral Reviews* 43 (2014): 48–73.

Fredrickson, B. L. "The Broaden-and-Build Theory of Positive Emotions." *Philosophical Transactions of the Royal Society of London, Series B: Biological Sciences,* 359, no. 1449 (2004): 1367–77.

———. "What Good Are Positive Emotions?" *Review of General Psychology* 2, no. 3 (1998): 300–19.

———, et al. "Positive Emotion Correlates of Meditation Practice: A Comparison of Mindfulness Meditation and Loving-kindness Meditation." *Mindfulness* 8, no. 6 (2017): 1623–33.

Friston, K. "The History of the Future of the Bayesian Brain." *NeuroImage* 62, no. 2 (2012): 1230–33.

Fronsdal, G. *The Dhammapada: A New Translation of the Buddhist Classic with Annotations.* Boulder, CO: Shambhala Publications, 2006.

Gailliot, M. T., et al. "Self-Control Relies on Glucose as a Limited Energy Source: Willpower Is More Than a Metaphor." *Journal of Personality and Social Psychology* 92, no. 2 (2007): 325.

Galati, et al. "Multiple Reference Frames Used by the Human Brain for Spatial Perception and Memory." *Experimental Brain Research* 206, no. 2 (2010), 109–20.

Gallagher, S. "Philosophical Conceptions of the Self: Implications for Cognitive Science." *Trends in Cognitive Sciences* 4, no. 1 (2000): 14–21.

Geertz, A. W. "When Cognitive Scientists Become Religious, Science Is in Trouble: On Neurotheology from a Philosophy of Science Perspective." *Religion* 39, no. 4 (2009): 319–24.

Gellhorn, E., and W. F. Kiely. "Mystical States of Consciousness: Neurophysiological and Clinical Aspects." *Journal of Nervous and Mental Disease* 154, no. 6 (1972): 399–405.

Germer, C. *The Mindful Path to Self-Compassion: Freeing Yourself from Destructive Thoughts and Emotions.* New York: Guilford Press, 2009.

———, and K. D. Neff. "Self-Compassion in Clinical Practice." *Journal of Clinical Psychology* 69, no. 8 (2013): 856–67.

Gilbert, P. *Compassion Focused Therapy: Distinctive Features.* London: Routledge, 2010.

———. "Introducing Compassion-Focused Therapy." *Advances in Psychiatric Treatment* 15, no. 3 (2009): 199–208.

———. "The Origins and Nature of Compassion Focused Therapy." *British Journal of Clinical Psychology* 53, no. 1 (2014): 6–41.

Gillihan, S. J., and M. J. Farah. "Is Self Special? A Critical Review of Evidence from Experimental Psychology and Cognitive Neuroscience." *Psychological Bulletin* 131, no. 1 (2005): 76.

Gleig, A. *American Dharma: Buddhism Beyond Modernity.* New Haven, CT: Yale University Press, 2019.

Goldstein, J. *The Experience of Insight: A Simple and Direct Guide to Buddhist Meditation.* Boulder, CO: Shambhala Publications, 2017.

———. *Mindfulness: A Practical Guide to Awakening.* Boulder, CO: Sounds True, 2013.

Goleman, D., and R. J. Davidson. *Altered Traits: Science Reveals How Meditation Changes Your Mind, Brain, and Body.* New York: Penguin, 2017.

Gombrich, R. F. *What the Buddha Thought.* Sheffield, UK: Equinox, 2009.

Grabovac, A. "The Stages of Insight: Clinical Relevance for Mindfulness-Based Interventions." *Mindfulness* 6, no. 3 (2015): 589–600.

Grosmark, A. D., and G. Buzsáki. "Diversity in Neural Firing Dynamics Supports Both Rigid and Learned Hippocampal Sequences." *Science* 351, no. 6280 (2016): 1440–43.

Grossenbacher, P. "Buddhism and the Brain: An Empirical Approach to Spirituality." Paper prepared for "Continuity + Change: Perspectives on Science and Religion," June 3–7, 2006, in Philadelphia, PA. https://www.scribd.com/document/283480254/Buddhism-and-the-Brain.

Gross, R. M. *Buddhism After Patriarchy: A Feminist History, Analysis, and Reconstruction of Buddhism.* Albany: SUNY Press, 1993.

Habas, C., et al. "Distinct Cerebellar Contributions to Intrinsic Connectivity Networks." *Journal of Neuroscience* 29, no. 26 (2009): 8586–94.

Halifax, J. *Standing at the Edge: Finding Freedom Where Fear and Courage Meet.* New York: Flatiron Books, 2018.

Hamlin, J. K., et al. "Three-Month-Olds Show a Negativity Bias in Their Social Evaluations." *Developmental Science* 13, no. 6 (2010): 923–29.

Hanh, T. N. *Being Peace.* Berkeley, CA: Parallax Press, 2008.

———. *Inside the Now: Meditations on Time.* Berkeley, CA: Parallax Press, 2015.

———. *The World We Have: A Buddhist Approach to Peace and Ecology.* Berkeley, CA: Parallax Press, 2004.

Hanson, R. *Buddha's Brain: The Practical Neuroscience of Happiness, Love, and Wisdom.* Oakland, CA: New Harbinger Publications, 2009.

———. *Hardwiring Happiness: The New Brain Science of Contentment, Calm, and Confidence.* New York: Harmony Books, 2013.

———, and F. Hanson. *Resilient: How to Grow an Unshakable Core of Calm, Strength, and Happiness.* New York: Harmony Books, 2018.

Hansotia, P. "A Neurologist Looks at Mind and Brain: 'The Enchanted Loom.'" *Clinical Medicine & Research* 1, no. 4 (2003): 327–32.

Harkness, K. L., et al. "Stress Sensitivity and Stress Sensitization in Psychopathology: An Introduction to the Special Section." *Journal of Abnormal Psychology* 124 (2015): 1.

Harris, A. *Conscious: A Brief Guide to the Fundamental Mystery of the Mind.* New York: Harper, 2019.

Harris, S. *Waking Up: A Guide to Spirituality Without Religion.* New York: Simon & Schuster, 2014.

Hayes, S. *The Act in Context: The Canonical Papers of Steven C. Hayes.* New York: Routledge, 2015.

Herculano-Houzel, S. "The Remarkable, Yet Not Extraordinary, Human Brain as a Scaled-Up Primate Brain and Its Associated Cost." *Proceedings of the National Academy of Sciences* 109, Supplement 1 (2012): 10661–68.

Hill, K. R., et al. "Co-residence Patterns in Hunter-Gatherer Societies Show Unique Human Social Structure." *Science* 331, no. 6022 (2011): 1286–89.

Hilton, L., et al. "Mindfulness Meditation for Chronic Pain: Systematic Review and Meta-analysis." *Annals of Behavioral Medicine* 51, no. 2 (2016): 199–213.

Hofmann, S., et al. "Loving-kindness and Compassion Meditation: Potential for Psychological Interventions." *Clinical Psychology Review* 31, no. 7 (2011): 1126–32.

Hölzel, B. K., et al. "How Does Mindfulness Meditation Work? Proposing Mechanisms of Action from a Conceptual and Neural Perspective." *Perspectives on Psychological Science* 6, no. 6 (2011): 537–59.

———, et al. "Investigation of Mindfulness Meditation Practitioners with Voxel-Based Morphometry." *Social Cognitive and Affective Neuroscience* 3 (2008): 55–61.

Hood R. W., et al. *The Psychology of Religion: An Empirical Approach,* 5th ed. New York: Guilford Press, 2018.

Hu, X., et al. "Unlearning Implicit Social Biases During Sleep." *Science* 348, no. 6238 (2015): 1013–15.

Huber, D., et al. "Vasopressin and Oxytocin Excite Distinct Neuronal Populations in the Central Amygdala." *Science* 308, no. 5719 (2005): 245–48.

Hung, L. W., et al. "Gating of Social Reward by Oxytocin in the Ventral Tegmental Area." *Science* 357, no. 6358 (2017): 1406–11.

Huxley, A. *The Perennial Philosophy.* Toronto: McClelland & Stewart, 2014.

Hyman, S. E., et al. "Neural Mechanisms of Addiction: The Role of Reward-Related Learning and Memory." *Annual Review of Neuroscience* 29, no. 1 (2006): 565–98.

Jastrzebski, A. K. "The Neuroscience of Spirituality." *Pastoral Psychology* 67 (2018): 515–24.

Johnsen, T. J., and O. Friborg. "The Effects of Cognitive Behavioral Therapy as an Anti-depressive Treatment Is [*sic*] Falling: A Meta-analysis." *Psychological Bulletin* 141, no. 4 (2015): 747.

Johnstone, B., et al. "Right Parietal Lobe-Related 'Selflessness' as the Neuropsychological Basis of Spiritual Transcendence." *International Journal for the Psychology of Religion* 22, no. 4 (2012): 267–84.

Jones, S. *There Is Nothing to Fix: Becoming Whole Through Radical Self-Acceptance.* Somerville, MA: LAKE Publications, 2019.

Josipovic, Z. "Neural Correlates of Nondual Awareness in Meditation." *Annals of the New York Academy of Sciences* 1307, no. 1 (2014): 9–18.

———, and B. J. Baars. "What Can Neuroscience Learn from Contemplative Practices?" *Frontiers in Psychology* 6 (2015): 1731.

Kalu Rinpoche and the Dalai Lama. *Luminous Mind: The Way of the Buddha.* Somerville, MA: Wisdom Publications, 1993.

Kandel, E. R. *In Search of Memory: The Emergence of a New Science of Mind.* New York: W. W. Norton, 2007.

Karlsson, M. P., and L. M. Frank. "Awake Replay of Remote Experiences in the Hippocampus." *Nature Neuroscience* 12, no. 7 (2009): 913–18.

Keltner, D. *Born to Be Good: The Science of a Meaningful Life.* New York: W. W. Norton, 2009.

Kempermann, G. "Youth Culture in the Adult Brain." *Science* 335, no. 6073 (2012): 1175–76.

———, et al. "Human Adult Neurogenesis: Evidence and Remaining Questions." *Cell Stem Cell* 23, no. 1 (2018): 25–30.

Keuken, M. C., et al. "Large Scale Structure-Function Mappings of the Human Subcortex." *Scientific Reports* 8, no. 1 (2018): 15854.

Key, B., et al. "Insects Cannot Tell Us Anything About Subjective Experience or the Origin of Consciousness." *Proceedings of the National Academy of Sciences* 113, no. 27 (2016): E3813.

Kiken, L. G., et al. "From a State to a Trait: Trajectories of State Mindfulness in Meditation During Intervention Predict Changes in Trait Mindfulness." *Personality and Individual Differences* 81 (2015): 41–46.

Killingsworth, M. A., and D. T. Gilbert. "A Wandering Mind Is an Unhappy Mind." *Science* 330, no. 6006 (2010): 932.

Koch, C., et al. "Neural Correlates of Consciousness: Progress and Problems." *Nature Reviews Neuroscience* 17, no. 5 (2016): 307–21.

Kok, B. E., and B. L. Fredrickson. "Upward Spirals of the Heart: Autonomic Flexibility, as Indexed by Vagal Tone, Reciprocally and Prospectively Predicts Positive Emotions and Social Connectedness." *Biological Psychology* 85, no. 3 (2010): 432–36.

Kornfield, J. *After the Ecstasy, the Laundry.* New York: Bantam, 2000.

———. *A Path with Heart: A Guide Through the Perils and Promises of Spiritual Life.* New York: Bantam, 2009.

Kraft, D. *Buddha's Map: His Original Teachings on Awakening, Ease, and Insight in the Heart of Meditation.* Grass Valley, CA: Blue Dolphin Publishing, 2013.

Kral, T. R. A., et al. "Impact of Short- and Long-Term Mindfulness Meditation Training on Amygdala Reactivity to Emotional Stimuli." *NeuroImage* 181 (2018): 301–13.

Kreibig, S. D. "Autonomic Nervous System Activity in Emotion: A Review." *Biological Psychology* 84, no. 3 (2010): 394–421.

Kringelbach, M. L., and K. C. Berridge. "Neuroscience of Reward, Motivation, and Drive." In *Recent Developments in Neuroscience Research on Human Motivation*, edited by K. Sung-il et al. Bingley, UK: Emerald Group Publishing, 2016, pp. 23–35.

Kritman, M., et al. "Oxytocin in the Amygdala and Not the Prefrontal Cortex Enhances Fear and Impairs Extinction in the Juvenile Rat." *Neurobiology of Learning and Memory* 141 (2017): 179–88.

Langner, R., and S. B. Eickhoff. "Sustaining Attention to Simple Tasks: A Meta-analytic Review of the Neural Mechanisms of Vigilant Attention." *Psychological Bulletin* 139, no. 4 (2013): 870.

Laricchiuta, D., and L. Petrosini. "Individual Differences in Response to Positive and Negative Stimuli: Endocannabinoid-Based Insight on Approach and Avoidance Behaviors." *Frontiers in Systems Neuroscience* 8 (2014): 238.

Lazar, S. W., et al. "Functional Brain Mapping of the Relaxation Response and Meditation." *Neuroreport* 11, no. 7 (2000): 1581–85.

———, et al. "Meditation Experience Is Associated with Increased Cortical Thickness." *Neuroreport* 16 (2005): 1893–97.

Leary, M. R. *The Curse of the Self: Self-Awareness, Egotism, and the Quality of Human Life.* New York: Oxford University Press, 2007.

———, et al. "Allo-inclusive Identity: Incorporating the Social and Natural Worlds into One's Sense of Self." In *Decade of Behavior. Transcending Self-Interest: Psychological Explorations of the Quiet Ego*, edited by H. A. Wayment and J. J. Bauer. Washington, DC: American Psychological Association, 2008, pp. 137–47.

Lee, T. M., et al. "Distinct Neural Activity Associated with Focused-Attention Meditation and Loving-kindness Meditation." *PLoS One* 7, no. 8 (2012): e40054.

Legrand, D., and P. Ruby. "What Is Self-Specific? Theoretical Investigation and Critical Review of Neuroimaging Results." *Psychological Review* 116 (2009): 252.

Lent, R., et al. "How Many Neurons Do You Have? Some Dogmas of Quantitative Neuroscience Under Revision." *European Journal of Neuroscience* 35, no. 1 (2012): 1–9.

Leung, M. K., et al. "Increased Gray Matter Volume in the Right Angular and Posterior Parahippocampal Gyri in Loving-kindness Meditators." *Social Cognitive and Affective Neuroscience* 8, no. 1 (2012): 34–39.

Lieberman, M. D. *Social: Why Our Brains Are Wired to Connect.* New York: Oxford University Press, 2013.

———, and N. I. Eisenberger. "Pains and Pleasures of Social Life." *Science* 323, no. 5916 (2009): 890–91.

Lindahl, J. R., et al. "The Varieties of Contemplative Experience: A Mixed-Methods Study of Meditation-Related Challenges in Western Buddhists." *PLoS One* 12, no. 5 (2017): e0176239.

Linehan, M. *Cognitive-Behavioral Treatment of Borderline Personality Disorder*. New York: Guilford Press, 2018.

Lippelt, D. P., et al. "Focused Attention, Open Monitoring and Loving Kindness Meditation: Effects on Attention, Conflict Monitoring, and Creativity—A Review." *Frontiers in Psychology* 5 (2014): 1083.

Liu, Y., et al. "Oxytocin Modulates Social Value Representations in the Amygdala." *Nature Neuroscience* 22, no. 4 (2019): 633.

Loizzo, J. J., et al., eds. *Advances in Contemplative Psychotherapy: Accelerating Healing and Transformation*. New York: Routledge, 2017.

Löwel, S., and W. Singer. "Selection of Intrinsic Horizontal Connections in the Visual Cortex by Correlated Neuronal Activity." *Science* 255, no. 5041 (1992): 209–12.

Loy, D. *Ecodharma: Buddhist Teachings for the Ecological Crisis*. Somerville, MA: Wisdom Publications, 2019.

Lupien, S. J., et al. "Beyond the Stress Concept: Allostatic Load—A Developmental Biological and Cognitive Perspective." In *Developmental Psychopathology*, vol. 2: *Developmental Neuroscience*, 2nd ed., edited by D. Cicchetti and D. Cohen. Hoboken, NJ: Wiley, 2006, pp. 578–628.

Lutz, A., et al. "Altered Anterior Insula Activation During Anticipation and Experience of Painful Stimuli in Expert Meditators." *NeuroImage* 64 (2013): 538–46.

———, et al. "Long-Term Meditators Self-Induce High-Amplitude Gamma Synchrony During Mental Practice." *PNAS* 101 (2004): 16369–73.

Madan, C. R. "Toward a Common Theory for Learning from Reward, Affect, and Motivation: The SIMON Framework." *Frontiers in Systems Neuroscience* 7 (2013): 59.

Maharaj, N., et al. *I Am That: Talks with Sri Nisargadatta Maharaj*, translated by M. Frydman. Durham, NC: Acorn Press, 1973.

Mahone, M. C., et al. "fMRI During Transcendental Meditation Practice." *Brain and Cognition* 123 (2018): 30–33.

Manuello, J., et al. "Mindfulness Meditation and Consciousness: An Integrative Neuroscientific Perspective." *Consciousness and Cognition* 40 (2016): 67–78.

Martin, K. C., and E. M. Schuman. "Opting In or Out of the Network." *Science* 350, no. 6267 (2015): 1477–78.

Mascaro, J. S., et al. "The Neural Mediators of Kindness-Based Meditation: A Theoretical Model." *Frontiers in Psychology* 6 (2015): 109.

Maslow, A. H. *Religions, Values, and Peak-Experiences*, vol. 35. Columbus: Ohio State University Press, 1964.

Mather, J. A. "Cephalopod Consciousness: Behavioural Evidence." *Consciousness and Cognition* 17, no. 1 (2008): 37–48.

Matsuo, N., et al. "Spine-Type-Specific Recruitment of Newly Synthesized AMPA Receptors with Learning." *Science* 319, no. 5866 (2008): 1104–7.

McDonald, R. J., and N. S. Hong. "How Does a Specific Learning and Memory System in the Mammalian Brain Gain Control of Behavior?" *Hippocampus* 23, no. 11 (2013): 1084–102.

McGaugh, J. L. "Memory: A Century of Consolidation." *Science* 287, no. 5451 (2000): 248–51.

McMahan, D. L., and E. Braun, eds. *Meditation, Buddhism, and Science.* New York: Oxford University Press, 2017.

Menon, V. "Salience Network." In *Brain Mapping: An Encyclopedic Reference*, vol. 2, edited by A. W. Toga. Cambridge, MA: Academic Press, 2015, pp. 597–611.

Merton, T. *In the Dark Before Dawn: New Selected Poems*, edited by L. R. Szabo. New York: New Directions Publishing, 2005.

Meyer-Lindenberg, A. "Impact of Prosocial Neuropeptides on Human Brain Function." *Progress in Brain Research* 170 (2008): 463–70.

Mitchell, S. *Tao Te Ching: A New English Version.* New York: Harper Perennial Modern Classics, 1988.

Moore, S. R., and R. A. Depue. "Neurobehavioral Foundation of Environmental Reactivity." *Psychological Bulletin* 142, no. 2 (2016): 107.

Mosig, Y. D. "Conceptions of the Self in Western and Eastern Psychology." *Journal of Theoretical and Philosophical Psychology* 26, no. 1–2 (2006): 3.

Muir, J. *My First Summer in the Sierra.* Illustrated Anniversary Edition. Boston: Houghton Mifflin Harcourt, 2011.

Muller, R. A. *Now: The Physics of Time.* New York: W. W. Norton, 2016.

Mullette-Gillman, O., and S. A. Huettel. "Neural Substrates of Contingency Learning and Executive Control: Dissociating Physical, Valuative, and Behavioral Changes." *Frontiers in Human Neuroscience* 3 (2009): 23.

Nadel, L., et al. "Memory Formation, Consolidation and Transformation." *Neuroscience & Biobehavioral Reviews* 36, no. 7 (2012): 1640–45.

Nader, K., et al. "Fear Memories Require Protein Synthesis in the Amygdala for Reconsolidation After Retrieval." *Nature* 406, no. 6797 (2000): 722.

Nanamoli, B. *The Path of Purification: The Classic Manual of Buddhist Doctrine and Meditation.* Kandy, Sri Lanka: Buddhist Publication Society, 1991.

Naumann, R. K., et al. "The Reptilian Brain." *Current Biology* 25, no. 8 (2015): R317–21.

Nechvatal, J. M., and D. M. Lyons. "Coping Changes the Brain." *Frontiers in Behavioral Neuroscience* 7 (2013): 13.

Neff, K. *Self-Compassion: The Proven Power of Being Kind to Yourself.* New York: William Morrow, 2011.

———, and K. A. Dahm. "Self-Compassion: What It Is, What It Does, and How It Relates to Mindfulness." In *Handbook of Mindfulness and Self-Regulation*, edited by B. D. Ostafin et al. New York: Springer, 2015, pp. 121–37.

Newberg, A. B. "The Neuroscientific Study of Spiritual Practices." *Frontiers in Psychology* 5 (2014): 215.

———. *Principles of Neurotheology.* Farnham, UK: Ashgate Publishing, 2010.

———, et al. "A Case Series Study of the Neurophysiological Effects of Altered States of Mind During Intense Islamic Prayer." *Journal of Physiology–Paris* 109, no. 4–6 (2015): 214–20.

————, et al. "Cerebral Blood Flow During Meditative Prayer: Preliminary Findings and Methodological Issues." *Perceptual and Motor Skills* 97, no. 2 (2003): 625–30.

————, et al. "The Measurement of Regional Cerebral Blood Flow During the Complex Cognitive Task of Meditation: A Preliminary SPECT Study." *Psychiatry Research: Neuroimaging* 106, no. 2 (2001): 113–22.

————, and J. Iversen. "The Neural Basis of the Complex Mental Task of Meditation: Neurotransmitter and Neurochemical Considerations." *Medical Hypotheses* 61, no. 2 (2003): 282–91.

Newen, A., et al., eds. *The Oxford Handbook of 4E Cognition.* New York: Oxford University Press, 2018.

Northoff, G., and F. Bermpohl. "Cortical Midline Structures and the Self." *Trends in Cognitive Sciences* 8, no. 3 (2004): 102–7.

Oakley, B., et al., eds. *Pathological Altruism.* New York: Oxford University Press, 2011.

Oh, M., et al. "Watermaze Learning Enhances Excitability of CA1 Pyramidal Neurons." *Journal of Neurophysiology* 90, no. 4 (2003): 2171–79.

Ott, U., et al. "Brain Structure and Meditation: How Spiritual Practice Shapes the Brain." In *Neuroscience, Consciousness and Spirituality,* edited by H. Walach et al. Berlin: Springer, Dordrecht, 2011, pp. 119–28.

Owens, L. R., and J. Syedullah. *Radical Dharma: Talking Race, Love, and Liberation.* Berkeley, CA: North Atlantic Books, 2016.

Packard, M. G., and L. Cahill. "Affective Modulation of Multiple Memory Systems." *Current Opinion in Neurobiology* 11, no. 6 (2001): 752–56.

Paller, K. A. "Memory Consolidation: Systems." *Encyclopedia of Neuroscience* 1 (2009): 741–49.

Palmo, A. T. *Reflections on a Mountain Lake: Teachings on Practical Buddhism.* Boulder, CO: Shambhala Publications, 2002.

Panksepp, J. *Affective Neuroscience: The Foundations of Human and Animal Emotions.* New York: Oxford University Press, 1998.

Paolicelli, R. C., et al. "Synaptic Pruning by Microglia Is Necessary for Normal Brain Development." *Science* 333, no. 6048 (2011), 1456–58.

Pasanno, A., and A. Amaro. *The Island.* Redwood Valley, CA: Abhayagiri Monastic Foundation, 2009.

Petersen, S. E., and M. I. Posner. "The Attention System of the Human Brain: 20 Years After." *Annual Review of Neuroscience* 35 (2012): 73–89.

Pollan, M. *How to Change Your Mind: What the New Science of Psychedelics Teaches Us About Consciousness, Dying, Addiction, Depression, and Transcendence.* New York: Penguin Books, 2018.

Porges, S. W. *The Polyvagal Theory: Neurophysiological Foundations of Emotions, Attachment, Communication, and Self-Regulation.* New York: W. W. Norton, 2011.

————, and C. S. Carter. "Polyvagal Theory and the Social Engagement System." In *Complementary and Integrative Treatments in Psychiatric Practice,* edited by P. L. Gerbarg et al. New York: American Psychiatric Association Publishing, 2017, pp. 221–39.

Posner, M. I., and S. E. Petersen. "The Attention System of the Human Brain." *Annual Review of Neuroscience* 13, no. 1 (1990): 25–42.

Prendergast, J. *The Deep Heart: Our Portal to Presence.* Boulder, CO: Sounds True, 2019.

Preston, S. D. "The Rewarding Nature of Social Contact." *Science* 357, no. 6358 (2017): 1353–54.

Pritz, M. B. "Crocodilian Forebrain: Evolution and Development." *Integrative and Comparative Biology* 55, no. 6 (2015): 949–61.

Quiroga, R. Q. "Neural Representations Across Species." *Science* 363, no. 6434 (2019): 1388–89.

Radke, S., et al. "Oxytocin Reduces Amygdala Responses During Threat Approach." *Psychoneuroendocrinology* 79 (2017): 160–6.

Raichle, M. E. "The Restless Brain: How Intrinsic Activity Organizes Brain Function." *Philosophical Transactions of the Royal Society of London, Series B: Biological Sciences* 370, no. 1668 (2015): 20140172.

———, et al. "A Default Mode of Brain Function." *Proceedings of the National Academy of Sciences* 98, no. 2 (2001): 676–82.

Ranganath, C., et al. "Working Memory Maintenance Contributes to Long-Term Memory Formation: Neural and Behavioral Evidence." *Journal of Cognitive Neuroscience* 17, no. 7 (2005): 994–1010.

RecoveryDharma.org. *Recovery Dharma: How to Use Buddhist Practices and Principles to Heal the Suffering of Addiction.* 2019.

Ricard, M. *Happiness: A Guide to Developing Life's Most Important Skill.* London: Atlantic Books, 2015.

———. *On the Path to Enlightenment: Heart Advice from the Great Tibetan Masters.* Boulder, CO: Shambhala Publications, 2013.

———, et al. *The Quantum and the Lotus: A Journey to the Frontiers Where Science and Buddhism Meet.* New York: Three Rivers Press, 2001.

Rothschild, B. *The Body Remembers: The Psychophysiology of Trauma and Trauma Treatment.* New York: W. W. Norton, 2000.

Roxin, A., et al. "On the Distribution of Firing Rates in Networks of Cortical Neurons." *Journal of Neuroscience* 31, no. 45 (2011): 16217–26.

Rozin, P., and E. B. Royzman. "Negativity Bias, Negativity Dominance, and Contagion." *Personality and Social Psychology Review* 5, no. (2001): 296–320.

Sahn, S., and S. T. Sŏnsa. *Only Don't Know: Selected Teaching Letters of Zen Master Seung Sahn.* Boulder, CO: Shambhala Publications, 1999.

Salzberg, S. *Lovingkindness: The Revolutionary Art of Happiness.* Boulder, CO: Shambhala Publications, 2004.

———. *Real Love: The Art of Mindful Connection.* New York: Flatiron Books, 2017.

Sapolsky, R. M. *Why Zebras Don't Get Ulcers: The Acclaimed Guide to Stress, Stress-Related Diseases, and Coping.* New York: Holt Paperbacks, 2004.

Sara, S. J., and M. Segal. "Plasticity of Sensory Responses of Locus Coeruleus Neurons in the Behaving Rat: Implications for Cognition." *Progress in Brain Research* 88 (1991): 571–85.

Schaper, D., ed. *40-Day Journey with Howard Thurman*. Minneapolis: Augsburg Books, 2009.

Schore, A. N. *Affect Regulation and the Origin of the Self: The Neurobiology of Emotional Development*. New York: Routledge, 2015.

Schwartz, J. M., et al. "Quantum Physics in Neuroscience and Psychology: A Neurophysical Model of Mind-Brain Interaction." *Philosophical Transactions of the Royal Society of London, Series B: Biological Sciences* 360, no. 1458 (2005): 1309–27.

Schweiger, D., et al. "Opioid Receptor Blockade and Warmth-Liking: Effects on Interpersonal Trust and Frontal Asymmetry." *Social Cognitive and Affective Neuroscience* 9, no. 10 (2013): 1608–15.

Seeley, W. W., et al. "Dissociable Intrinsic Connectivity Networks for Salience Processing and Executive Control." *Journal of Neuroscience* 27, no. 9 (2007): 2349–56.

Segal, Z., et al. *Mindfulness-Based Cognitive Therapy for Depression*, 2nd ed. New York: Guilford Press, 2018.

Semple, B. D., et al. "Brain Development in Rodents and Humans: Identifying Benchmarks of Maturation and Vulnerability to Injury Across Species." *Progress in Neurobiology* 106 (2013): 1–16.

Seth, A. K., et al. "An Interoceptive Predictive Coding Model of Conscious Presence." *Frontiers in Psychology* 2 (2012): 395.

Shiota, M. N., et al. "Beyond Happiness: Building a Science of Discrete Positive Emotions." *American Psychologist* 72, no. 7 (2017): 617.

Shors, T. J. "Memory Traces of Trace Memories: Neurogenesis, Synaptogenesis and Awareness." *Trends in Neurosciences* 27, no. 5 (2004): 250–56.

Shrobe, R., and K. Wu. *Don't-Know Mind: The Spirit of Korean Zen*. Boulder, CO: Shambhala Publications, 2004.

Siegel, D. *Aware: The Science and Practice of Presence, The Groundbreaking Meditation Practice*. New York: Penguin, 2018.

———. *The Mindful Brain*. New York: W. W. Norton, 2007.

Sin, N. L., and S. Lyubomirsky. "Enhancing Well-Being and Alleviating Depressive Symptoms with Positive Psychology Interventions: A Practice-Friendly Meta-analysis." *Journal of Clinical Psychology* 65, no. 5 (2009): 467–87.

Smallwood, J., and J. Andrews-Hanna. "Not All Minds That Wander Are Lost: The Importance of a Balanced Perspective on the Mind-Wandering State." *Frontiers in Psychology* 4 (2013): 441.

Smith, H. "Is There a Perennial Philosophy?" *Journal of the American Academy of Religion* 55, no. 3 (1987): 553–66.

Sneddon, L. U. "Evolution of Nociception in Vertebrates: Comparative Analysis of Lower Vertebrates." *Brain Research Reviews* 46, no. 2 (2004): 123–30.

Sneve, M. H., et al. "Mechanisms Underlying Encoding of Short-Lived Versus Durable Episodic Memories." *Journal of Neuroscience* 35, no. 13 (2015): 5202–12.

Snyder, S., and T. Rasmussen. *Practicing the Jhānas: Traditional Concentration Meditation as Presented by the Venerable Pa Auk Sayada*. Boulder, CO: Shambhala Publications, 2009.

Sobota, R., et al. "Oxytocin Reduces Amygdala Activity, Increases Social Interactions, and Reduces Anxiety-Like Behavior Irrespective of NMDAR Antagonism." *Behavioral Neuroscience* 129, no. 4 (2015): 389.

Soeng, M. *The Heart of the Universe: Exploring the Heart Sutra.* New York: Simon & Schuster, 2010.

Sofer, O. J. *Say What You Mean: A Mindful Approach to Nonviolent Communication.* Boulder, CO: Shambhala Publications, 2018.

Sokolov, A., et al. "The Cerebellum: Adaptive Prediction for Movement and Cognition." *Trends in Cognitive Sciences* 21, no. 5 (2017): 313–32.

Spalding, K. L., et al. "Dynamics of Hippocampal Neurogenesis in Adult Humans." *Cell* 153, no. 6 (2013): 1219–27.

Stafford, W. *The Way It Is: New and Selected Poems.* Minneapolis: Graywolf Press, 1999.

Szyf, M., et al. "The Social Environment and the Epigenome." *Environmental and Molecular Mutagenesis* 49, no. 1 (2008), 46–60.

Tabibnia, G., and M. D. Lieberman. "Fairness and Cooperation Are Rewarding: Evidence from Social Cognitive Neuroscience." *Annals of the New York Academy of Sciences* 1118, no. 1 (2007): 90–101.

Tabibnia, G., and D. Radecki. "Resilience Training That Can Change the Brain." *Consulting Psychology Journal: Practice and Research* 70 (2018): 59.

Taft, M. *The Mindful Geek: Secular Meditation for Smart Skeptics.* Oakland, CA: Cephalopod Rex, 2015.

Takeuchi, T., et al. "The Synaptic Plasticity and Memory Hypothesis: Encoding, Storage and Persistence." *Philosophical Transactions of the Royal Society of London, Series B, Biological Sciences* 369, no. 1633 (2014): 1–14.

Talmi, D. "Enhanced Emotional Memory: Cognitive and Neural Mechanisms." *Current Directions in Psychological Science* 22, no. 6 (2013): 430–36.

Tang, Y., et al. "Short-Term Meditation Training Improves Attention and Self-Regulation." *Proceedings of the National Academy of Sciences* 104, no. 43 (2007): 17152–56.

Tannen, D. *You Just Don't Understand: Women and Men in Conversation.* New York: William Morrow, 1990.

Tarlaci, S. "Why We Need Quantum Physics for Cognitive Neuroscience." *NeuroQuantology* 8, no. 1 (2010): 66–76.

Taylor, S. E. "Tend and Befriend Theory." Chapter 2 of *Handbook of Theories of Social Psychology*, vol. 1, edited by P. A. M. Van Lange et al. London: Sage Publications, 2011.

Teasdale, J., and S. Zindel. *The Mindful Way Through Depression: Freeing Yourself from Chronic Unhappiness.* New York: Guilford Press, 2007.

Thānissaro, B. *The Wings to Awakening.* Barre, MA: Dhamma Dana Publications, 1996.

Thompson, E. *Mind in Life: Biology, Phenomenology, and the Sciences of Mind.* Cambridge, MA: Harvard University Press, 2010.

———. "Neurophenomenology and Contemplative Experience." In *The Oxford Handbook of Religion and Science,* edited by Philip Clayton. New York: Oxford University Press, 2006.

———. *Waking, Dreaming, Being: Self and Consciousness in Neuroscience, Meditation, and Philosophy.* New York: Columbia University Press, 2014.

Thubten, A. *No Self, No Problem: Awakening to Our True Nature.* Boulder, CO: Shambhala Publications, 2013.

Tononi, G., et al. "Integrated Information Theory: From Consciousness to Its Physical Substrate." *Nature Reviews Neuroscience* 17 (2016): 450–61.

Torrisi, S. J., et al. "Advancing Understanding of Affect Labeling with Dynamic Causal Modeling." *NeuroImage* 82 (2013): 481–88.

Trautwein, F. M., et al. "Decentering the Self? Reduced Bias in Self- Versus Other-Related Processing in Long-Term Practitioners of Loving-Kindness Meditation." *Frontiers in Psychology* 7 (2016): 1785.

Treleaven, D. A. *Trauma-Sensitive Mindfulness: Practices for Safe and Transformative Healing.* New York: W. W. Norton, 2018.

Trivers, R. L. "The Evolution of Reciprocal Altruism." *Quarterly Review of Biology* 46, no. 1 (1971): 35–57.

Tully, K., and V. Y. Bolshakov. "Emotional Enhancement of Memory: How Norepinephrine Enables Synaptic Plasticity." *Molecular Brain* 3, no. 1 (2010): 15.

Uhlhaas, P. J., et al. "Neural Synchrony and the Development of Cortical Networks." *Trends in Cognitive Sciences* 14, no. 2 (2010): 72–80.

Ulfig, N., et al. "Ontogeny of the Human Amygdala." *Annals of the New York Academy of Sciences* 985, no. 1 (2003): 22–33.

Underwood, E. "Lifelong Memories May Reside in Nets Around Brain Cells." *Science* 350, no. 6260 (2015): 491–92.

Vago, D. R., and F. Zeidan. "The Brain on Silent: Mind Wandering, Mindful Awareness, and States of Mental Tranquility." *Annals of the New York Academy of Sciences* 1373, no. 1 (2016): 96–113.

Vaish, A., et al. "Not All Emotions Are Created Equal: The Negativity Bias in Social-Emotional Development." *Psychological Bulletin* 134, no. 3 (2008): 383.

Varela, F. J. "Neurophenomenology: A Methodological Remedy for the Hard Problem." *Journal of Consciousness Studies* 3, no. 4 (1996): 330–49.

———, et al. *The Embodied Mind: Cognitive Science and Human Experience.* Cambridge, MA: MIT Press, 2017.

Vieten, C., and S. Scammell. *Spiritual and Religious Competencies in Clinical Practice: Guidelines for Psychotherapists and Mental Health Professionals.* New York: New Harbinger Publications, 2015.

———, et al. "Future Directions in Meditation Research: Recommendations for Expanding the Field of Contemplative Science." *PLoS One* 13, no. 11 (2018): e0205740.

Walach, H., et al. *Neuroscience, Consciousness and Spirituality*, vol. 1. Berlin: Springer Science & Business Media, 2011.

Wallace, B. A. *Mind in the Balance: Meditation in Science, Buddhism, and Christianity.* New York: Columbia University Press, 2014.

———, and S. L. Shapiro. "Mental Balance and Well-Being: Building Bridges Between Buddhism and Western Psychology." *American Psychologist* 61, no. 7 (2006): 690.

Watson, G. *Buddhism AND.* Oxford, UK: Mud Pie Books, 2019.

Watts, A. W. *The Book: On the Taboo Against Knowing Who You Are.* New York: Vintage Books, 2011.

Weingast, M. *The First Free Women: Poems of the Early Buddhist Nuns.* Boulder, CO: Shambhala Publications, 2020.

Weker, M. "Searching for Neurobiological Foundations of Faith and Religion." *Studia Humana* 5, no. 4 (2016): 57–63.

Welwood, J. "Principles of Inner Work: Psychological and Spiritual." *Journal of Transpersonal Psychology* 16, no. 1 (1984): 63–73.

Whitlock, J. R., et al., "Learning Induces Long-Term Potentiation in the Hippocampus." *Science* 313, no. 5790 (2006): 1093–97.

Williams, A. K., et al. *Radical Dharma: Talking Race, Love, and Liberation.* Berkeley, CA: North Atlantic Books, 2016.

Wilson, D. S., and E. O. Wilson. "Rethinking the Theoretical Foundation of Sociobiology." *Quarterly Review of Biology* 82, no. 4 (2007): 327–48.

Winnicott, D. W. "Primary Maternal Preoccupation." In *The Maternal Lineage: Identification, Desire, and Transgenerational Issues,* edited by P. Mariotti. New York: Routledge, 2012, pp. 59–66.

Winston, D. *The Little Book of Being: Practices and Guidance for Uncovering Your Natural Awareness.* Boulder, CO: Sounds True, 2019.

Wright, R. *Why Buddhism Is True: The Science and Philosophy of Meditation and Enlightenment.* New York: Simon & Schuster, 2017.

Xiankuan (Donald Sloane). *Six Pathways to Happiness: Mindfulness and Psychology in Chinese Buddhism,* vol. 1. Parker, CO: Outskirts Press, 2019.

Yaden, D., et al. "The Varieties of Self-Transcendent Experience." *Review of General Psychology* 21, no. 2 (2017): 143–60.

Yogis, J. *All Our Waves Are Water: Stumbling Toward Enlightenment and the Perfect Ride.* New York: Harper Wave, 2017.

———. *Saltwater Buddha: A Surfer's Quest to Find Zen on the Sea.* Somerville, MA: Wisdom Publications, 2009.

Yuan, J., et al. "Diversity in the Mechanisms of Neuronal Cell Death." *Neuron* 40, no. 2 (2003): 401–13.

Zaehle, T., et al. "The Neural Basis of the Egocentric and Allocentric Spatial Frame of Reference." *Brain Research* 1137 (2007): 92–103.

INDEX

ABOUT THE AUTHOR

Rick Hanson, PhD, is a psychologist, senior fellow of the Greater Good Science Center at UC Berkeley, and *New York Times* bestselling author. His books have been published in twenty-eight languages and include *Neurodharma, Resilient, Hardwiring Happiness, Just One Thing, Buddha's Brain,* and *Mother Nurture*—with more than 900,000 copies in English alone. Founder of the Wellspring Institute for Neuroscience and Contemplative Wisdom, he has been an invited speaker at Google, NASA, Oxford, and Harvard, and taught in meditation centers worldwide. He has several online offerings—including the *Neurodharma* experiential program—and more than 150,000 people receive his free weekly newsletter. He and his wife live in Northern California and have two adult children. He enjoys being in wilderness and taking a break from emails.

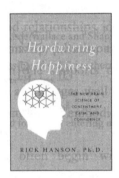